Negative Taxes and

the Poverty Problem

Studies of Government Finance

TITLES PUBLISHED

Federal Fiscal Policy in the Postwar Recessions, by Wilfred Lewis, Jr.

Federal Tax Treatment of State and Local Securities, by David J. Ott and Allan H. Meltzer.

Federal Tax Treatment of Income from Oil and Gas, by Stephen L. McDonald.

Federal Tax Treatment of the Family, by Harold M. Groves.

The Role of Direct and Indirect Taxes in the Federal Revenue System, John F. Due, Editor. A Report of the National Bureau of Economic Research and the Brookings Institution (Princeton University Press).

The Individual Income Tax, by Richard Goode.

Federal Tax Treatment of Foreign Income, by Lawrence B. Krause and Kenneth W. Dam.

Measuring Benefits of Government Investments, Robert Dorfman, Editor.

Federal Budget Policy, by David J. Ott and Attiat F. Ott.

Financing State and Local Governments, by James A. Maxwell.

Essays in Fiscal Federalism, Richard A. Musgrave, Editor.

Economics of the Property Tax, by Dick Netzer.

A Capital Budget Statement for the U.S. Government, by Maynard S. Comiez.

Foreign Tax Policies and Economic Growth, E. Gordon Keith, Editor. A Report of the National Bureau of Economic Research and the Brookings Institution (Columbia University Press).

Defense Purchases and Regional Growth, by Roger E. Bolton.

Federal Budget Projections, by Gerhard Colm and Peter Wagner. A Report of the National Planning Association and the Brookings Institution.

Corporate Dividend Policy, by John A. Brittain.

Federal Estate and Gift Taxes, by Carl S. Shoup.

Federal Tax Policy, by Joseph A. Pechman.

Economic Behavior of the Affluent, by Robin Barlow, Harvey E. Brazer, and James N. Morgan.

Intergovernmental Fiscal Relations in the United States, by George F. Break.

Studies in the Economics of Income Maintenance, Otto Eckstein, Editor.

Trusts and Estate Taxation, by Gerald R. Jantscher.

Negative Taxes and the Poverty Problem, by Christopher Green.

Negative Taxes and

the Poverty Problem

CHRISTOPHER GREEN

A background paper prepared for a conference
of experts held June 8-9, 1966, together
with a summary of the conference discussion

Studies of Government Finance

THE BROOKINGS INSTITUTION

WASHINGTON, D.C.

THE BROOKINGS INSTITUTION is an independent organization devoted to nonpartisan research, education, and publication in
economics, government, foreign policy, and the social sciences
generally. Its principal purposes are to aid in the development of sound public
policies and to promote public understanding of issues of national importance.

The Institution was founded December 8, 1927, to merge the activities of
the Institute for Government Research, founded in 1916, the Institute of
Economics, founded in 1922, and the Robert Brookings Graduate School of
Economics and Government, founded in 1924.

The general administration of the Institution is the responsibility of a
self-perpetuating Board of Trustees. The trustees are likewise charged with
maintaining the independence of the staff and fostering the most favorable
conditions for creative research and education. The immediate direction of
the policies, program, and staff of the Institution is vested in the President,
assisted by the program directors and an advisory council, chosen from the
professional staff of the Institution.

In publishing a study, the Institution presents it as a competent treatment
of a subject worthy of public consideration. The interpretations and conclusions in such publications are those of the author or authors and do not
purport to represent the views of the other staff members, officers, or trustees
of the Brookings Institution.

Foreword

IN THE PAST FEW YEARS, increasing attention has been given to the idea of using the tax system as a possible method of helping families who are below the poverty levels. The traditional method has been through public welfare and other direct payments (for example, old-age assistance, aid to families with dependent children, and so on). These programs reach specific categories of families, but provide little or no assistance to a large number of poor persons. While the welfare system and the tax system developed in response to different pressures, it has been increasingly recognized that one may be regarded as an extension of the other. Direct assistance to persons with low incomes is an extension of progression into the lowest brackets, with negative rather than positive rates.

This volume on negative taxes by Professor Christopher Green, now of the economics faculty of North Carolina State University, was originally prepared as a doctoral dissertation at the University of Wisconsin. It was used as the background paper for a conference of experts held at the Brookings Institution on June 8 and 9, 1966. The conference discussion is summarized in Chapter X and a list of the conference participants is given on pages 177-78.

The author wishes to acknowledge a great intellectual and personal debt to Robert J. Lampman, who suggested the topic and acted as guide and critic throughout the study. He is also indebted to Harold M. Groves and Burton A. Weisbrod for their extensive comments on major sections of the manuscript. Comments by the Reading Committee, consisting of Jesse Burkhead, Otto Eckstein, and Rashi Fein, and by Joseph A. Pechman were extremely helpful in putting the manuscript into final form. Numerous technical problems were worked out in discussions with Joseph Bell, Michael D. Bird, Gerard M. Brannon, Edwin T. Burton III, James M. Lyday, Benjamin A. Okner, David J. Ott, Floyd O. Reeves, Heather L. Ross, Gabriel G. Rudney, and Walter Williams. Lenore A. Epstein, Joseph A. Kershaw, Robert A. Levine, Ida C. Merriam, Mollie Orshansky, Alvin Schorr, James Tobin, and Harold W. Watts gave up valuable time to discuss related matters. Several typists—Edna Breedlove, Lynnette Jones, Alice Wilcox, and Peggy Snyder—were especially helpful during the early stages of the background paper. Virginia D. Parker edited the manuscript and Florence Robinson prepared the index.

The author is grateful for permission to use tabulations based on the Survey of Consumer Expenditures of the Bureau of Labor Statistics which were made by the Office of Tax Analysis of the U. S. Treasury Department. He also wishes to express appreciation to the National Science Foundation and the Office of Economic Opportunity for financial assistance during the preparation of this study. A research position with the Wisconsin Institute for Research on Poverty enabled him to prepare the volume for publication.

This book is part of the Brookings series of Studies of Government Finance, a special program of research and education in taxation and government expenditures at the federal, state, and local levels. It was sponsored by the National Committee on Government Finance, which was established in 1960, and supported with funds provided by the Ford Foundation.

Robert D. Calkins
President

June 1967
Washington, D.C.

Studies of Government Finance

Studies of Government Finance is a special program of research and education in taxation and government expenditures at the federal, state, and local levels. This program is under the supervision of the National Committee on Government Finance appointed by the trustees of the Brookings Institution, and is supported by a special grant from the Ford Foundation.

MEMBERS OF THE ADVISORY COMMITTEE

Contents

Text Tables

Figures

Appendix Tables

CHAPTER I

Introduction

SINCE THE DEPRESSION of the 1930's, public programs to improve standards of living have received increasing support in the United States. The most well-established and far-reaching of the federal programs are public assistance to the traditional categories of the poor—the aged, the disabled, and dependent children—and the wage-related social security and unemployment insurance programs. More recently, with the start of the war on poverty, programs were introduced to provide opportunities for better training and education of the poor.

While these programs have helped to reduce poverty and its accompanying social and economic problems, about one-fifth of the U. S. population still ekes out a living on an income below the so-called poverty line—the amount of income recognized in the United States as that required to maintain a decent standard of living. And of this fifth of a nation, a surprisingly large proportion of the very poor families receive no direct assistance other than the public services available to everyone, whether rich or poor.

In recent years, there have been a series of proposals to supplement or complement the present programs by using the federal tax system to close all or part of the poverty gap—that is, the gap between the income of poor families and the income they need to move above the poverty line. The proponents of these proposals are in favor of extending the income tax system into the lowest income

1

brackets through the adoption of negative, rather than positive, tax rates. By making payments based on negative tax rates to persons who have incomes below some specified line and by collecting positive taxes from persons with incomes above that line, the government could operate a single system for the giving and taking of income. Some advocates of these proposals also believe that such a system might increase work incentives by removing many poor persons now receiving public assistance from what amounts to a 100 percent tax bracket, since many payments under these programs are reduced by a dollar for each dollar earned.

In this volume, these tax-transfer proposals are called "transfer-by-taxation." Although the transfer-by-taxation plans differ in detail, most are distinguished from present public transfer programs by: (1) the focus on closing the poverty gap; (2) the emphasis upon income—usually related to the size of the family—in determining whether a given unit is eligible for allowances, rather than upon basing eligibility on such characteristics as age, physical disability, work history, or dependent children; and (3) the degree to which the tax system is used as a vehicle for transferring income.

In general, the plans are of two basic types. One, social dividend taxation, would fill the whole poverty gap and substantially alter the entire income distribution. The second, negative rates taxation (more commonly, but less precisely, known as negative income taxation), would close a portion of the poverty gap. Other proposals do not fit neatly into either of these types, but have some features of one or the other or of both types.

This book explores major proposals for use of tax allowances to narrow the poverty gap; compares them to each other and to present programs; analyzes costs for programs with different tax rates, breakeven levels of income, and family sizes; describes alternative methods of administering and financing the plans; and evaluates the effects of minimum income guarantees on incentives to work and on the birth rate.

Poverty in the United States

Two general, but fundamental, assumptions underlie this study of negative taxes: There is still a serious poverty problem in the United States in spite of continuing efforts during the past several decades to do away with it. More and more, society as a whole seems willing to try new ways aimed at reducing and eventually eliminating the remaining hard core of poverty. Although the extent and nature of poverty are not extensively analyzed here, a brief review of statistics on the subject serves as useful background for subsequent discussion.[1]

There were about 35.3 million "poor" persons in 1963 and 34.1 million in 1964.[2] Thus about one-fifth of the people in the United States are poor. How poor are they? The poverty index of the Social Security Administration (SSA) defines a nonfarm family of four persons as "poor" if its 1963 income was less than $3,130. For smaller and larger families, the poverty index differential is about $500 a person. What would it take to raise the income of these persons so that they would no longer be poor? As estimated by Mollie Orshansky, the poor needed $28.8 billion to cover their basic requirements in 1963. Since the poor in that year had an income of $17.3 billion, the deficit, or poverty income gap, was $11.5 billion.[3]

The continued rapid growth of personal income since 1963 has undoubtedly narrowed the poverty income gap. But other changes also could have affected the gap. Disposable income has increased as a result of changes in the income tax but decreased because of extra social security taxes; prices have increased as a result of inflation but decreased because of excise tax cuts; and the need for dollars by the aged has been reduced by the new Medicare program.

Table 1-1 shows that poverty was not confined to a few demographic groups. The poor are found in big and small families, in rural and urban areas, among the young and the aged, among the employed as well as the unemployed. As Table 1-1 shows, the chances of being poor are substantially higher than average if the family is not white or is large; or if the head of the family is old or

[1] I have relied for most of these statistics on detailed analyses reported by Mollie Orshansky of the Division of Research and Statistics, Social Security Administration.

[2] Orshansky, "Who's Who Among the Poor: A Demographic View of Poverty," *Social Security Bulletin*, Vol. 28 (July 1965), p. 4. These figures are based on a poverty index developed by the Social Security Administration of the Department of Health, Education, and Welfare.

[3] Orshansky, "Counting the Poor: Another Look at the Poverty Profile," *Social Security Bulletin*, Vol. 28 (January 1965), pp. 9 and 13.

TABLE 1-1. Characteristics of Poor Families, 1963[a]

Characteristic	Number of Poor Families (Millions)	Poor Families as Percent of All U.S. Families	Percentage Distribution of All Poor Families
All poor families	7.2	15	100
Residence:			
Farm	.7	23	10
Nonfarm	6.5	15	90
Race of head:			
White	5.2	12	72
Nonwhite	2.0	42	28
Age of head:			
14–24 years	.7	26	10
25–54 years	4.0	13	54
55–64 years	1.0	13	14
65 years and over	1.5	24	22
Type of family:			
Husband and wife	5.0	12	70
Wife in paid labor force	.9	7	13
Wife not in paid labor force	4.1	15	57
Other male head	.2	17	3
Female head	2.0	40	27
Size of family:			
Two persons	2.5	16	34
Three persons	1.0	11	14
Four persons	1.0	10	14
Five persons	.9	14	13
Six persons	.6	19	9
Seven persons or more	1.2	35	16
Related children under age 18:			
None	2.4	13	34
One	1.1	12	15
Two	1.0	11	13
Three	1.0	17	14
Four	.6	23	9
Five	.5	36	7
Six	.6	49	8
Earners in family:			
None	2.0	53	27
One	3.3	16	46
Two	1.5	9	21
Three or more	.4	7	6
Employment status and occupation of head:			
Not in labor force[b]	3.0	34	42
Unemployed	.4	28	6
Employed	3.7	10	52
Professional, technical, and kindred	.1	3	2
Farmers and farm managers	.5	29	8
Managers, officials, proprietors (nonfarm)	.3	5	4
Clerical, sales, and kindred	.2	4	3
Craftsmen, operatives, and kindred	1.2	8	17
Service, including private household	.6	20	8
Laborers (except mining)	.7	30	10
Work experience of head in 1963 (civilians):			
Worked	4.6	11	64
Worked at full-time jobs—	3.6	10	50
Worked 50 or more weeks	2.0	7	28
Worked at part-time jobs	1.0	36	14
Did not work	2.6	38	36

Source: Based on Mollie Orshansky, "Counting the Poor: Another Look at the Poverty Profile," *Social Security Bulletin*, Vol. 28 (January 1965), Table 2, p. 12. Miss Orshansky's data were derived from special tabulations by the Bureau of the Census for the Social Security Administration.

[a] Poor families, defined in the text, are those with incomes below the SSA "economy level" or poverty index.

[b] Includes approximately 900,000 family heads in the Armed Forces, of whom about 100,000 have incomes under $3,000.

a female, or is not in the labor force. But, in 1963, the heads of two million poor families worked from 50 to 52 weeks; 70 percent of the poor families were husband and wife families; 72 percent of the poor families were white; and the heads of 54 percent of the poor families were between 25 and 54 years of age.[4]

Since these figures overstated the number of poor by not accounting for assets and understated the number by omitting the "hidden poor,"[5] Miss Orshansky later attempted to make a rough adjustment for these factors. When allowance is made for the increased consumption power that would arise if all the assets were used over the aged family's remaining expected years of life, the number of aged families and unrelated individuals in poverty is reduced by only 500,000—from 5.2 million to 4.7 million.[6] However, there were 2.9 million hidden poor to offset this figure.[7]

The data indicate that disadvantages are associated with certain demographic characteristics. But the pervasive character of poverty amid affluence—although the poor are often hidden from sight, as Harrington has observed[8]—undoubtedly explains why a broad-ranging war has been declared on poverty. If poverty were confined to a homogenous group, a multifaceted antipoverty program would be less necessary.

Unique Features of an Income-Conditioned Plan

Present public transfer programs vary in coverage, eligibility for benefits, and type of benefit. These differences in such programs

[4] When Miss Orshansky followed up her "Counting the Poor" (*op. cit.*) article with that on "Who's Who Among the Poor" (*op. cit.*), which concentrated on the demographic aspect of poverty, her later findings reinforced her earlier conclusions as to the particularly disadvantaged position of the aged, children in broken families, children in large families, and the nonwhite family whatever its make-up.

[5] "Who's Who Among the Poor," *op cit.*, p. 5. The "hidden poor" are defined as "individuals or subfamily members with own income below the poverty level but living in a family above the poverty line. A subfamily represents a married couple with or without children or a parent and 1 or more children under age 18 residing in a family as relatives of the head." These persons are of interest because programs aimed at reducing poverty might bring out of "hiding" a number of persons potentially poor, but presently not counted as poor.

[6] *Ibid.*, p. 13. In taking account of assets, Miss Orshansky was limited by insufficient data to analysis of the assets of the aged.

[7] *Ibid.*, Table 1, p. 5.

[8] Michael Harrington, *The Other America* (New York: Macmillan, 1926), pp. 2-4.

as social insurance, public assistance, veterans' benefits, and special subsidies largely reflect differences in philosophy. For example, the social insurance programs are based on what amounts to a contract between the employee and the government, with coverage extended to almost all wage earners. Eligibility for benefits is not based on whether a person is or is not poor. Instead, eligibility is confined to persons who are retired or unemployed through no fault of their own or who in some way are handicapped, either because of old age or because a family's main wage earner has been disabled or has died. With the exception of health benefits, the payments for these present social insurance programs are in cash.

In contrast to the social insurance programs, public assistance is designed to meet the "needs" of some of the poor where need is measured in terms of a means test. For public assistance, a line is drawn between those persons who are able and expected to work, and those persons who are not. Most public assistance has not been aimed at helping poor families headed by an able-bodied earner. Work relief, retraining, and minimum wage legislation have been the order of the day for the able-bodied. Public assistance cat-egories pinpoint families that are unlikely to have an able-bodied person who is expected to work. Thus, the two most important pub-lic assistance programs are old-age assistance and aid to dependent children. The general assistance (or "relief") program is an exception to the rule regarding the able-bodied poor, but the number of per-sons currently receiving general assistance is small, indicating that they are exceptions that tend to prove the rule (Chapter III). Public assistance benefits may be in cash or in kind—that is, they may in-clude housing, food, counseling, etc., as well as cash.

Coverage under the program for veterans is based on the status as a veteran. Eligibility for benefits is sometimes, but not always, based on need. Some of the benefits are in cash, others are pay-ments-in-kind in the form of medical and educational services. In the United States, the veterans' program is the only public transfer program of the federal government which is so clearly based on sta-tus. In other countries, an aged person or a dependent child auto-matically qualifies for a "demogrant"—that is, a payment based on demographic status.

Beyond the public transfer programs, numerous public expendi-tures are designed to provide for such "social wants" as public health and for "merit wants" such as education, medical care, and housing.[9] Public programs also pay subsidies to producers on the basis of social needs (for example, airline subsidies) or preferred occupations (for example, farm subsidies). These programs are outside the scope of this book, but warrant mention to help illustrate that public programs making cash payments and payments-in-kind to individual households and firms embody many different philosophies.

The rationale of transfer-by-taxation differs from present public transfer, service, and subsidy programs in that coverage is universal and all payments are in cash. Benefits are determined under a transfer-by-taxation plan with no attention paid to why a person or family is poor. As a matter of "right," everyone has access to the benefits, which are conditioned only upon the level of the person's or family's income. This contrasts especially with the view implicit in the public assistance and unemployment compensation programs that, in providing assistance, society must be protected against the loafer—the person who can work but is unwilling to do so. The refusal to draw a line between the able-bodied poor and those persons with some form of disability seems to be at the heart of the difference between transfer-by-taxation and present income maintenance programs, especially public assistance. And unlike some of the public transfer programs, transfer-by-taxation is designed to supplement the earnings of the working poor. Of course, a transfer-by-taxation plan could include a provision that individuals, or families with heads who are able but unwilling to work, are not eligible to receive transfer-by-taxation allowances. However, such a provision is rarely contemplated in negative tax proposals.

Transfer-by-taxation seems to differ from the public assistance programs in another way by taking an aggregate approach to poverty. It concentrates on closing the poverty gap by transferring income from those with higher incomes to those who are poor. While public assistance contributes to the alleviation of poverty (Chapter

---

[9] Social wants have been defined as "those wants satisfied by services that must be consumed in equal amounts by all. People who do not pay for the services cannot be excluded from the benefits that result." Merit wants were defined as wants "that could be serviced through the market but are not, since consumers choose to spend their money on other things." Budgetary action is taken to correct individual choice. See Richard A. Musgrave, *The Theory of Public Finance* (New York: McGraw-Hill, 1959), pp. 8-9.

II), its emphasis—as indicated by the role of the social worker—is upon the individual and the reasons why he or she is poor.[10]

Transfer-by-taxation has a superficial similarity to a minimum wage law, but there are important differences. Explicit in a minimum wage law is the philosophical view that no one should work for less than a specified amount. Implied, then, is some notion of a minimum income. However, a minimum wage law not only fails to touch families without an earning member, it may also backfire if unemployment is produced because the minimum wage guarantees hourly earnings in excess of the value of the product of some workers.[11] In contrast, the proposed tax-transfer plans can guarantee a minimum income without creating the involuntary unemployment often associated with minimum wages.

The transfer-by-taxation proposals contrast with—but are certainly not incompatible with—the antipoverty programs originating under the Economic Opportunity Act. The programs under the Economic Opportunity Act are aimed at making the poor more productive future earners; the transfer-by-taxation proposals would give dollars directly to the poor. Thus transfer-by-taxation can be considered as a complement of the antipoverty programs; and, as a complement, it could open up a new front in the war on poverty. It is not inconsistent to provide money income for the poor and at the

[10] For a discussion of the role of the social worker—which may be defined broadly as the art of helping people to help themselves to cope more effectively with their problems—see Helen H. Perlman, *Social Casework: A Problem Solving Process* (Chicago: University of Chicago Press, 1957); Rex A. Skidmore and Milton G. Thackeray, *Introduction to Social Work* (New York: Meredith Publishing Co., 1964); Herbert H. Stroup, *Social Work: An Introduction to the Field* (New York: American Book Company, 1953).

[11] The classic debate on the employment effects of higher wages is that between Lester, Machlup, and Stigler. Richard A. Lester, "Shortcomings of Marginal Analysis for Wage-Employment Problems," *American Economic Review*, Vol. 36 (March 1946), pp. 63-82. George Stigler, "The Economics of Minimum Wage Legislation," *American Economic Review*, Vol. 36 (June 1946), pp. 358-65. Fritz Machlup, "Marginal Analysis and Empirical Research," *American Economic Review*, Vol. 36 (September 1946), pp. 519-54. Lester's Reply and Rejoinders by Stigler and Machlup are in the *American Economic Review*, Vol. 37 (March 1947). Also see Fred Blum, "Marginalism and Economic Policy: A Comment," *American Economic Review*, Vol. 37 (September 1947), pp. 645-52. More recent work has been done by John Peterson in "Employment Effects of Minimum Wages, 1938-1950," *Journal of Political Economy*, Vol. 65 (October 1957), pp. 412-30; and "Research Needs in Minimum Wage Theory," *Southern Economic Journal*, Vol. 29 (July 1962), pp. 1-9.

same time to make government expenditures for raising the productivity of the poor. An important purpose of transfer-by-taxation and other income maintenance schemes is to break the vicious circle of poor education, low productivity, and low income. Transfer-by-taxation also embodies the principle that the poor can be trusted to allocate their own funds without government supervision. Those who support transfer-by-taxation believe that public programs should increase individual freedom of choice and reduce impediments to the operation of the market system.

Transfer-by-Taxation and Progressive Taxation

Use of the federal income tax system to close the poverty gap would imply that society will go beyond the ability-to-pay justification for progressive income taxation. Under transfer-by-taxation, the income tax system would be used directly to reduce income inequality, although such reduction may not be the main objective of a given transfer-by-taxation plan. This raises serious philosophical issues that have been debated at length.[12] While these issues generally will be by-passed in this book, two comments are warranted.

The ability-to-pay principle is not necessarily incompatible with a plan for reducing economic inequality directly. True, some early proponents of the ability-to-pay principle held that it is not the function of the income tax system to reduce economic inequality; that social reform should be effected through government expenditures and not by taxation.[13] By extending tax rates below zero to

[12] See E. R. A. Seligman, *Progressive Taxation in Theory and Practice,* publication of the American Economic Association, Vol. 9, Nos. 1 and 2 (1894); Henry C. Simons, *Personal Income Taxation* (Chicago: University of Chicago Press, 1938); Elmer F. Fagan, "Recent and Contemporary Theories of Progressive Taxation," *Journal of Political Economy,* Vol. 46 (August 1938), pp. 457-98; Walter J. Blum and Harry Kalven, Jr., *The Uneasy Case for Progressive Taxation* (Chicago: University of Chicago Press, 1953); Harold M. Groves, "Toward a Social Theory of Progressive Taxation," *National Tax Journal,* Vol. 9 (March 1956), pp. 27-34.

[13] Seligman, *op. cit.,* p. 69. Simons, *op. cit.,* p. 16, is roundly critical of Seligman's argument that expenditure, but not taxation, is the tool for improving income distribution. However, Simons did not reach the conclusion that the tax system should redistribute income directly through the process of transferring income.

negative levels, the income tax system can reduce income inequality through transfers. Early proponents of the ability-to-pay principle excluded from the list of services to be paid for out of income taxes the service of providing a guaranteed minimum income. But once this service is included, it is hard to avoid the conclusion that the ability-to-pay principle is inseparable from at least one form of reduction in economic inequality—that is, cutting off the lower end of the income distribution.

The relationship between transfer-by-taxation and the progression issue can be considered in another way. This approach begins by noting that the personal exemptions in the present income tax system add an element of progressivity that would remain even if the graduated marginal rates were abandoned in favor of a single income tax rate. The main justification for personal exemptions stems from the view that only "clear income" is taxable, that providing the basic necessities of life is a cost to be deducted from gross income in arriving at net (taxable) income. Transfer-by-taxation adds the view that the tax system should, in the absence of taxable income, make refunds in some proportion to the failure of a family to achieve a clear income. A similar proposal is to give each taxpayer and dependent a tax credit which is equal to, or some fraction of, the costs of subsistence. Possibly transfer-by-taxation may add a dimension to the concept of personal exemptions which has not been contemplated by the proponents of a clear-income basis for income taxation. But this new dimension is a logical extension of the clear-income concept. Proponents claim that transfer-by-taxation avoids the "stigma" attached to allowances viewed simply as a subsidy to social outcasts, and rest their case on the added protection or economic security afforded every family by an income tax system with rates which do not stop at zero.[14]

The Main Issues

A summary of the main issues discussed in Chapters II through IX—the section of this book which served as a background paper for the Brookings conference of experts—falls roughly into two

[14] The case for transfer-by-taxation does not rest only on the modicum of economic security that it affords to every family. The discussion in Chapter III suggests that it may be the most efficient way to reduce the poverty income gap.

parts. Chapters II and III develop the relevance of transfer-by-taxation to the present scene. Chapters IV through IX deal directly with transfer-by-taxation plans, without, however, advocating one type of plan in preference to another. The main issues, in brief, follow:

1. The existing system of monetary transfer payments closes about three-fifths of the before-transfer poverty gap. In doing so, about one-third of the families who had been poor before the transfers are pulled out of poverty. Some of the remaining two-thirds receive transfer income that closes less than 50 percent of that group's before-transfer poverty gap.

2. There are several alternative ways further to reduce the poverty gap. The present social insurance and public assistance programs could be broadened to contribute more in filling the poverty gap. However, since public assistance is directed only to the disadvantaged poor in specific categories and social insurance is related to wages in the United States, the nature of these programs seriously limits their effectiveness as antipoverty tools. Family allowances have a good deal in common with transfer-by-taxation—especially the social dividend type of transfer, which would fill the whole poverty gap. The main difference is that payment of such allowances is limited to families with children.

3. All transfer-by-taxation plans have in common at least three basic variables. Each has a guaranteed minimum level of income; a "tax" rate at which allowances are reduced for each dollar of increase in before-allowance income; and a breakeven level of income at which the allowance is reduced to zero. The magnitudes of two of these variables determine the magnitude of the third, and transfer-by-taxation plans differ to the extent that the three magnitudes differ. In fact, these comments extend to any type of proposal assuring a minimum income to everyone.

4. A negative rates taxation plan would not necessitate any major changes in the present positive individual income tax system. A social dividend plan, however, would be so expensive, and would pay net allowances to so many persons who now pay taxes, that the present individual income tax system would have to undergo major changes.

5. The income measure used for determining the level of negative rates taxation allowances should reflect a welfare concept of

income. The family's money income more nearly approximates a welfare definition than does adjusted gross income—the definition which is now used for income tax purposes. Financing a social dividend plan would require a tax base considerably broader than the present definition of taxable income.

6. The tax unit used for determining eligibility for transfer-by-taxation allowances should reflect a welfare unit. The family would seem to be a better approximation of the basic welfare unit than the present tax unit which is composed of the individual and his or her dependents.

7. The problems involving determination of eligibility for allowances, the timing of allowance payments, and administration of allowance payments are difficult but it is by no means impossible to solve them.

8. Evidence on the probable effects of representative transfer-by-taxation plans on work incentives and on birth rates is inconclusive. Most of the studies of the effects of high tax rates on work incentives are based on upper income groups. It is not clear that the findings would carry over to groups with low incomes. The probable effect of such a tax plan upon the total birth rate is small, although there might be an initial stimulus to the birth rate among poor families.

9. Representative plans for negative rates taxation would cost from $5 billion to $9 billion a year. A typical social dividend plan would cost about $30 billion annually. There is no wholly satisfactory way to eliminate the income gap of poor families in the United States. Raising revenues only to match the $12 billion poverty gap would not prove to be an undue economic burden. But to close the gap completely would undoubtedly require far more than $12 billion in transfer-by-taxation allowances. Filling the gap would require an effective tax on before-allowance income at a 100 percent rate and, therefore, would encourage many earners to reduce their work effort. This difficulty cannot be avoided by using any one of the alternative income maintenance programs such as public assistance or social insurance.

In Chapter X, the summary of discussion at the conference of experts held at the Brookings Institution in June 1966 further points up the major issues in transfer-by-taxation. The conference participants agreed generally that some form of income-conditioned grant is desirable. By this, they meant a grant not restricted to the poor with specified categories of disadvantages such as age, illness, or inability to seek work. While the conferees recognized that a negative tax device is neither a simple means, nor a wholly satisfactory one, for improving the existing income maintenance system, many of them favored further study and adoption of such a device.

CHAPTER II

How Transfer Payments
Can Alleviate Poverty

PUBLIC TRANSFER PAYMENTS may properly be thought of as "negative taxes." Similarly, taxes paid could be thought of as "negative transfers"—at least when such taxes directly reduce disposable income. The concepts of negative taxes and negative transfers follow from a broad view of the relation of the public treasury to the individual family unit. Just as government in the United States has constructed an intricate and varied system for raising revenues, it has also developed a varied system for transferring income to certain population groups. Although the two systems usually are not related directly, it is useful to consider a family's net account with government.

Transfer Payments and the Extent of Poverty

A first step in this study is to seek some understanding of what present monetary transfer programs in the United States do to reduce poverty and what effect taxes have upon the extent of poverty. The present system of public transfers has been important in keeping many families out of poverty and in reducing the before-transfer "income gap" (that is, the difference between a family's earnings

14

and its poverty line) of many more poor families. Most public transfers are made under one of the following social welfare programs: old-age, survivors, disability, and health insurance; unemployment compensation; public assistance; and veterans' compensation and pensions.

The estimates in Tables 2-1 through 2-4 understate what is presently done for the poor in three ways. First, the estimates exclude all nonmonetary benefits. For example, some poor families are provided with income-in-kind in the form of surplus food and medical services. In addition, there are vocational training programs and the newly created community programs established under the Economic Opportunity Act. Training programs (some of which include subsistence payments) and community programs are designed to increase future income by raising the productivity of the poor and by increasing their ability to cope with the complexities and demands of modern society.

A second reason for understatement is that the estimates are based on data from the Survey of Consumer Expenditures made by the Bureau of Labor Statistics (BLS) in 1960-61. This BLS Survey provides the only recent data on what the public transfer programs do separately and as a whole for poor families and individuals. The use of 1961 data on transfer payments understates the present contribution, in absolute terms at least, of the public transfer programs in meeting the needs of the poor. For example, total public monetary transfer payments amounted to $36.6 billion in fiscal year 1965 compared with $29.4 billion in fiscal year 1961.[1]

Third, almost any survey of family income is subject to underreporting, and public transfer income is no exception to the rule. For example, the BLS Survey shows receipts of only $2.6 billion in public assistance and $2.7 billion in unemployment compensation. However, the Social Security Administration (SSA) reports that in 1961 public assistance benefits amounted to $4.1 billion and unemployment compensation to $4.0 billion.[2] The figures of the Social

---

[1] U. S. Department of Health, Education, and Welfare (HEW), *Social Security Bulletin*, Vol. 28 (October 1965), Table 1, p. 4. Public monetary transfers include social insurance, public assistance less vendor medical payments, and veterans' pensions and compensation. The figures also include administrative costs of the programs.

[2] HEW, *Social Security Bulletin*, Vol. 29 (June 1966), Tables 14 and 17, pp. 34 and 38.

Security Administration include administrative costs and other items such as vendor medical payments in public assistance and expenses of the U. S. Employment Service in unemployment compensation, which are not included in the BLS estimates. But this does not completely explain the difference between the two sets of figures.

Effect of Transfer Payments on the Number of Poor Families

How many families are taken out of poverty by the U.S. system of transfer payments? Table 2-1 shows that in 1961 there were 13.6 million families with 38.5 million persons who were classed as poor before income was transferred.[3] Thus, in 1961, almost 25 percent of all families had to be classified as poor on the basis of their before-transfer income. After receiving transfer income, 8.9 million families with 27.2 million persons were still poor. Transfer payments had the effect in 1961 of raising 4.7 million families (11.3 million persons) out of poverty. Transfer payments reduced the number of poor families by 35 percent and the number of poor persons by 29 percent. Overall, transfers lowered the percentage of all poor families to all families in the country from 25 to 16 percent. Clearly, then, the transfer system plays an important role in reducing the incidence of poverty.

Table 2-1 also shows that the incidence of poverty is not uniform for all family sizes. Very small and very large families (those with one, two, and six or more persons to the family) are much more likely to be poor than medium-sized families of three to five members. Furthermore, the role played by transfer payments in keeping families out of poverty is not uniform for all family sizes. Line 5 of Table 2-1 shows that transfer payments did a better job of raising small families out of poverty than they did in raising larger families out of poverty. For family sizes of one to three members, the reduction of poor families ranged from 33 to 46 percent. For families with four or more members, the reduction in poverty ranged from 26 down to 16 percent. It may be that the present bet-

[3] Adjusted gross income (AGI) was used as a proxy for before-transfer or factor income. The tables, based on the BLS survey, produced estimates of types of income and numbers of families by family size and by both money income and AGI income classes. The poverty lines adopted, as noted in Table 2-1, are $1,500 for a single member or head of family and $500 for each additional member of the family.

TABLE 2-1. Effect of Transfer Payments in Reducing Poverty, 1961[a]
(Number of families and persons in thousands)

Type of Family	Members in Family Unit						Total Families	Total Persons in Families
	One	Two	Three	Four	Five	Six or More		
(1) All families in population	8,488	16,656	9,805	9,019	5,621	5,715	55,304	175,401
(2) Before-transfer poor families	3,971	4,596	1,443	833	816	1,937	13,596	38,463
(3) After-transfer poor families	2,643	2,499	878	627	603	1,628	8,878	27,194
(4) Families made nonpoor by transfers, (2)–(3)	1,328	2,097	565	206	213	309	4,718	11,269
(5) Percentage reduction in poor families, [(4)÷(2)]×100	33.4	45.6	39.1	24.7	26.1	15.9	34.7	29.3
(6) Before-transfer poor as percentage of all families, [(2)÷(1)]×100	46.8	27.6	14.7	9.2	14.5	33.9	24.6	21.9
(7) After-transfer poor as percentage of all families, [(3)÷(1)]×100	31.0	15.0	8.9	6.9	10.7	28.5	16.1	15.5

Source: Data from U. S. Department of the Treasury, Office of Tax Analysis, based on special tabulations of the Survey of Consumer Expenditures, 1960–61, of the Bureau of Labor Statistics, U. S. Department of Labor.

[a] Poverty lines are $1,500 for a single member or head of family and $500 for each additional member of the family.

ter record of help for small families is a result of the importance in the present transfer system of the old-age, survivors, disability, and health insurance.

How many poor families receive transfer income of some kind? Unfortunately, it is not possible to answer this question directly. The BLS data give numbers of families receiving broad classes of transfers such as the following: (1) "public benefits and pensions"— including old-age, survivors and disability insurance (OASDI), other public and private pensions (received mainly by former government employees), unemployment compensation, and workmen's compensation; (2) public and private relief—including public assistance, private nonfamily assistance, and interfamily cash gifts; and (3) veterans' compensation and pensions. Undoubtedly there is overlapping; for example, some beneficiaries of OASDI also received public assistance or veterans' pensions.

Table 2-2 shows that a minimum of 8.3 million and a maximum of 13.6 million before-transfer poor families received transfer payments. The corresponding figures for the after-transfer poor are 4.4 million and 8.0 million families. Lines 6, 7, and 8 show what percentage of the poor received a particular class of transfer payment. Of those families who were poor before receiving transfer income, 61 percent received public benefits and pensions, 35 percent received relief of some sort, and 10 percent received veterans' compensation or pensions. The number of after-transfer poor receiving public benefits and pensions, relief, and veterans' compensation and pensions was 49 percent, 36 percent, and 5 percent, respectively. Of those families who were made nonpoor by transfer, 84 percent re-

TABLE 2-2. Number of Families Receiving Transfer Income, 1961[a]

Families	Public Benefits and Pensions (1)	Public and Private Relief (2)	Veterans' Pensions and Compensation (3)	Range of Totals[b] (4)
Receiving transfer income (in thousands):				
(1) All receiving transfers	17,712	14,117	3,634	17,712–35,463
(2) Before-transfer poor	8,346	4,800	1,396	8,346–13,596
(3) After-transfer poor	4,382	3,195	424	4,382– 8,001
(4) Made nonpoor by transfers	3,964	1,605	972	4,718
Percentage receiving transfer income:				
(5) All receiving transfers	32.0	25.5	6.6	32.0– 64.1
(6) Before-transfer poor	61.4	35.3	10.3	61.4–100.0
(7) After-transfer poor	49.3	36.0	4.8	49.3– 90.1
(8) Made nonpoor by transfers	84.0	34.0	20.6	100.0

Source: U.S. Treasury Department, Office of Tax Analysis, based on special tabulations of the Survey of Consumer Expenditures, 1960–61, of the Bureau of Labor Statistics.
[a] See text for explanation of the types of transfers in the broad classes shown in columns 1, 2, and 3.
[b] There is overlapping in the totals since some of the families receive at least two of the three broad types of transfers.

ceived public benefits and pensions, 34 percent received relief, and 21 percent received veterans' payments.

Portion of Transfers Received by the Poor

What portion of total and specific transfer payments went to poor families? Table 2-3 shows that 51.2 percent of all transfer payments, public and private, were received by families who before receiving transfer income were poor. Thus, the nonpoor received 48.8 percent of total transfer payments. Only 23 percent of transfer income went to families who were still poor after receiving transfer income. If interfamily gifts were excluded from total transfer payments shown in the table, the percentage of transfer income going to the before-transfer poor would rise to 53.6 percent and that to the after-transfer poor would rise to 24.4 percent.

BEFORE-TRANSFER POOR. Table 2-3 also shows how each of the major public transfer programs contributed to the reduction of poverty. Line 6 shows what percentage of transfer payments went to families who were poor before they received transfers, with 93 percent shown for public and private assistance payments and 63 percent for OASDI payments.[4] These percentages make public assistance the most important transfer program per dollar expended from the point of view of the poor. Judged on the basis of the number of dollars expended on the poor, OASDI is the most important social welfare program. Line 6 indicates also that only 36 percent of unemployment compensation payments and 46 percent of veterans' pensions and compensation were received by families who were poor on a before-transfer basis. As shown in line 10, these two programs when combined accounted for less than 18 percent of all transfer payments received by the before-transfer poor, as contrasted with the contribution made by OASDI and public assistance, which together accounted for about 73 percent.

AFTER-TRANSFER POOR. Those who were still poor after transfers (that is, the poor measured on the basis of their total money income) received 23 percent of all transfer payments, and these also largely consisted of OASDI and public assistance payments (line 7, Table 2-3). Public assistance is the only major social welfare program with more than half of its payments (69 percent) going to the after-transfer poor.[5] Although only 24 percent of OASDI payments went to the after-transfer poor, such payments still accounted for almost half (47 percent) of transfer payments received by the after-transfer poor; and for this group, unemployment compensation and veterans' pensions and compensation together accounted for only about 12 percent of the transfer payments (line 11).

[4] The 7 percent of public assistance payments which was received by nonpoor families (on a before-transfer basis) may represent payments under aid to dependent children to foster parents and/or OAA payments to elderly persons living with nonpoor families.

[5] The fact that this figure is so much less than 100 percent is interesting in light of the fact that public assistance programs are not designed to provide payments which would raise family income to poverty line levels. However, a good number of aged persons who received OASDI transfers also received public assistance payments and together the two programs may raise aged families above the poverty line.

TABLE 2-3. Transfer Income Received from Major Programs, 1961

Transfer Payments	OASDI	Unem-ployment Compen-sation	Public Assis-tance[a]	Veterans' Pensions and Compen-sation	Other Trans-fers[b]	Totals
Payments (in $ million) Received by:						
(1) All families	12,145	2,684	2,591	3,226	6,413	27,059
(2) Before-transfer poor families	7,639	961	2,406	1,471	1,371	13,848
(3) After-transfer poor families	2,937	424	1,777	356	787	6,280
(4) Families made nonpoor by transfers	4,702	537	629	1,114	585	7,568
Percentage Total Transfers Received by:						
(5) All families	100.0	100.0	100.0	100.0	100.0	100.0
(6) Before-transfer poor families	62.9	35.8	92.9	45.6	22.4	51.2
(7) After-transfer poor families	24.2	15.8	68.6	11.0	12.3	23.2
(8) Families made nonpoor by transfers	38.7	20.0	24.3	34.5	9.1	28.0
Percentage Transfer Payment to Total Transfer Payments Received by:						
(9) All families	44.9	9.9	9.6	11.9	23.7	100.0
(10) Before-transfer poor families	55.2	6.9	17.4	10.6	9.4	100.0
(11) After-transfer poor families	46.8	6.7	28.3	5.7	12.5	100.0
(12) Families made nonpoor by transfers	62.1	7.1	8.3	14.7	7.7	100.0
(13) Percentage of transfers re-ceived by before-transfer poor families which con-tributed to making them non-poor, (4)÷(2)	61.5	55.9	26.1	75.7	42.7	54.7

Source: U.S. Treasury Department, Office of Tax Analysis, based on special tabulations of the Survey of Consumer Expenditures, 1960–61, of the Bureau of Labor Statistics.

[a] The BLS figures lump public and private assistance (for example, church charity) together. However, so much of the assistance actually is public assistance that it can be so described for purposes of this table.

[b] Other transfers include: old-age, survivors and disability insurance payments made under the railroad, federal civilian employee, and state and local employee programs. It also includes workmen's compensation and interfamily gifts. It does not include interest on state, local, or national debt.

THOSE MADE NONPOOR BY TRANSFERS. Overall, 28 percent of all transfer payments contributed to lifting families out of poverty, and this amounted to more than half of all transfer payments going to the before-transfer poor (lines 6, 7, and 8 of Table 2-3). This 55 percent, in dollar terms, was composed primarily of OASDI payments and secondarily of veterans' compensation and pensions (line 13). Over 60 percent of all transfers which contributed to making poor families nonpoor were made under the OASDI program.

Effect of Transfer Payments on the Poverty Gap

What do transfers add to the income of the poor? Table 2-4 provides some answers, again based on the BLS Survey of 1961 expenditures. Line 7 shows that transfer income was 48 percent of the total money income (TMI) of the before-transfer poor, 42 percent

TABLE 2-4. Amounts Added by Transfers to the Income of the Poor, 1961[a]

(*Dollar amounts in millions*)

Item	Before-Transfer Poor	After-Transfer Poor	Families Made Nonpoor by Transfers
(1) Income needed in order not to be poor	$32,734	$22,476	$10,258
(2) Before-transfer income[a]	14,764	8,582	6,182
(3) Before-transfer poverty gap, (1)–(2)	17,970	13,894	4,076
(4) Transfer income	13,848	6,280	7,568
(5) Total money income[b]	28,730	14,969	13,761
(6) Transfers as a percentage of before-transfer poverty gap, (4)÷(3)	77.0	45.2	185.7
(7) Transfers as a percentage of total money income, (4)÷(5)	48.2	42.0	55.0

Source: U.S. Treasury Department, Office of Tax Analysis, based on special tabulations of Survey of Consumer Expenditures, 1960–61, of the Bureau of Labor Statistics.

[a] Adjusted gross income (AGI) is used as a proxy for before-transfer income. Total AGI reported in the BLS Survey was $323.1 billion.

[b] Total money income (TMI) reported in the BLS Survey was $348.0 billion. Note that lines 2 and 4 do not add to line 5, since AGI plus transfer income does not necessarily equal TMI, although it is close to TMI.

of the TMI of the after-transfer poor, and 55 percent of the TMI of families made nonpoor by transfers. Line 6 shows that transfer income received by the before-transfer poor amounted to 77 percent of their poverty income gap.[6] Since some of these transfers raised family income above the poverty line level, transfers closed only about 60 percent of the before-transfer poverty income gap. Of those families still poor after receiving transfer income, transfers filled 45 percent of the poverty income gap. For those families made nonpoor by transfers, transfer income on the average was almost double the poverty income gap.

Of those lifted out of poverty, 85 percent were small families— that is, families with three or fewer members.[7] This bias in favor of

[6] Here "poverty income gap" signifies the difference between the poverty line and AGI.

[7] Small families made up 74 percent of the before-transfer poor.

small families is indicated in the following list showing transfers to the before-transfer poor as a percentage of the before-transfer poverty income gap for each family size:

Members in Family	Percent Poverty Gap
One	78
Two	104
Three	89
Four	79
Five	51
Six or more	40
All family sizes	77

Comparison of BLS and Census Estimates

The BLS estimates based on the Survey of Consumer Expenditures, 1960-61, in several respects do not agree with those derived from the data based on the Current Population Survey of the Bureau of the Census which is used by the Social Security Administration. Census data are available for 1961 and 1964. Thus, it is possible both to compare Census and BLS data for 1961 and to gauge the changes which would occur in the preceding tables if later BLS data had been available.[8]

The SSA estimate for the number of poor persons in 1961 is 38.1 million in 13.0 million poor households.[9] By 1964, the number of poor was down to 34.1 million persons in 11.9 million households, according to SSA figures; with a reduction, respectively, of 10.5 percent and 8.5 percent. If these percentages are applied to the BLS estimates of 27.2 million persons and 8.9 million families (Table 2-1, line 3), the number of BLS after-transfer poor persons and families, in 1964, would have dropped to 24.3 million and 8.1 million, respectively.

[8] Some of the following estimates based on Census data are my own; others are those of Mollie Orshansky. My estimates use poverty lines of $1,500 for an unrelated individual, $2,000 for a couple and $500 for each additional family member, rather than the poverty lines developed by the Social Security Administration. The SSA figures also take account of the income-in-kind of farmers; no such account is taken in my figures. The SSA poverty lines may be found in Mollie Orshansky, "Recounting the Poor—A Five-Year Review," *Social Security Bulletin*, Vol. 29 (April 1966), Table 1, p. 23.

[9] Orshansky, *ibid.*, p. 24. Households are Census families (composed of two or more persons) plus unrelated individuals.

The BLS after-transfer poor received total money income of about $15 billion (Table 2-4, line 5). The comparable Census figure for 1961 is $18.9 billion, and for 1964 is $16.8 billion. The BLS estimate of the poverty gap for 1961 is about $7.5 billion (Table 2-4, line 4). The Census estimate of the poverty gap, in 1961, is $15.0 billion; but by 1964 the Census poverty gap had been reduced to $12.3 billion.[10] A comparable reduction in the BLS estimate would produce a figure of $6.1 billion for 1964.

Data from Census for 1964 and from BLS for 1961 indicate that the poor received about a fourth of total OASDI benefits. However, whereas Census data indicate that the poor received about three-fifths of the combined total of unemployment compensation and public assistance payments, the BLS data indicate the fraction is only about two-fifths.[11]

Data of the BLS show that transfers, in 1961, were 42 percent of the total money income of the after-transfer poor. A Census estimate for 1961 is not available. However, Census data for 1964 indicate that transfers were about 40 percent of the money income of the poor.[12] The SSA figures also show that the three major public transfer programs (OASDI, unemployment compensation, and public assistance) made up 36 percent of the income of the poor.[13] The comparable figure from the BLS Survey is 35 percent.

The significant differences between the BLS and Census estimates are not easily bridged. However, some important ways in which the Census Survey differs from the BLS Survey can be pinned down. Differences in the definition of the family unit and in the time period to which the composition of the family and its income refer undoubtedly account for an important part of the varia-

[10] The Census figures for 1961 and 1964 money income are my estimates based on data in U. S. Bureau of the Census, *Current Population Reports,* Series P-60, No. 39, Table 5, p. 18 (for 1961), and Series P-60, No. 47, Table 4, p. 25 (for 1964). These are the sources also for the Census estimates of the poverty gap in 1961 and 1964.

[11] Mollie Orshansky, "More About the Poor in 1964," *Social Security Bulletin,* Vol. 29 (May 1966), p. 3. This could be attributed to the more widespread unemployment in 1961.

[12] Although a Census figure for total transfers received by the poor is not available, the Census data indicate that in 1964 earnings were 54 percent of the money income of the poor, which would leave about 6 percent for income from sources other than earnings and transfers.

[13] Orshansky, "More About the Poor in 1964," *op. cit.,* Table 11, p. 20.

tions in the estimates.[14] A brief discussion of these differences is given in Appendix A.

Taxes and the Extent of Poverty

Up to this point no consideration has been given to taxes. Yet a case can be made that some taxes, at least, can be viewed as "negative transfers." For example, do not personal income taxes reduce disposable income in the same way that unemployment compensation increases disposable income? Again, is there not a symmetry between the effect produced by social security contributions made by employees and that produced by the receipt of OASDI benefits? In both cases, the former can be considered as a negative transfer which reduces disposable income, and the latter as a negative tax which increases disposable income.

Taxes and Poverty Lines

For present purposes, taxes can be divided into two groups. One group of taxes is made up of those which reduce disposable income. Examples of such taxes are personal income taxes, poll taxes, personal property taxes, and the employee's share of social security taxes. The second group consists of those taxes which raise prices. That is, the incidence of the second group of taxes is upon consumers. Examples of taxes which are believed to raise prices are sales and excise taxes, business property taxes, the employer's share of the social security taxes, and the corporate income tax.[15]

Assume for the moment the validity of separating taxes into these two groups. What, then, is the relevance of this dichotomy to the discussion of poverty? It would seem to be that an increase or reduction in the taxes that affect prices would raise or lower the poverty line, whereas taxes which increase or decrease disposable income leave the poverty line, as presently calculated, unchanged. The poverty lines used by the Council of Economic Advisers (CEA) and the Social Security Administration (among others) are based on budget studies of the cost of minimum sufficient diets made by the Department of Agriculture. Hence, they reflect the prices of goods

---

[14] See T. Paul Schultz, *Statistics on the Size Distribution of Personal Income in the United States*, Joint Economic Committee, 88 Cong. 2 sess. (1964).

[15] How much they increase prices is another question.

and services needed to produce a "minimum decent" standard of living. They measure the income level, before income tax, above which most families, in fact, receive a nutritious diet.[16] To repeat, if some tax increases raise the prices of consumer goods and services, this increase would be reflected in the poverty lines. Thus, in principle, if a reduction in sales and excise taxes reduced consumer prices, it would reduce the poverty lines. Further, if an increase or decrease in taxes raised or lowered disposable income, but had no effect on prices, it should not change the poverty lines as presently calculated.

The official poverty lines are based on "required" total money income before taxes. If a family of four (with a $3,000 poverty line) has exactly $3,000 in money income and pays an income tax of $100, it has a disposable income (or money income after tax) of $2,900. Such a family is at the poverty line, since $3,000 in money income before tax equals the $3,000 poverty line. Now suppose there is an increase in income tax rates so that the family pays a $200 tax on its $3,000 money income. If there is no change in prices, the family is certainly worse off than before; since it was at the poverty line before the tax increase, one would expect it to be below the poverty line after the rise in taxes. Yet the family still has a money income before tax which just equals the poverty line of $3,000. Clearly, then, the poverty line should be based on money income after personal taxes (including the social security taxes). If this were the case, a tax change which reduced disposable income would push into poverty those families with disposable income, or money income after taxes, at or very close to the poverty line.

It is possible to estimate the increase in the number of poor families if the relevant income measure were changed to money income after taxes rather than before taxes. Table 2-5, based on the BLS Survey, shows that the number of after-transfer poor families on a basis of income after personal tax is 9,187,000—an increase of 309,000 families over the 8,878,000 after-transfer poor when money income is on a before-tax basis. Unfortunately, the BLS did

[16] For an interesting critique of the poverty lines used by the CEA and Miss Orshansky, see Rose D. Friedman, *Poverty: Definition and Perspective* (Washington: American Enterprise Institute, 1965), pp. 18-34. Rose Friedman's quarrel with them is based on the standards for an "adequate diet," and the multiplier of three times the cost of an "adequate diet" used in computing the poverty line.

not include social security taxes in "personal taxes." As Table 2-5 shows, an estimated 329,000 additional families would be in poverty if social security taxes paid by employees or self-employed persons were also subtracted from money income before taxes. Thus, the number of families in poverty on an after-tax basis with all personal taxes deducted rises by 638,000. This is 7 percent greater than the number of poor families on the basis of money income before tax.

How many poor families would be made nonpoor if they did not have to pay any taxes, direct or indirect? There is no straightforward way to answer this question. However, the question can be turned around: How many families would be pushed out of poverty if they were given a cash credit for all the taxes they now pay?

TABLE 2-5. The Number of Poor Families, Measured by Money Income After Taxes, 1961

(Number of families in thousands)

Effects of Different Types of Income Measures on Poor Families	Members in Poor Family						Total Poor Families
	One	Two	Three	Four	Five	Six	
(1) Number on basis of money income before tax	2,643	2,499	878	627	603	1,628	8,878
(2) Number on basis of money income after personal tax (except social security)	2,686	2,603	931	658	624	1,685	9,187
(3) Rise in number, (2)–(1)[a]	43	104	53	31	21	57	309
(4) Estimated additional number if social security taxes are deducted from money income[b]	20	97	35	70	32	75	329
(5) Rise in number if all personal taxes are deducted from money income, (3)+(4)	63	201	88	101	53	132	638

Source: U.S. Treasury Department, Office of Tax Analysis, based on special tabulations of the Survey of Consumer Expenditures, 1960–61, of the Bureau of Labor Statistics.
[a] The BLS tabulations include income distributions on the basis of income after personal tax (not including social security contributions).
[b] The formula used for calculating the additional poor families if social security contributions are subtracted from money income after personal taxes, but before social security contributions, is as follows:

$$V = \frac{PL - (PL - X)}{1,000}(Y)$$

where V = increase in the number of poor families,
PL = poverty line,
X = average social security contribution of families making such contributions in income bracket just above poverty line income,
Y = number of families in income bracket just above poverty line who made social security contributions,
1,000 = size of income bracket; it is assumed that families are evenly distributed over the whole income bracket.

Presented in this form, it is possible to calculate the number of families who no longer would be poor if they paid no taxes at all. The real problem, however, is to determine what percentage of their money income before taxes is used to pay direct and indirect taxes. Clearly, the taxes that reduce disposable income should be included at the rate at which they fall on income. But what about the taxes that raise prices? To what extent do they raise prices? When the impact of a tax is on sellers, is the incidence of the tax upon the consumers who pay for the goods or is it—as Earl Rolph believes—upon the incomes of the factors which produce the goods?[17]

Total Effective Tax Rate on the Income of the Poor

Richard Musgrave has calculated the effective rates of total taxes in 1954 for different income classes, with the results reproduced below.[18]

Spending Unit Income Class	Effective Total Tax Rate
Less than $2,000	26.9
$ 2,000– 3,000	28.3
3,000– 4,000	28.9
4,000– 5,000	29.8
5,000– 7,500	31.3
7,500– 10,000	33.0
More than 10,000	40.9
All Classes	32.9

Unfortunately, no comparable estimates based on Rolph's analysis of the incidence of indirect taxes are available. However, one would expect that effective total tax rates based on Rolph's views would show greater progressivity than those estimated by Musgrave. This expectation is caused by the proportional form of excise and sales

[17] Economists are not in agreement on the answers to these questions. One view is that sales taxes are passed on, at least in part, to consumers in the form of higher prices. Another view is that the incidence of sales taxes is upon factor incomes and that the burden of sales and excise taxes is similar to that of a proportional income tax. Appendix B briefly examines these two points of view, including those expressed by Earl Rolph, *The Theory of Fiscal Economics* (Berkeley: University of California Press, 1954).

[18] Richard A. Musgrave, "The Incidence of the Tax Structure and its Effects on Consumption," *Federal Tax Policy for Economic Growth and Stability,* papers submitted by panelists appearing before the Subcommittee on Tax Policy, Joint Committee on the Economic Report, 84 Cong. 1 sess. (1955), Table 2, p. 98.

taxes in the Rolph framework as opposed to their regressive form in the Musgrave analysis.

The Musgrave estimates indicate that there is little progressivity in the tax system as a whole through the low-income and middle-income classes. His estimates indicate that income classes which contain poor families are effectively taxed at a rate close to 30 percent of money income. Because regressive state-local taxes have risen sharply since 1954, it seems reasonable to assume that the present effective total tax rate on the total money income of poor families of all sizes is 30 percent. This assumption lacks scientific rigor and it sidesteps the Rolph view on incidence, but it allows a calculation of the reduction in the number of families in poverty if poor families were credited for the taxes they pay.

Table 2-6 indicates that 3.3 million families could be lifted out of poverty if their money incomes before taxes were raised 30 percent through a cash tax credit from which they would receive $4.5 billion. For purposes of comparison, totals for tax credits at other rates are as follows:

Tax Credit (Percent)	Families Lifted Out of Poverty (Thousands)	Total Tax Credit (Millions)
10	1,346	$1,497
20	2,425	2,994
40	4,001	5,988

These figures are rough, in part because of the assumptions about incidence upon which they are based. But accepting that they are subject to wide margins of error, they still show that an impressive number of poor families could be lifted out of poverty through use of a tax credit.

This type of tax credit has little merit as a means of improving income maintenance for the poor. Its great disadvantage is that the "poorest" poor get the least while the "best off" poor get the most. Because this tax credit is a percentage of total money income, the poor with the most money income would get a larger dollar credit than would the poor who have very little money income. In addition, the tax credit would create a "notch" problem. If only families with income below their poverty lines are eligible for a credit, families with income just above their poverty lines would increase their money income by reducing their income before the tax credit to

TABLE 2-6. Effects of a 30 Percent Cash Tax Credit on the Number of Poor Families, 1961

Item, by Members in Family	Family's Bracket for Money Income Before Tax					
	Under $1,000	$1,000– 1,999	$2,000– 2,999	$3,000– 3,999	$4,000– 4,999	Total
Number of Poor Families (thousands):						
One	1,405	1,238[a]				2,643
Two	445	2,054				2,499
Three	85	455	338[a]			878
Four	36	214	377			627
Five	38	153	225	187[a]		603
Six or more[b]	59	218	540	475	336[a]	1,628
Familes of all sizes						8,878
Number of Poor Families Lifted Out of Poverty by Tax Credit[c] (thousands):						
One		857				857
Two		949				949
Three		70	338			408
Four			261			261
Five			69	187		256
Six or more[b]				255	336	591
Families of all sizes						3,322
Tax Credit Received by Poor Families ($ millions):						
One	279	464				743
Two	82	947				1,029
Three	16	215	228			459
Four	d	103	289			392
Five	d	70	170	182		422
Six or more[b]	6	107	406	498	428	1,445
Families of All Sizes						$4,490

Source: U.S. Treasury Department, Office of Tax Analysis, based on special tabulations of Survey of Consumer Expenditures, 1960–61, of the Bureau of Labor Statistics.
[a] Number of poor families below mid-point of total money income bracket.
[b] Assumes an average of seven members in families with six or more persons.
[c] Reduction in poor families is based on assumption that families are evenly distributed throughout the income brackets.
[d] BLS data produce a negative result.

29

a level just below their poverty lines. For example, a family of four with $3,100 in earnings would receive less money income than a family of four with $2,700 earnings and an $810 tax credit. To avoid this, a partial tax credit would have to be extended to families with incomes above their poverty lines. If the tax credit for poor families were tapered off to zero as total money income approached the poverty line, the notch problem could be avoided.

Net Transfers

By combining some of the results of the investigation so far, it is possible to provide an overview of what the system of transfer and taxes did in 1961 to disposable income of families of different sizes with different amounts of before-transfer income. Here interest is confined, on the one hand, to those taxes which directly reduce disposable income—mainly personal taxes—and, on the other, to those taxes which were used to pay for the transfers. In the case of the former, because the BLS provides data on personal taxes and social security contributions of employees, it is these taxes which are subtracted from transfers in calculating "net transfers." (Net transfers are here defined as transfer payments minus taxes which reduce disposable income).

TABLE 2-7. Net Transfers Per Family, by Family Size and Before-Transfer Income, 1961[a]

Before-Transfer Income Class	Members in Family					
	One	Two	Three	Four	Five	Six or More
Under $1,000	$ 885	$1,374	$1,567	$1,741	$1,539	$2,000
$ 1,000– 1,999	619	1,084	935	667	577	810
2,000– 2,999	280	656	435	311	570	418
3,000– 3,999	— 97	392	113	46	169	389
4,000– 4,999	— 581	— 184	— 73	— 125	60	118
5,000– 5,999	— 863	— 467	— 463	— 389	— 343	— 65
6,000– 7,499	— 1,112	— 776	— 762	— 653	— 567	— 303
7,500– 9,999	— 1,193	—1,288	—1,030	—1,053	—1,104	— 579
10,000–14,999	— 2,684	—1,868	—1,863	—1,666	—1,529	—1,300
15,000 and over	—13,051	—5,831	—4,898	—3,772	—5,706	—2,545

Source: U.S. Treasury Department, Office of Tax Analysis, based on special tabulations of the Survey of Consumer Expenditures, 1960–61, of the Bureau of Labor Statistics.
[a] Net transfer is average transfer payment per family minus average personal taxes (including social security contributions) paid per family.

Table 2-7 shows that the dollar value of net transfers declined as before-transfer income rose, and generally rose as family size increased.[19] The breakeven point (that is, the point at which personal taxes equal transfers) was reached and passed in the $3,000-$4,000 bracket for single-member families; in the $4,000-$5,000 before-transfer income bracket for families with two, three, and four members; and in the $5,000-$6,000 bracket for five- and six-member families. Hence, the relationship between taxes and transfers roughly reflects the increased needs of the larger families.

Table 2-8 indicates how before-transfer income was changed by public and private transfers, and the additional effect of a 7 percent tax on after-transfer income required to pay for the public transfers.[20] The table shows information for each size of family in columns A, B, C, and D. In each case, column A shows transfer income as a percentage of the family's poverty line income. Column B indicates how much the 7 percent tax changes the distance from the poverty line. The net effect of transfers and the taxes which pay for them (column A minus column B) is shown in column C, which shows that the breakeven line is in the $5,000-$6,000 before-transfer income bracket for all except the one- and five-member families. Most families did not begin to pay "net" for the public transfer system until their incomes exceeded $5,000. Column D is the after-tax, after-transfer income as a percentage of the family's poverty line, and thus shows how the family stood in relation to its poverty line. Column D also indicates how average after-tax transfer income responded to an approximate $1,000 rise in before-transfer income. This is accomplished by observing for a family of a given size the percentages in column D for two successive income brackets. For example, for three-person families whose before-transfer income rose from under $1,000 to the $1,000-$2,000 bracket, after-tax and transfer income responded by rising on the average from 73 to

---

[19] An exception was the case of two-person families in low-income brackets. Their average net transfer was substantially higher than that of other family sizes for given levels of before-transfer income.

[20] Transfer payments made up 7 percent of total money income recorded in the BLS Survey. The tax rate on money income required to pay for the transfers would, therefore, have to average 7 percent. In Table 2-8, it is assumed that the tax rate for each family size and income bracket is 7 percent. This assumption is based on a rough guess about the regressivity and progressivity of the taxes out of which transfers are paid.

90 percent of the three-person family's poverty line. For the six-person family moving from the lowest to the next lowest income bracket the potential effects on incentives to work were great. A $1,000 increase in before-transfer income seems to have raised after-tax and transfer income by only 1 percentage point—from 48

TABLE 2-8. Effect of Private-Public Money Transfers and an Assumed 7 Percent Tax on After-Transfer Income, 1961

Before-Transfer Income Class	Percentages of Poverty Line Income for Different Family Sizes[a]											
	One Member				Two Members				Three Members			
	A	B	C	D	A	B	C	D	A	B	C	D
Under $1,000	59	5	54	71	70	6	64	79	64	5	59	73
$ 1,000– 2,000	48	10	38	130	52	9	43	116	37	7	30	90
2,000– 3,000	21	13	8	172	32	11	21	145	27	9	18	120
3,000– 4,000	18	17	1	232	29	14	15	188	18	11	7	148
4,000– 5,000	12	22	−10	288	19	17	2	228	15	14	1	180
5,000– 6,000	10	26	−16	345	18	20	− 2	271	10	16	− 6	214
6,000– 7,500	7	32	−25	418	9	24	−15	324	6	19	−13	254
7,500–10,000	2	40	−38	528	8	30	−22	404	11	25	−14	331
10,000–15,000	2	55	−53	728	3	40	−37	541	1	33	−32	442
15,000 and over	b	148	−148	1,978	6	85	−79	1,126	3	65	−62	866

Before-Transfer Income Class	Four Members				Five Members				Six or More Members			
	A	B	C	D	A	B	C	D	A	B	C	D
Under $1,000	60	5	55	62	41	3	38	44	47	4	43	48
$ 1,000– 2,000	25	5	20	71	20	4	16	59	18	4	14	49
2,000– 3,000	24	8	16	101	26	7	19	91	17	5	12	67
3,000– 4,000	13	9	4	122	11	8	3	105	14	6	8	86
4,000– 5,000	20	11	9	152	11	10	1	130	9	8	1	102
5,000– 6,000	6	13	− 7	178	16	11	5	150	6	9	− 3	120
6,000– 7,500	5	16	−11	212	5	14	− 9	182	6	11	− 5	144
7,500–10,000	5	20	−15	272	4	18	−14	234	6	14	− 8	181
10,000–15,000	7	28	−21	372	4	24	−20	310	3	19	−16	248
15,000 and over	1	47	−46	622	5	50	−45	666	b	32	−32	414

Source: U.S. Treasury Department, Office of Tax Analysis, based on special tabulations of the Survey of Consumer Expenditures, 1960–61, of the Bureau of Labor Statistics.
[a] The columns headed A, B, C, and D have the following meanings:
A means after-transfer income less before-transfer income, or transfers as a percentage of poverty line income for the family size.
B means 7 percent of after-transfer income as a percentage of poverty line income.
C means (A) minus (B), or net transfers as a percentage of poverty line income.
D means after-transfer, after-tax income as a percentage of poverty line income.
[b] Information not available.

to 49 percent of poverty line income. There is no obvious explanation for this result. One conceivable explanation is that many large families with no income receive public assistance. As earnings (before-transfer income) increase, public assistance payments are reduced by one dollar for each dollar of increase in earnings. Where this happens, after-transfer income will equal before-transfer income.

In Summary

The estimates from the BLS Survey of Consumer Expenditures indicate that public transfer payments are an important source of income of the poor. A majority of the poor families receive one or another form of transfer payment. Transfers equaled 77 percent of the before-transfer poverty gap, filled about 60 percent of that gap, and closed 45 percent of the poverty gap of the after-transfer poor. The before-transfer poor received about half and the after-transfer poor about a quarter of total transfer payments.

If poverty lines had been based on income after taxes rather than before taxes, over 600,000 additional families would have been classed as poor in 1961. The total tax load (direct and indirect) of poor families may be as high as 30 percent of their income. A cash tax credit for taxes paid would significantly reduce the number of poor families, but would do least for the poorest of the poor. On the average, families do not begin to pay net for the public transfer system until their incomes exceed $5,000.

CHAPTER III

Other Types of Income Maintenance

ALTERNATIVE METHODS for improving the present income maintenance system in the United States may be preferred to reliance upon transfer-by-taxation. Some of these are examined in this chapter under three broad categories. First is the possibility of making major improvements in the public assistance programs. Next is social insurance as an approach to more extensive income maintenance. And, finally, there are family allowances. One alternative that is not discussed is the possibility of raising the minimum wage and extending its coverage. This alternative might help some of the working poor, a group receiving less than minimal support from the present transfer programs. However, it would be of limited use to the poor who were working part time, and no use to the poor in a household without an employed member.

Public Assistance

Roots of the present system of public assistance lie deep in Anglo-American history. State assistance to the poor began in the Elizabethan period, commencing with the Act of 1563. However, there were strict limitations on such assistance. English settlers in

America brought with them the Elizabethan principle that those who could support themselves, or secure support from relatives, were not eligible for public relief. Moreover, the poor were treated as if poverty was their own fault and, because there was little or no attempt to distinguish between causes of poverty, all the poor were lumped together. Later, during the latter half of the nineteenth century as social understanding increased, certain categories of the poor were defined and treated apart from other poor. This was accompanied by increased state assistance to local governments for relief purposes.[1]

During the Great Depression of the 1930's, local and state relief agencies in the United States were not able to cope with the thousands of previously self-supporting workers who were unemployed and who, with their families, required assistance. Thus the responsibility for providing funds for relief, which up to then had rested with local authorities, shifted to the federal government. At first, the federal government through the Reconstruction Finance Corporation and later through the Federal Emergency Relief Administration made loans to the states. Then, in 1935, Congress passed the Social Security Act. In addition to establishing two social insurance programs, that Act defines three categories of relief based on means tests. These are old-age assistance (OAA), aid to dependent children (ADC), and aid to the blind (AB). Under the 1935 Act, the federal government makes grants-in-aid to the states based on predetermined formulas. However, control over the programs has remained with the individual states.

The federal public assistance programs now in existence include the three established under the Social Security Act and a newer one, aid to the permanently and totally disabled (APTD). There is also a program completely financed by state and local governments called general assistance. The hallmark of the public assistance programs, except for the general assistance program, is that they are designed partially to meet the needs of such categories of the poor as the aged and the blind, and to carry on the tradition of refusing to support the able-bodied (employable) poor.[2] Although the number of

[1] Lewis Meriam, *Relief and Social Security* (Washington: Brookings Institution, 1946), pp. 7-9.

[2] This is beginning to change as certain states have broadened eligibility for aid to dependent children. By December 1964, there were 18 states which made

families receiving public assistance has grown, only about a third of the poor families and a fourth of the poor persons received public assistance in 1963.[3] This could be caused by failure to fall into one of the prescribed categories which are eligible for assistance. It may also be affected by the level of the family's assets and income,[4] the existence of relatives upon whom responsibility for support can be placed, or failure to meet residence requirements. Or a family may be too "proud" to accept a form of assistance to which it feels a social stigma is attached.

Undoubtedly, before receiving public assistance, most recipients are among the "poorest" poor. However, there is evidence that a large number of very poor families receive no assistance at all. About 30 percent of the poor families have money incomes which are less than half the family's poverty line; but of these poor families, only about a fourth or a fifth appear to have received public assistance. More than two-thirds of the recipients of public assistance appear to have total money incomes (including public assistance) which exceed 50 percent of the family's poverty line income.[5]

The existence of a large number of very poor families receiving

ADC payments to families with an unemployed parent. U. S. Department of Health, Education, and Welfare (HEW), *Welfare in Review*, Statistical Supplement, 1965, Table 4, p. 6.

[3] Mollie Orshansky estimates on the basis of data from the Bureau of the Census that there were 30.4 million persons in 7.4 million poor families and 4.9 million poor unrelated individuals in 1963. Orshansky, "Who's Who Among the Poor: A Demographic View of Poverty," *Social Security Bulletin*, Vol. 28 (July 1965), p. 4. In December 1963, there were 4.1 million families and about 8 million persons receiving public assistance. The number of families receiving public assistance in 1936 and 1947 were 2.8 and 3.2 million, respectively. It should be noted that public assistance figures are on a monthly basis. To the extent there is movement on and off the welfare rolls, the number of families or persons who received relief during a given year will exceed the largest monthly figure.

[4] Public assistance "requirements" are usually well below the poverty lines.

[5] The evidence for these statements is obtained from tabulations of the Survey of Consumer Expenditures, 1960-61, of the Bureau of Labor Statistics (BLS) of the U. S. Department of Labor. These tabulations were made for the Office of Tax Analysis, U. S. Department of the Treasury. The BLS data indicate that there were 8.9 million poor families in 1961 and that 2.4 million had incomes which were less than 50 percent of their poverty line. Although the BLS reports that 1.6 million after-transfer poor families received public assistance in 1961, only about 500,000 had after-transfer incomes less than 50 percent of their poverty line income. However, it is quite likely that some families were too "proud" to admit to the interviewer that they received public assistance.

no public assistance should not come as a great surprise to persons who are familiar with the public assistance programs.[6] Over 75 percent of public assistance recipients are in one of two categories: they are aged or they are dependent children—many in broken families. In December 1965, this group was made up of 2,127,000 recipients of old-age assistance and 4,457,000 recipients of aid to dependent children (in 1,069,000 families).[7] Another category includes 670,000 recipients who were blind or totally disabled.[8] However, the evidence concerning who is poor in the United States indicates that poverty is not confined to particular categories of people. There must be millions of poor families who are not eligible for any of these categorical forms of public assistance.[9]

There is, however, general assistance—a carryover from the pre-1930 system of relief—which still is completely financed at the state or local levels of government. Unlike the other public assistance programs, general assistance is available to indigent individuals and families in general, not just to certain categories of the poor. In December 1936, there were 1.5 million general assistance cases receiving an annual total of $439 million. In December 1965, there were 310,000 general assistance cases with a total of 677,000 recipients receiving an annual total of $260 million.[10] These figures indicate that general assistance is much less important than it once was. This may result from several factors: (1) Many prospective general assistance recipients have moved out of poverty as prosperity has developed. (2) Some general assistance recipients are classified in one or another of the federally assisted categories. And (3) the states show less willingness to finance general assistance and greater willingness to rely heavily on those public assistance programs that are financed substantially by the federal government.

Could the public assistance programs be modified to contribute

[6] Note that some poor families may be recipients of other forms of transfer payment. However, their total money income was still less than 50 percent of the poverty line income

[7] In 1962, the program for aid to dependent children (ADC) became aid to families of dependent children (AFDC).

[8] HEW, *Social Security Bulletin*, Vol. 29 (April 1966), Table M-16, p. 59.

[9] See Chapter I, especially Table 1-1.

[10] HEW, *Social Security Bulletin*, Vol. 29 (April 1966), Table M-16, p. 59. The average number of persons to a "case" is not given, but since many recipient families are likely to be of the father-mother-plus-children variety, it seems reasonable to assume an average of four persons per case.

much more to the alleviation of poverty?[11] Clearly, the present public assistance programs are a form of income maintenance; they represent society's way of saying no one is going to starve to death. That is to say, if a family has absolutely no way to meet basic survival needs, and if private assistance is not forthcoming, some form of assistance usually will be made available. The federally supported public assistance programs go somewhat further in that certain categories of the poor—if they are willing to swallow their pride and apply for public assistance—are more or less assured a minimum income, even if that minimum is well below generally accepted poverty lines.

If more is to be done for the poor through public assistance, either the present categories for eligibility must be broadened, new categories created, all categories eliminated, or much more emphasis placed on general assistance. In any case, more can be done simply by providing minimum levels of assistance.

One category which might be broadened usefully is that of the family with dependent children. This present category could be broadened by allowing all poor families with children to receive AFDC payments—not just those families in which the father is absent from the family.[12] Two new subcategories that might be created are: (1) poor families having a head who is unemployed but not eligible for, or no longer receiving unemployment insurance, and (2) poor families having a head who is employed but in desperate need of a supplement to earnings. (At present, a few states, including New York, will supplement the wages of poor persons applying for and otherwise eligible for relief.)[13] If elimination of all categories is the chosen route, public assistance could be made available to all families whose income is low enough to place them in great need. Placing greater emphasis upon the present general assistance program has a very real drawback in that such assistance

[11] One recent view on this issue is in HEW, Report of the Advisory Council on Public Welfare, *Having the Power, We Have the Duty* (June 1966).

[12] Some states already have broadened eligibility to receive AFDC payments to include families with an unemployed father.

[13] The supplementation is made out of the funds of the general assistance program. See Duncan M. MacIntyre, *Public Assistance: Too Much or Too Little?* (Ithaca: New York State School of Industrial and Labor Relations, Cornell University, December 1964), pp. 50-51.

now is financed solely by the states. One possible improvement along this line would be to have the federal government help in financing general assistance.[14]

Neither federal financing of general assistance nor federal financing of new categories of assistance may be enough to make the public assistance approach a good alternative to transfer-by-taxation. There are now tremendous differences among the states as to local residence requirements and the amounts of assistance payments to the poor—amounts that cannot be accounted for simply by differences in the cost of living. Even if public assistance were standardized by providing for greater federal control over the administration of the programs—including the elimination of local residence requirements—a basic question would remain. Can public assistance ever be so modified that its recipient will not feel that being on relief is a social stigma? Moreover, the personal touch added in principle by the client-welfare worker relationship has not worked out in practice. Welfare workers rather than spending most of their time providing services to clients often spend at least half of their time on paperwork concerning payments and checking to see whether their clients still qualify for assistance.[15] The time problem might be remedied by hiring more welfare workers. But so long as the welfare worker must "snoop" into his client's private life as a check on indigence and other conditions for eligibility, the service function of the social worker is likely to be undercut by mutual distrust.

Even if eligibility for public assistance were broadened, increased federal funds made available, unjustified differences in state standards eliminated, and the client-welfare worker relationship improved, the public assistance programs would still be burdened by a fatal weakness. That weakness is the effective 100 percent "tax rate" on the earnings of welfare recipients. Under the present programs, welfare payments are reduced dollar-for-dollar as earnings

[14] Possibly if one of the plans for federal sharing of revenues with the states were adopted, part of the funds could be earmarked for general assistance. For a description of such a plan, see Edwin Dale, "Subsidizing the States," *New Republic* (November 28, 1964), pp. 11-12.

[15] For an interesting discussion of the present administration of public assistance, see Edgar May, *The Wasted Americans* (New York: Harper and Row, 1964), pp. 106-14.

rise.[16] This means that up to the point at which the assistance payment is reduced to zero there is no economic gain from work. For the earner whose work effort is not likely to reward him with an income substantially in excess of the public assistance income he would receive if he earned nothing, the present budgeting arrangement creates an enormous potential—and in many cases probably actual—incentive not to work.

Assuming work is distasteful, this 100 percent "tax rate" would become a more serious problem if public assistance were extended to cover the employable poor. Now most public assistance is received by categories of the poor among whom the potential for work is limited. But if public assistance were broadened in order to aid the working poor, the 100 percent rate could do a good deal of damage to worker incentives. It certainly would be undesirable to fill in the poverty gap by reducing the work incentives of the poor, thereby raising the before-transfer poverty income gap. Moreover, the 100 percent rate might induce employers to reduce the wages of workers eligible to receive public assistance supplements to their earnings.

In summary, improving public assistance as an antipoverty measure would seem to require, at the very least, action to:

1.   Broaden or eliminate special categories of recipients in order to reach a much larger number of poor families.

2.   Increase federal financing.

3.   Reduce assistance payments at a rate substantially less than a dollar for each dollar earned.

4.   Improve the client-welfare worker relationship.

5.   Minimize the social stigma presently attached to receiving relief.

[16] There have been experiments in Denver and Cleveland with something less than a 100 percent rate. The Denver experiment is discussed in the first section of Chapter VIII. Also 1962 and 1965 amendments to the public assistance section of the Social Security Act *permit* the states to disregard some earning in the calculation of need. A state may now disregard or exempt the first $20 and half of the next $60 of the monthly earnings of a recipient of old-age assistance or aid to the permanently and totally disabled. The exemption under the aid to families of dependent children (AFDC) program is $50 of earnings per child per month, but not more than $150 in the same family. However, very few states have adopted these measures.

Social Insurance

Another possible way to improve income maintenance in the United States is to broaden the social insurance system. The major programs in the U.S. social insurance system now are: (1) provision of benefits to the aged, survivors of insured workers, and disabled workers (OASDI); (2) health insurance for the aged under Medicare; (3) unemployment compensation; and (4) workmen's compensation. These programs have broad coverage. Under OASDI, the coverage of workers is now almost universal, although at present benefits are not.[17] About 80 percent of all wage and salary workers are covered by unemployment compensation.[18] Yet, in 1963, there were 5.2 million aged poor persons in 4.1 million poor households headed by an aged person.[19] In March 1964, there were 1.9 million persons in 400,000 poor families headed by an unemployed person.[20] About a quarter of the 4.2 million unemployed persons in that month were in poor households.[21]

The aged poor and the unemployed poor could be lifted out of poverty without adding any additional programs to the existing social insurance system. It would be necessary to raise OASDI benefits and to extend the benefits to all aged persons and survivors regardless of their own or their spouse's previous work experience. It would also be necessary to extend unemployment compensation to all workers, raise the minimum benefits to levels above the poverty line, and abolish the limit on the period during which an unemployed person is eligible to receive benefits. If these changes had been implemen'ed in 1962, there would have been, in 1963, something closer to 5.4 million rather than to 7.4 million poor families, as reported by the Bureau of the Census, and as many as 2.5 million fewer poor unrelated individuals.[22] However, this approach is

[17] *European Social Security Systems,* Paper No. 7, Economic Policies and Practices, Joint Economic Committee, 89 Cong. 1 sess. (1965), p. 43.
[18] *Ibid.,* p. 50.
[19] Mollie Orshansky, "Who's Who Among the Poor," *op. cit.,* pp. 12-13.
[20] *Ibid,* Table C, p. 28. This does not include unemployed unrelated individuals.
[21] *Ibid.,* pp. 21-22.
[22] The figure might exceed 2.5 million depending upon the number of unrelated individuals (figure not given by Orshansky) who were poor because they were un-

expensive inasmuch as increased payment could not be confined to the aged and unemployed poor. The benefits of nonpoor persons and families in these categories would also have to be raised.[23]

Since most of the poor are in households with heads who are neither aged nor defined as unemployed, the existing social insurance system is limited in the contribution it can make toward reducing the poverty that currently exists in the United States. Experience with the Western European social security systems—most of them broader than in the United States—suggests one moderate line of advance. In addition to programs comparable to those of the United States mentioned above, the European systems usually include health and sickness insurance, maternity benefits, and family allowances.[24] Of these systems, however, only family allowances (payments to mothers or fathers with dependent children) would materially reduce the number of poor families in the United States. Since only family allowances of this group are an important means of improving the income maintenance system, they are given separate treatment in this chapter.

Two aspects of the social insurance approach adopted in both Western Europe and the United States limit the effectiveness of social insurance as an antipoverty measure. One is that social insurance systems are composed of a limited number of programs covering a limited number of categories of the population. There are always likely to be families who fall between such categories, but it would be difficult to insure against this eventuality. The second is the emphasis placed on wage-related insurance systems. All

employed. Incidentally, it should be noted that in order to have eliminated the aged and the unemployed from the ranks of the poor by means of increased OASDI and unemployment compensation benefits, it would have been necessary, in some cases, for the benefits per unit of time to have exceeded average past earnings per unit of time.

[23] At the Brookings Institution conference on negative taxes, one participant said that the Department of Health, Education, and Welfare has estimated that an additional $11 billion would be needed to get half of the aged poor out of poverty. The aged poor who have a $3 billion poverty gap would receive only a third of the $11 billion, some of which would put some of the aged poor above the poverty line. Most of the nonpoor who would receive additional benefits now fall into the recently defined "near poor" group. The poverty lines for the "near poor" are approximately a third higher than those defining the poor. See Mollie Orshansky, "Recounting the Poor," *Social Security Bulletin*, Vol. 29 (April 1966), Table 1, p. 23.

[24] *European Social Security Systems, op. cit.,* p. 1

of the U.S. social insurance programs—though not all of the European programs—are financed through taxes on wages and salaries and/or on employer payrolls. Usually the monetary benefits of a particular social insurance program are related to the amount paid into the program; this amount, in turn, is related to the worker's level of earnings. An exception is the family allowance, where the amount received is usually independent of income.[25] While the ratio of benefits to earnings is often higher for low earners than high earners, it is always a fraction of earnings. Therefore, the wage-related approach will fail to assure against poverty if a worker's earnings are below the poverty line. Also the wage-related approach has limitations in that not all family or household units have a present or past earner.

The foregoing comments should not be taken to preclude the possibility that the social insurance approach might be extended in such a way as to insure against poverty. In fact, one writer recently claimed that the social security system in the United States (including public assistance) has evolved over the past twenty years in the direction of a basic minimum income.[26] How such an evolution might culminate in a social security system that guarantees against indigence is illustrated by the New Zealand system of social security which is described briefly below.

In 1938, New Zealand inaugurated a single comprehensive social security system.[27] New Zealand's Social Security Act of 1938 combined into a single program, aimed at insuring everyone against want, several pension plans that until then had formed the basis of the country's social insurance system. In addition, the new act filled in gaps in the earlier system and included a national health service. The present social security system insures against poverty by making monetary payments to all families with income below a certain level. These grants include benefits for age (persons 60 years or

[25] However, in France, family allowances are directly related to earnings; and in Denmark they are inversely related to the family's income.

[26] Eveline Burns, "Social Security in Evolution: Towards What?", *Proceedings of the Seventeenth Annual Meeting of the Industrial Relations Research Association* (Chicago: December 1964), p. 20.

[27] Meriam, *op. cit.,* p. 515. Also see John B. Condliffe, *The Welfare State in New Zealand* (London: George Allen and Unwin Ltd., 1959), pp. 293-322, and C. Weststrate, *Portrait of a Modern Mixed Economy: New Zealand* (Wellington: New Zealand University Press, 1959), pp. 80-119.

older); for widows, orphans, invalids, and minors; and for unemployment and sickness. In addition, there are emergency benefits for anyone who is in need but is not eligible for any other type of monetary benefit.[28]

Both eligibility for and the level of these benefits are conditioned upon an income means test. Essentially the means test provides that full benefits are payable if the family's income is below a stated level. For each pound of income in excess of the prescribed level, benefits are reduced by one pound. The level of income which is allowed before reduction of benefits varies among programs. In 1960, age, widow's, and invalid's benefits could be received in full if an individual's annual income was no greater than $390. The comparable figure for orphans was $130 a year. Unreduced unemployment and sickness benefits were payable if the recipient's income was below $7.50 a week. There is no limit on the duration of receipt of unemployment benefits.[29]

In addition to the benefits conditioned by income, three forms of benefit, or demogrant, are paid irrespective of the level of income. One is a superannuation benefit paid to all persons over the age of 65. Another is the family benefit paid to any father or mother with a child under 16 years of age; this is a flat amount for each child. The third form is a health benefit, available to all, which includes medical, pharmaceutical, hospital, and maternity service.[30]

The rates at which the income-conditioned benefits are taken away are shown in Figure 3-1. The rate schedule is a combination of a zero and a 100 percent rate. In Figure 3-1, age benefits are used to provide an illustration of how benefits vary with the level of income. In 1960, a single person eligible for age benefits could receive up to $390 a year without reduction in the basic age benefit of $552.50.[31] For each dollar of before-benefit income in excess of $390, age benefits are reduced by a dollar. This is indicated by the 45° line beginning at point B and ending at point C in Figure 3-1. Age benefits are reduced to zero when before-benefit income

[28] *New Zealand Official Yearbook* (Wellington: Public Printer, 1961), pp. 174-88.

[29] *Ibid.,* pp. 176-77. The amounts of benefits are given in U.S. dollars rather than pounds for convenience in comparing the systems. The conversion ratio of U. S. dollars for New Zealand pounds averaged $2.50 in 1960. *Currency Yearbook, 1964-65* (New York: Pick Publishing Corp., 1965), p. 360.

[30] Condliffe, *op. cit.,* pp. 301-04.

[31] *Yearbook, op. cit.,* p. 178.

FIGURE 3-1. New Zealand System of Income-Conditioned Age Benefits, 1960

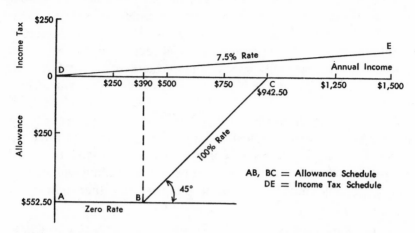

reaches $942.50. It is not clear whether the 100 percent take-away rate has adversely affected the incentives of benefit recipients. However, it does not seem to have reduced the average amount of work done per worker.[32]

The New Zealand social security system is financed mainly by a nominal registration fee and a flat income tax of 7.5 percent on before-benefit income without exemptions.[33] There are no employer and employee payroll taxes as in the United States. In Figure 3-1, line *DE* represents the 7.5 percent income tax rate. The vertical distance between line *DE* and any point on the horizontal before-benefit income axis is the tax paid in order to finance the social security system.[34]

[32] Weststrate, *op. cit.*, pp. 110-12. Weststrate says that the taxation required to finance the New Zealand social security programs may actually induce a person to work harder in order to make up for what is lost in taxes. Weststrate does not specifically raise the question of whether an effective 100 percent penalty rate on earnings causes a substitution of leisure for work. However, he indicates that most persons during their earning period do not receive regular benefits supplementing their income. This would minimize the extent of the incentive problem. With respect to the aged, Weststrate indicates that it is "practically certain" that the age benefit reduces work effort. Evidently this reduction is due to the high rate at which benefits are reduced for each dollar of earnings.

[33] Condliffe, *op. cit.*, p. 300.

[34] In Figure 3-1, the effective tax rate on income between $390 and $942.50 is 107.5 percent (100 percent penalty rate on each dollar increase in income plus the 7.5 percent social security income tax).

In 1959-60, New Zealand's social security benefits (monetary and nonmonetary) totaled $287 million, or 11 percent of national income. Forty percent of government expenditures were for social security programs.[35] Revenues from the social security income tax amounted to almost 80 percent of social security costs. The shortfall between the revenues specifically earmarked for the Social Security Fund and required revenues is made up from general revenues.[36]

The comprehensiveness of the New Zealand social security system probably is not matched by any other nation of the Western world. Certainly it stands in contrast to the U.S. welfare system. With its inauguration, New Zealand became a leading welfare state and a possible model for social planners in other nations.

Family Allowances

Family allowances, which have been adopted by many nations, have been defined as "systematic payments made to families with dependent children, either by employers or by the government, for the primary purpose of promoting the welfare of such children."[37] The rationale for family allowances is that the modern industrial system fails to accommodate differences in family size. Originally, family allowances usually were provided under a voluntary system in which an employer entered into an agreement with his employees; or in some cases family allowances were compulsory only within a particular region. Around 1930, however, governments began to assume control over the family allowance programs and the voluntary aspects often were replaced by a more general and compulsory system. By 1957, some thirty nations had one or another form of family allowance. Now, the United States is the only Western industrialized nation with no system of family allowances.

In 1964, the United States had about 4.5 million poor families with children, including 15 million children and 24 million persons. Thus, about 70 percent of the 34 million poor persons were in fam-

---

[35] *Yearbook, op. cit.*, pp. 745, 754-55.
[36] *Ibid.*, pp. 174-75.
[37] The definition is that of James Vadakin, and the following discussion of family allowances is largely based on his book, *Family Allowances* (Miami: University of Miami Press, 1958), pp. 1-26 *passim*.

ilies with children, and 22 percent of all children were in poor families.[38] A family allowance system, then, represents one logical approach to the reduction of poverty in the United States.[39]

Family allowance systems differ from country to country.[40] Some of the main differences—and questions raised by them—are with respect to:

1. Family eligibility: Should all families with children receive allowances? Or only workers' families? Or only families with per capita incomes less than some given level? Should family allowances begin only with the second child? What should be the maximum or minimum age for which children are eligible to receive allowances?

2. Rates of allowances: Should the rates be proportional, progressive, or regressive with respect to income and the number of children in the family?

3. Source of revenue: Should family allowances be paid out of revenues raised by special taxes, such as an employer payroll tax, or be paid out of general revenues?

Family allowance systems, whatever form they take, have been criticized mainly on the basis of some or all of four possibilities: (1) Such allowances may tend to increase the birth rate, especially among poorer families. (2) The allowances may not be spent on children. (3) The allowances may tend to depress wages. (4) A large portion of the total family allowance payments would go to families who by no stretch of the imagination are poor.

Family allowances have been supported, as well as attacked, on the ground that they will raise the birth rate. Strong support for family allowances is found in European countries (for example, France and Sweden) which from the end of World War I have been trying to raise their birth rates. However, there is little or no statistical evidence that family allowances affect the birth rate, and James Vadakin states that "family allowances are quite ineffective as a device for increasing the birth rate."[41] At any rate, with few exceptions

[38] Mollie Orshansky, "Who's Who Among the Poor," *op. cit.,* p. 4.

[39] Family allowances, in practice, are confined to families with children. In principle, it would seem allowances could be made to all members of all families. However, this discussion is confined to the approach taken in practice.

[40] For detailed discussion of differences, see Vadakin, *op. cit.,* pp. 41-45.

[41] *Ibid.,* p. 120

(Germany and Italy in the 1930's are two), the primary reason for starting family allowance programs has been to enhance the well-being of existing children.[42]

Also there seems to be no specific evidence to support the argument in opposition to family allowances that they may not be spent on the needs of children. And I have found no evidence to support the supposition that there may simply be a substitution in which family allowances pay for those goods and services which before had been bought with earnings. Canada, which now has a popular system of family allowances, has made surveys aimed at determining the uses to which the allowances have been put. The findings indicate that family allowances are spent on children. While it is uncertain whether the allowances are spent on the real needs of the children, it is clear that an "unusually high proportion of the families in all the studies spent their allowance checks for clothing, food, and medical care."[43] Usually, checks are made out to the mother rather than to the father on the assumption that the mother is more likely to see that the allowances are spent on the children.

The validity of the third objection—that family allowances tend to depress wages—seems to depend heavily on the method of financing family allowances and the level of family allowances. In France, where there is a heavy 16.75 percent employer payroll tax,[44] there is little question that family allowances have had a depressing influence on wages. Moreover, the level of family allowances is so high there that it is not unusual for a French worker with a large family to receive as much in allowances as he receives in wages. This may adversely affect work incentives as well as create employer resistance to wage increases.[45]

In Canada, where family allowances are paid out of general revenues, wages have been rising and their increase does not seem to have been retarded by the allowances. This may be caused, in part, by the general prosperity in Canada since adoption of family

[42] *Ibid.,* p. 92

[43] *Ibid.,* p. 82. This, however, does not prove that family allowances actually provided for additional spending to meet the needs of children. The allowances may simply have substituted for resources that otherwise would have been used to meet the needs of children.

[44] *Ibid.,* p. 43. This tax also covers maternity, housing, and prenatal programs.

[45] *Ibid.,* pp. 130-35.

allowances in 1944.[46] But there is reason for believing that financing from general revenues is less likely to depress wages than is an employer payroll tax. When family allowances are financed out of general revenues, an employer is less likely to use family allowances as an argument against granting wage increases when collective bargaining takes place.[47] Moreover, financing from general revenues is not likely to increase employers' costs. In Canada, too, family allowances are much smaller in relation to wages than in France.[48] This may well undercut the Canadian employers' opposition to wage increases on the grounds that workers already receive substantial family allowances. Also there is no indication that Canadian family allowances adversely affect incentives to work.[49]

The fourth objection to family allowances, especially as they would relate to poverty in the United States, is that they would be received by millions of families who were already quite well off. That is, as a measure against poverty, family allowances might well be considered inefficient. They might involve more redistribution of income than is required to meet the problem of poverty in the United States. To the extent that family allowances are desired not so much as a poverty measure but as a measure to redistribute income toward children, especially those in the lower half of the income distribution, this criticism becomes less valid.[50] Moreover, it is possible to copy Denmark in varying family allowance payments inversely with income, and discontinuing them altogether after a certain level of income is reached.

Estimates have been made of the cost of a family allowance system in the United States. The cost, if all families were included, would be $7.8 billion if each payment were $10 per month per child. If the same level of payments were made to parents whose

[46] *Ibid.,* p. 130

[47] *Ibid.,* p. 49. This is, in part, a problem in incidence theory.

[48] Canada's system is not based on wages, but its payments are low for such a high-income country. There the monthly allowance, in 1955, was $6 for a child under 10 and $8 for a child 10-15 years of age. In France, in 1955, family allowances were 22 percent of the mean monthly wage for the second child and 33 percent of the mean monthly wage for the third and each additional child per month. *Ibid.,* pp. 42-43.

[49] *Ibid.,* p. 136.

[50] If family allowances are paid out of general taxation, upper income recipients are likely to pay more in taxes to finance the allowances than they actually receive in allowances.

income is less than the value of their personal tax exemptions and deductions, the cost would be $1.9 billion. In this case, family allowances—like transfer-by-taxation allowances—would be income-conditioned benefits. For these same families, a payment of $30 a month for each child would cost $5.7 billion a year.[51]

[51] Patricia McGuire, "Family Allowances in the United States" (unpublished paper of Office of Policy Planning and Research, U. S. Department of Labor, April 1964), pp. 25-26. Note that this would create a "notch" problem such as that discussed in Chapter II in connection with cash tax credits.

CHAPTER IV

The Development of the Transfer-by-Taxation Idea

THE PROVISION OF INCOME to all families or persons with income below some specified level is not a new idea. An early example is the Speenhamland system of relief, inaugurated in Berkshire, in 1795 and copied widely throughout England in subsequent years. The Speenhamland system fixed a scale of relief proportioned to the price of wheat and the size of the applicant's family, and offered to give relief to all laborers whose wages were insufficient to provide subsistence. Unfortunately, that system created an incentive for employers to reduce wages and increasingly to throw the cost of a laborer's subsistence upon local taxpayers.[1] The Poor Law of 1834 abolished the Speenhamland system and provided that the able-bodied poor could receive relief only if they entered a poor house.[2] The failure of this first experiment with a guaranteed minimum income left as a legacy to the future grave doubts about the workability of any plan that provides a minimum income to all citizens.

[1] Karl Polanyi, *The Great Transformation* (New York: Rinehart, 1957), Chap. 7, pp. 77-85. The industrial revolution and the rising price of food due to the war with the French had produced a situation in which many laborers received a wage that hardly provided for subsistence.

[2] This is what has been termed "indoor" relief.

After Speenhamland, the guaranteed minimum income, as a practical proposal within the context of the capitalist system, seems to have disappeared until about the time of World War II. This is not to say that the idea died.[3] But for all practical purposes the proposals and subsequent programs advocated by Western social reformers and planners were more limited, and dealt mainly with problems created by an industrial society. Some of these programs were discussed in the preceding chapter. When the guaranteed minimum proposal appeared again it was in a form rather closely linked with the income tax system. Whatever earlier origins transfer-by-taxation may have had, its real history begins with the changes wrought by the Great Depression of the 1930's and World War II.

Social Dividend Taxation

During World War II, the Englishwoman, Lady Juliette Evangeline Rhys-Williams, proposed a comprehensive social insurance system which would include every man, woman, and child.[4] Essentially, the scheme consisted of a merger between the social insurance and income tax systems. According to Lady Rhys-Williams, all welfare services operated by the state should be combined into a single comprehensive system with benefits payable to all citizens, and not only to those who need help. The Rhys-Williams proposal grew, in part, out of discontent with the propensity of the existing unemployment insurance system to create a disincentive to work. In *Something to Look Forward To,* Lady Rhys-Williams wrote: "The lion in the path of curing want by means of insurance is the fact that if the standard of unemployment pay is raised to a level at which real want is banished, . . . then the advantages of working for

[3] In *The Economics of Welfare,* first published in 1920, A. C. Pigou discusses the idea of a national minimum standard of living and its effect on national output, or what Pigou calls the "national dividend." Pigou does not have any specific plan in mind, but he does recognize that a plan which simply brings people's income up to a prearranged standard will have deleterious effects on aggregate output. A. C. Pigou, *The Economics of Welfare* (4th ed.; London: Macmillan, 1952), pp. 720-28 and pp. 758-67.

[4] Lady Rhys-Williams, *Something to Look Forward To* (London: MacDonald, 1943). See also her later book, *Taxation and Incentive* (New York: Oxford University Press, 1953), pp. 121-37.

wages largely disappear."[5] The solution to this problem seemed to her to lie in the abandonment of the existing social insurance system with its philosophy that the state only helps the destitute and the sick, and its replacement by one based on "the democratic principle that the state owes precisely the same benefits to every one of its citizens." The employed and healthy should receive benefits just as the unemployed and the sick received them. However, Lady Rhys-Williams would have excluded from the provisions of her scheme the able-bodied unemployed who refused to accept jobs offered them.[6]

Under the Rhys-Williams scheme, a "social dividend" would be paid weekly to every man, woman, and child, though the amount varied with sex and age.[7] The social dividend would not be financed by an employee payroll tax, but rather by a proportional tax on all income, which at the time would have necessitated a rate close to 40 percent.[8] A surtax, starting on incomes above £600, would raise revenues required to finance other government expenditures. This two-tax approach reflects an assumption underlying the Rhys-Williams proposal. The assumption is that the "relationship between the citizen and the State falls into two parts, which ought to be kept distinct from one another from the financial point of view." On the one hand are the "dues" which are used to pay for the time-honored government services of justice, order, defense, government administration, national debt, and public works. On the other hand are the social services which Lady Rhys-Williams described as "merely a convenient arrangement whereby the citizen makes use of the central (or local) government machinery to provide himself and his family with goods and services, or benefits required to fulfill his personal needs, and which, without such arrangement, he would have to provide out of his private purse."[9]

[5] As quoted in *Taxation and Incentive*, p. 121. This reflects the fact that where the real wage is not substantially above a "minimum acceptable living wage," unemployment insurance is caught between the vices of creating work disincentives or providing too little to live on.

[6] *Taxation and Incentive, op. cit.*, pp. 121 and 123.

[7] *Ibid.*, pp. 128-37. Lady Rhys-Williams subsequently modified the original plan several times to meet certain criticisms. Essentially, no change in the basic proposal was made by the modifications. They were mainly in the form of changes in the levels of benefits and taxes and the degree to which social welfare programs, then existing in Great Britain, would be pre-empted by the proposal.

[8] *Ibid.*, p. 124. The tax rate would have been 7s. 6d. per £1.

[9] *Ibid.*, pp. 137-38.

At the time when the Rhys-Williams plan was proposed, family allowances were being seriously considered by the British government.[10] The Rhys-Williams social dividend scheme and family allowances have one characteristic in common: payments are made to families regardless of need. They differ in that family allowances are generally restricted to families with children, whereas the Rhys-Williams social dividend is available to all families and individuals. They differ, too, in that the Rhys-Williams plan explicitly ties the welfare system to the tax system. By adjusting the tax system so as to include direct payments to families, the Rhys-Williams plan was providing for negative as well as positive taxes.[11]

Lady Rhys-Williams' concept of a social dividend is of the sort which, in this study, is called "social dividend taxation." Social dividend taxation may be defined as a tax-transfer system in which every family begins the year with an income guarantee from the government. The guarantee can take either of two forms: (1) The family will receive cash payments of a given level at regular intervals during the year. Or (2), at the end of the year, the income guarantee will be subtracted from the family's tax liability in calculating the family's "net" tax payment. The essence of social dividend taxation is that it combines negative and positive taxes in such a way as to build a floor under the income of every family. It requires the tax system to raise revenues to finance the guaranteed minimum income to everybody as well as to finance other public services.

The proposal made by Lady Rhys-Williams never attracted a great deal of support in Great Britain or other North Atlantic nations. However, the simplicity of her approach to the elimination of poverty has attracted the attention of a few postwar writers. C. E. Ayres briefly mentions a similar plan; Robert R. Shutz, in a doctoral dissertation, developed a plan similar in most respects to the Rhys-Williams plan; Eveline Burns, of the Columbia University School of Social Work, recently proposed that the United States adopt a plan similar to that proposed by Lady Rhys-Williams; and

---

[10] *Ibid.*, p. 121. As it turned out, Great Britain never adopted the Rhys-Williams proposal but it did adopt allowances for families with two or more children.

[11] The view that transfers might be thought of as negative taxes was held by Hugh Dalton, Chancellor of the Exchequer, in the postwar Labour government. Hugh Dalton, *Principles of Public Finance* (4th ed.; London: Rutledge, 1957), pp. 148-49.

more recently D. B. Smith, a Canadian manufacturer, proposed a type of social dividend plan to eliminate poverty in Canada.[12]

Ayres does not present a comprehensive plan, but he suggests the relevance of a "social dividend" plan for an industrialized nation such as the United States. He would have every member of the community receive a "basic independent income, the same for all, and just sufficient to cover the 'minimum of subsistence'." The necessary revenues would be raised by a tax on earned income. Ayres notes that taxpayers receive a subsidy through exemptions for their dependents, and that it is only a step from tax deductions or exemptions to direct payment.[13]

Shutz's plan, which he calls "continuous taxation," is designed —as are those of Rhys-Williams and Ayres—to eliminate poverty. Shutz recognizes that to pay poor families the difference between their incomes and the minimum incomes necessary to meet minimum budget requirements would cause a reduction in productivity among those whose incomes were below, or near, the guaranteed income level.[14] Like Lady Rhys-Williams, Shutz would guarantee income payments to all families and finance the guarantee through a tax on all income. Unlike Lady Rhys-Williams, he does not formally distinguish between the social welfare functions of government and the more orthodox functions of defense, order, justice, and so on. Shutz' income tax schedule, which is quite progressive, would cover

[12] C. E. Ayres, *The Industrial Economy* (Boston: Houghton-Mifflin, 1952), pp. 263-64; Robert Rudolph Shutz, "Transfer Payments and Income Inequality" (unpublished doctoral dissertation, University of California, 1952); Eveline Burns, "Social Security in Evolution: Towards What?", *Proceedings of the Seventeenth Annual Meeting of the Industrial Relations Research Association* (Chicago: December 1964), pp. 20-28; and D. B. Smith, "A Simplified Approach to Social Welfare," *Canadian Tax Journal*, Vol. 13 (May-June 1965), pp. 260-65.

[13] Ayres, *op. cit.*, p. 263.

[14] A system which would pay families the difference between their incomes and a "Federally Guaranteed Minimum Income" of $3,000 has been advocated by Edward E. Schwartz of the University of Chicago School of Social Work in "A Way to End the Means Test," *Social Work*, Vol. 9 (July 1964), pp. 3-12. Schwartz does not seem to be especially moved about the potential work disincentives created by such a program. However, he does offer a modification of his program to reduce the potential disincentives. Robert Theobald has also suggested bringing all incomes up to a predetermined level. To mitigate somewhat the potential work disincentive effects, he would add a "premium" equal to some (small) percentage of earnings. See Robert Theobald, *Free Men and Free Markets* (New York: C. N. Potter, 1963), Appendix, pp. 192-97. Theobald has also edited a book entitled *The Guaranteed Income: Next Step in Economic Evolution?* (Garden City, N.Y.: Doubleday, 1966).

both the cost of his plan and other expenditures to which the revenues of the income tax are usually allocated.[15]

D. B. Smith's plan would provide $1,000 for every adult (persons over 21 years of age) and $200 for every person 21 years old and under. The rationale for this proposal is that "our society is changing so fast that it passes large numbers of our citizens by." Those passed by represent "overwhelming personal disasters," each an "infinitesimal part of a national disaster in the making." According to Smith, the Canadian welfare programs can be rationalized by adopting his approach and eliminating present welfare programs, including farm and other subsidies.[16]

To finance the $12 billion cost of his plan, Smith would apply a flat 40 percent tax rate to personal income (less imputed income). All other government expenditures would be financed by other taxes. But this would not be a major break with current experience, since Canada's federal government "is redistributing each year an amount close to that collected as personal income taxes."[17] Interestingly, Smith would "peg" the cost of his plan to a specific percentage of personal income. According to Smith, if per capita income rose in the future, as it undoubtedly would, the minimum income guarantee could also rise and/or the increased revenues could be used to finance some other desirable welfare plan—for example, health services.[18]

The Smith proposal is probably the simplest of the social dividend plans described here. However, all the plans are basically similar in that they guarantee all citizens a minimum income consistent with minimum "livable" budget costs. Because the guarantee is given to all families, not just poor ones, the cost of each proposed program is large. In each case, the average tax rates on income would run to about 40 percent.[19]

---

[15] Shutz estimated the gross cost of his plan, based on 1945 income and population, at $69 billion, with a net transfer or actual cost of the program estimated at $23 billion.

[16] Smith, op. cit., pp. 260-61. Smith uses the word "welfare" broadly, to include social insurance, pensions, and unemployment insurance as well as "relief" or "public assistance."

[17] Ibid.

[18] Ibid., p. 262. But per capita income might not rise if the 40 percent rate acts as a major disincentive to work.

[19] Lady Rhys-Williams' tax of 7s. 6d. on each £ of income would be at a rate of about 37.5 percent compared with Smith's 40 percent rate. Shutz would utilize

Negative Income Taxation

One way to avoid the necessarily heavy cost of a social dividend plan without creating major disincentives to work is to confine the programs to the poor and fill only part of their poverty income gap. This is the essence of negative income taxation.[20] This form of taxation in a sense is a watered-down version of social dividend taxation. It is aimed at the poor, it would meet some of the cash needs of the poor, and its limited coverage reflects recognition that the poor are a dwindling minority in the United States.

The two main proponents of negative income taxation in the United States are Milton Friedman and Robert J. Lampman.[21] However, they are by no means the only economists who have suggested that the income tax rates be extended beyond zero to negative levels in order to pay negative taxes (or transfers) to low-income families. Before the appearance of Friedman's *Capitalism and Freedom,* Earl Rolph and George Break in their textbook *Public Finance* had suggested such an approach if a "nation-wide program of assistance to all low-income groups" is thought desirable. Basic to the plan would be a "critical income level" for each family size at which neither taxes would be paid nor subsidies received. "Above

---

rates beginning with 21 percent on the first dollar of income in excess of the guarantee, and rates would run on up to 79.9 percent on incomes in excess of $200,000.

[20] In this historical chapter, the popular term "negative income taxation" is used. Earlier and in subsequent chapters I use the more accurate term "negative rates taxation." The focus of these plans is not on negative income but on the poverty income gap.

[21] I am not aware of negative income tax plans proposed by persons outside the United States. The plan suggested by Milton Friedman in *Capitalism and Freedom* (Chicago: University of Chicago Press, 1962), incidentally, originated in lectures by Friedman at Wabash College in 1956. Correspondence with Friedman, Walter Heller, William Vickrey, and Louis Shere turned up the fact that there had been some discussion of the idea during the 1940's, and that the subject had been informally discussed by some members, including Heller and Vickrey, then of the Division of Tax Research, Treasury Department. There is no evidence, however, that a paper on the subject was prepared in the Division of Tax Research. That the idea was in the air in the 1940's is illustrated by a passage in an article by George Stigler, who says that "there is great attractiveness in the proposal that we extend the personal income tax to the lowest income brackets with negative rates in these brackets." See Stigler, "The Economics of Minimum Wage Legislation," *American Economic Review,* Vol. 36 (June 1946), p. 365. (I am grateful to James Simler for bringing this passage to my attention.)

this level taxes would be paid (as is now the case), and below it money subsidies, computed as a percentage of the amount by which actual family income fell short of the critical level, would be received."[22] A similar idea is mentioned by James Buchanan, who stated that taxes could be imposed on those considered to be "receiving excessively high incomes, and the proceeds would be used to pay subsidies (negative taxes) to those considered to be receiving excessively low incomes."[23]

In *Capitalism and Freedom,* Milton Friedman proposed a negative income tax as an alternative to present welfare programs.[24] He would apply a 50 percent rate to the unused tax exemptions and deductions of families with no taxable income. On the supposition that families with no taxable income are poor, or very nearly poor, society could be assured that it was building a floor under the income of poor families and not subsidizing families which were not poor.

Briefly, Friedman's plan would work as follows: Each head of a family and his dependents would continue to receive the $600 exemption and a standard deduction.[25] If the family's total value of exemptions and deductions ($3,000, for example) exceeded its adjusted gross income (say $2,000) by $1,000, the family would receive "negative taxes" totaling $500 from the Treasury. Friedman says of his plan:

The advantages of this arrangement are clear! It is directed specifically at the problem of poverty. It gives help in the form most useful to the individual, namely, cash. It is general and could be substituted for the host of special measures now in effect. It makes explicit the cost borne by society. It operates outside the market. Like any other measures to alleviate poverty, it reduces the incentives of those helped to help themselves, but it does not eliminate that incentive entirely, as a system

[22] Earl Rolph and George Break, *Public Finance* (New York: Ronald Press, 1961), p. 404.
[23] James Buchanan, *The Public Finances* (Homewood, Illinois: Richard D. Irwin, Inc., 1960), pp. 157-58.
[24] *Op. cit.,* pp. 191-94.
[25] When Friedman wrote in 1961-62, the standard deduction was 10 percent of a family's adjusted gross income. However, under the 1964 Tax Law revision the 10 percent standard deduction was changed to a minimum standard deduction of $300 for the filer and $100 for each of his dependents.

of supplementing incomes up to some fixed minimum would. An extra dollar earned always means more money available for expenditure.[26]

Robert J. Lampman differs from Friedman in suggesting negative income taxes as only one of the approaches to the reduction of poverty.[27] Lampman notes that the really poor families—especially those with children—do not receive the "full force" of personal exemptions and deductions. By applying a tax rate (or rates) to unused exemptions and deductions, as Friedman has suggested, the present tax system could more fully realize the equity characteristics of its present allowance of personal exemptions and deductions.[28] However, Lampman stops short of Friedman's view that the negative income tax should replace existing social welfare programs (including farm subsidies and public housing). Lampman's view is that the negative income tax is both a supplement and a complement to the existing welfare programs, although he believes that it would, and should, reduce the public assistance programs.[29]

In a recent paper, Lampman explored the philosophy behind and the mechanics of a negative income tax.[30] There he says: the poor need help; the present income tax discriminates against the poor (for example, neither a family of four with no income nor a family of four with a $3,000 income pays any income tax); cuts in the tax rate or increases in the dollar value of exemptions and standard deductions do almost nothing for the poor; and a good deal more equity could be produced in the tax system if negative tax rates were added to it.[31] But equity presumably would be produced with a 14 percent tax rate (the rate at present for the lowest bracket). If more than equity is to be produced—that is, if welfare is to be of prime importance—the negative tax rate would have to be

[26] *Op. cit.*, p. 192.

[27] Lampman, "Prognosis for Poverty," *Proceedings of 57th Annual Conference of the National Tax Association* (Pittsburgh: September 1964), pp. 71-81. See also his "Approaches to the Reduction of Poverty," *American Economic Review, Papers and Proceedings*, Vol. 55 (May 1965), pp. 521-29.

[28] Lampman, "Approaches to the Reduction of Poverty," *op. cit.*, pp. 526-27.

[29] Based on my conversations with Robert J. Lampman.

[30] Lampman, "Negative Rates Income Taxation" (unpublished paper prepared for the Office of Economic Opportunity, August 1965).

[31] *Ibid.*, pp. 2-4. References to Lampman's views in the rest of this paragraph are from my conversations with him. The equity issue is explained and analyzed in Chapter VI.

FIGURE 4-1. The Tobin Plan for a Basic Income Allowance (Family of Four)

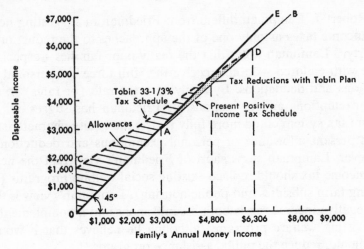

closer to 50 percent than to 14 percent. It is Lampman's view that if the negative tax rate (or rates) is to be above 25 percent, the poverty income gap should be substituted for unused exemptions and deductions as the negative tax base. His reasoning is that once equity plays second fiddle to welfare or antipoverty goals, the argument that negative tax rates would further rationalize the individual income tax system is weakened. It would be preferable then to use the poverty income gap as a base instead of unused exemptions and deductions because the poverty income gap would produce greater equity in the treatment of poor families of different sizes.

In still another recent paper, James Tobin developed a basic income allowance proposal which might be considered a cross between negative income taxation and social dividend taxation.[32] Essentially the Tobin plan consists of a basic allowance of $400 per year for every man, woman, and child. The way his plan would

[32] James Tobin, "Improving the Economic Status of the Negro," *Daedalus*, Vol. 94 (Fall 1965), pp. 889-95. Tobin sets an upper limit of $2,700 for a family. A family of six would receive a $2,400 basic allowance. The seventh and eighth members would receive $150 apiece. After the eighth member, no additional allowances would be provided. Tobin would exclude beneficiaries of old-age, survivors, and disability insurance (OASDI) from the plan on the basis that they should be assured a minimum of $400 each.

affect a family of four is shown in Figure 4-1. A tax unit, under his plan, is subject to a 33⅓ percent tax rate on income other than the allowance ($1,600 in this case) as shown by *CD* in Figure 4-1. What is unique about the plan is that Tobin is able to merge the negative tax with the present positive tax system. He does so by providing that the 33⅓ percent rate applies only up to the income level ($6,306 for a family of four) where the net tax[33] under the Tobin system equals the tax liability of the present positive tax system. After that income level (shown by point *D*), the present tax schedule (curve *ADB*) applies. Tobin thereby assures that no one would pay more taxes than he is presently paying.

The net cost of the Tobin plan is about $14 billion.[34] Tobin evidently assumes that $14 billion is modest enough to be financed out of the rising revenues produced by the growth of the economy.

In Conclusion

Negative income taxation does not really differ in principle from social dividend taxation. But each raises different issues and problems. It is fair to say (1) that negative taxation is an offshoot of social dividend taxation and (2) that negative taxation is a much less "radical" proposal—mainly because it is confined to a minority segment of society and it is much less expensive. Negative income taxation, as it has been presented by Friedman and Lampman, represents a means to attack existing poverty with a minimum of income redistribution. Negative income taxation is also a means whereby the poor would benefit from tax cuts if the tax cuts included an increase in the negative tax rate or a rise in personal exemptions. In this age of Keynesian economic policy, income tax cuts are an important fiscal weapon. Yet it is clear that the poor do not benefit directly from either a fall in (positive) income tax rates or a rise in the level of personal exemptions and deductions. For these reasons, adoption of the negative income tax approach seems more likely in the United States than does the social dividend taxation approach.

[33] Net tax is the basic allowance minus the income tax liability. This may be positive or negative.
[34] Tobin's estimate is based on income tax data for 1962. The net cost includes an estimate of the resultant reduction in tax revenues.

CHAPTER V

The Common Features of Transfer-by-Taxation Plans

THE DIFFERENT TYPES of transfer-by-taxation plans which were discussed in the preceding chapter are basically similar. Furthermore, all transfer-by-taxation contains three basic variables: (1) a guaranteed minimum level of income that varies with family size or family composition or both; (2) a tax rate or rates applied against a tax base; and (3) a breakeven level of income where the tax liability equals the allowance guarantee. Any two of these variables determine the outcome of the third.

The Basic Variables

The interrelationships of these three variables of transfer-by-taxation can be clarified by simple illustrations. If a family is guaranteed $3,000 and a tax rate of 50 percent is applied against the family's income (excluding the guaranteed allowance), the breakeven level of income will be $6,000 for the family. That is, at $6,000 the family's income tax liability of $3,000 (.50 times $6,000) equals the guaranteed allowance of $3,000. Suppose it were desirable to make the family's breakeven level of income $3,000 and to guarantee $1,500. The transfer-by-taxation tax rate would be 50 percent—or some combination of rates which averaged 50 percent on $3,000 of family income. Finally, a break-even level of income of $3,000 and a 25 percent tax rate would mean an income guarantee of $750 (.25 times $3,000). Only if the guarantee is $750 is the net allowance[1] reduced to zero by a flat 25 percent tax rate when income reaches $3,000.[2]

Once it becomes clear that the essentials of transfer-by-taxation can be reduced to three basic variables, it is easy to understand why there is, in principle, no difference between the Rhys-Williams social dividend plan, the Lampman or Friedman negative rates taxation plans, and the Tobin plan which is a cross between the two types.[3] The only important difference between these plans lies in the magnitude of the guaranteed minimum income or allowance, the level of the tax rate, and the breakeven level of income.

All the social dividend schemes described in Chapter IV begin with the choice of a guaranteed minimum income (which varies with family size) and the choice of an income tax rate which will finance the plan. These choices determine the magnitude of the third variable, the breakeven level of income. In simple algebraic terms:

(5-1) $Y_g/t_s = R$

where Y_g = guaranteed minimum income,

t_s = social dividend tax rate,

R = the breakeven level of income—or the level of income at which the net allowance is reduced to zero.

The righthand side of equation 5-1 may be thought of as the "outcome" of sociopolitical decisions involving the magnitudes on the lefthand side of the equation. This does not mean that in social dividend taxation the breakeven level of income, R, is not a matter of concern for policy makers. It simply means that social dividend taxation is characterized by an emphasis upon a guaranteed minimum income and a tax schedule which reduces the guarantee to zero at

[1] The net allowance is equal to the guaranteed allowance less the tax on the family's income.

[2] Throughout this discussion, "income" refers to the family's income excluding the allowance.

[3] For details of these plans, see Chapter IV and the sources cited there.

some point. This is true of the Tobin plan which differs from social dividend taxation in its more modest proportions and in its failure to specify how the cost is to be financed. It is also true of tax credit schemes which would convert the personal exemptions under present tax systems into a credit financed by a tax on income.

The emphasis in negative rates taxation is somewhat different. A breakeven level of income is first determined. In the case of Friedman's plan, the breakeven level of income is the value of exemptions and deductions allowed a family; for the plan by Lampman it is the family's poverty line. When the breakeven level of income is combined with a negative tax schedule, a guaranteed minimum income level is determined. The equation for negative rates taxation might be written as:

$$(5\text{-}2) \qquad R t_n = Y_g,$$

where $\qquad t_n =$ the negative tax rate (or rates)

and R and Y_g are the same as in equation 5-1 above.

The negative rates taxation equation might also have been written as:

$$(5\text{-}3) \qquad Y_g / R = t_n.$$

The emphasis here is upon a breakeven level of income and a guaranteed minimum income. The outcome is the negative tax rate. It is difficult to say whether proponents of a negative rates plan, after having chosen a breakeven level of income, put more emphasis on the negative tax rate or upon the guaranteed minimum income. The answer probably is "both equally."

The tax base, at first glance, would seem to differentiate negative rates taxation from social dividend taxation or the Tobin plan. In negative rates taxation, the tax base is the gap between some "standard"—such as the value of personal exemptions and minimum standard deductions (hereafter EX-MSD) allowed a family or the family's poverty line—and the family's income. In social dividend taxation and in the Tobin plan the tax base is the family's income before allowance. In fact, this difference is superficial. For example, it is easy to show that a negative rates plan which fills X percent of a family's poverty income gap is the same as a plan which guarantees a minimum income equal to X percent of the family's poverty line and taxes the family's income at an X percent

TABLE 5-1. Allowance for a Family of Four Under Two Transfer-by-Taxation Plans

Type of Plan	Family's Income Before Allowance				
	$ 0	$ 500	$1,000	$2,000	$3,000
Negative Rates Taxation:					
(1) Poverty income gap or unused EX-MSD[a]	$3,000	$2,500	$2,000	$1,000	$ 0
(2) Allowance based on 40% of poverty gap or unused EX-MSD	1,200	1,000	800	400	0
Social Dividend:					
(3) Basic allowance guarantee of $1,200 (equal to 40% of poverty line)	1,200	1,200	1,200	1,200	1,200
(4) Tax liability with 40% income tax rate	0	200	400	800	1,200
(5) Net allowance, (3)–(4)	1,200	1,000	800	400	0

[a] Both the Lampman poverty line and the value of exemptions and minimum standard deductions (EX-MSD) are $3,000 for a family of four.

rate. This is shown in Table 5-1. The first plan shows what happens under a typical negative rates taxation plan with a negative tax rate of 40 percent applied against the family's poverty income gap or the family's unused EX-MSD. The second resembles a social dividend plan in that it guarantees a family of four $1,200 (40 percent of $3,000) and taxes the family's income at a 40 percent rate. Lines 2 and 5 show that both plans, given the family's income, produce identical results.[4]

The Similarity of Transfer-by-Taxation and Other Minimum Income Plans

It is interesting to consider whether any plan which guarantees a minimum income differs, in principle, from a transfer-by-taxation plan. That is, if a plan completely unrelated to the tax system is devised, will it not in substance be the same as a transfer-by-taxation plan? The answer would seem to be yes. If, as an example, some federal bureau were established with the duty of assuring all families a minimum income, it would necessarily have to implement a

[4] The similarity between negative rates taxation and social dividend taxation is further illustrated by comparing their allowance formulas (Appendix C).

plan consisting of a "tax rate" and a breakeven level of income in addition to the guaranteed minimum. This is because the bureau would be forced to decide on a rate at which the guaranteed allowances are reduced as a family's income rises. Once this is determined, the rate (or rates) in conjunction with the guarantee will determine a breakeven level of income. In addition, the bureau would have to secure financing in some form, even though the means of financing might be completely unrelated to the plan itself.

Some writers, as noted in Chapter IV, have proposed raising the income of families with income deficiencies to some predetermined level.[5] This effectively means equating the minimum income guarantee and the breakeven level of income. The outcome is a 100 percent tax rate on the negative taxable income of allowance recipients. Sometimes modifications are made in order to mitigate the potential disincentive to work produced by a 100 percent tax on earned income. One modification takes the form of an allowance premium equal to some percentage of the family's earned income.[6] If a family is guaranteed $3,000 and has earnings of $2,000, it might be allowed $1,000 (which would fill the gap) plus some percentage of its earned income. The difficulty with this modification is that it produces what tax experts call a "notch" problem. That is, it is possible for some families, whose before-allowance income made them worse off than some other families, to have a higher after-allowance income than that of previously better-off families. For example, suppose two four-member families have, respectively, $2,000 and $3,200 of income before an allowance is made.[7] Assume the guaranteed minimum income for a four-person family is $3,000. The $3,200 family does not qualify for any allowance because its before-tax income is above the guarantee. The $2,000 family qualifies for a $1,000 allowance plus a premium of, say, 20 percent of its $2,000 earnings. Its after-tax and after-allowance income is $3,400.

This notch problem can be remedied by extending eligibility for receiving an allowance to families whose before-tax income is above the guaranteed minimum income level. Schwartz, one of the

[5] See Edward E. Schwartz, "A Way to End the Means Test," *Social Work*, Vol. 9 (July 1964), pp. 3-12; Robert Theobald, ed., *Free Men and Free Markets* (New York: C. N. Potter, 1963), Appendix, pp. 192-97.

[6] This approach is taken by Theobald, *op. cit.*

[7] It is assumed for simplicity that the income of these families is composed solely of earnings.

proponents of the fill-the-gap approach, has suggested such a remedy. Under his modified plan, outlined in Table 5-2, as earned income rises, the allowance falls until a breakeven point is reached at $4,000. This plan, aside from the progressivity in the tax schedule, is equivalent to a social dividend plan with a $3,000 guarantee and a 75 percent tax rate on income below the breakeven level of income.

TABLE 5-2. The Schwartz Plan[a]

Earned Income	Tax on Income (Percent)	Allowance	Total Income
$ 0– 999	60	$3,000–2,400	$3,000–3,399
1,000–1,999	70	2,399–1,700	3,399–3,699
2,000–2,999	80	1,699– 900	3,699–3,899
3,000–3,999	90	899– 0	3,899–3,999
4,000–4,499	100	0	4,000–4,499

Source: Edward Schwartz, "A Way to End the Means Test," *Social Work*, Vol. 9 (July 1964), page 9.
[a] Guarantees a minimum income of $3,000 to all families.

In sum, simply filling the gap is equivalent to a negative rates plan with a 100 percent negative tax rate. If the disincentive effect of such a plan is to be avoided without producing a notch problem, the fill-the-gap plan resembles a social dividend plan. The same analysis may be applied to public assistance, social insurance, and family allowance programs designed to guarantee a minimum income.[8] Although this study is confined to transfer-by-taxation plans, such a limitation is not necessary except to the extent that it reduces the number of specific plans to be examined.

[8] A recent guaranteed minimum income proposal appears in U. S. Department of Health, Education, and Welfare, Advisory Council on Public Welfare, *Having the Power, We Have the Duty* (June 1966).

CHAPTER VI

Breakeven Lines and
Tax Schedules

AN IMPORTANT QUESTION, in constructing a transfer-by-taxation plan, is how the positive and negative rates are to be combined. In probably the simplest of the transfer-by-taxation plans—the Friedman negative rates plan[1]—there is mutual exclusion between the positive and negative rate schedules. That is to say, there is no overlap in the sense that a recipient of net allowances would also be a taxpayer.[2] This mutual exclusion is possible because Friedman made the existence of unused exemptions and deductions the criterion for eligibility to receive allowances. The relationship between the Friedman negative rates plan (with a 50 percent negative rate) and the existing positive income tax system is shown in Figure 6-1. The shaded area between line AB and the horizontal axis represents the negative rates allowances paid to four-person families with varying levels of income. The slope of the line AB represents a single 50 percent negative tax rate. Curve CD shows the positive tax

[1] See Milton Friedman, *Capitalism and Freedom* (Chicago: University of Chicago Press, 1962), pp. 191-93.
[2] This abstracts from the question of the definition of income and the eligible tax unit for negative rates taxation purposes.

68

FIGURE 6-1. Mutual Exclusion and Overlap Under Various Transfer-by-Taxation Plans (Family of Four)

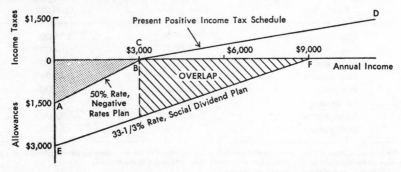

schedule which comes into play at or above the $3,000 money income level.[3]

Mutual exclusion is not possible when transfer-by-taxation plans are designed to eliminate poverty by guaranteeing an income equal to or greater than the poverty line levels of income.[4] This is illustrated by line *EF* in Figure 6-1 which represents a social dividend of $3,000 and a 33⅓ percent social dividend tax levied against income in order to finance the plan. To avoid paying net allowances to present taxpayers, exemptions and minimum standard deductions (referred to hereinafter as EX-MSD) would have to be raised to the breakeven levels of income. However, some proponents of social dividend taxation (such as Lady Rhys-Williams) believe the social dividend system has its own job to do, and overlap with the positive income tax system is not considered undesirable.

Breakeven Lines in Negative Rates Taxation

The proposals for negative rates taxation would apply a negative rate or set of rates to the unused portion (if any) of a taxpayer's exemptions and deductions or to his poverty income gap. Does it make a difference whether the value of EX-MSD or poverty lines are chosen as the breakeven income levels? Table 6-1 indicates

---

[3] Where it begins depends upon the level of adjusted gross income. Adjusted gross income is not necessarily the same as money income.

[4] The conditions for mutual exclusion are that $Y_g/t \leq Y_e$, where Y_g is the income guarantee, t is the negative tax rate, and Y_e is the level of tax exempt income.

TABLE 6-1. Poverty Lines Compared to Exemptions and Deductions, by Family Size[a]

Family Size	Poverty Line	EX-MSD[b]
One person	$1,500	$ 900
Two persons	2,000	1,600
Three persons	2,500	2,300
Four persons	3,000	3,000
Five persons	3,500	3,700
Six persons	4,000	4,400
Seven persons	4,500	5,100
Eight persons	5,000	5,800

[a] It is assumed that the size of the family equals the person who files the tax return (or head of family) plus the number of his dependents. See description of poverty lines in footnote 5, this chapter.
[b] Exemptions and minimum standard deductions.

how, for families of different sizes, the value of EX-MSD compares with poverty lines.[5] The divergences between the two are especially apparent for very small and very large families.

Criteria for Choosing the Breakeven Lines

At least three criteria are relevant in choosing between EX-MSD and the poverty line in approaching negative rates taxation. The first criterion is to assure that as many as possible of the poor are covered by the plan. This is the "efficiency" criterion or objective. Does efficiency with regard to a negative rates plan imply that those who are not poor should be excluded from receiving allowances? There is little question that the main—if not the only—objective of a negative rates plan is to meet some of the income needs of the poor. Thus the major proportion of benefits should go directly to the poor. However, if it were necessary to provide allowances to those who are not poor in order to help the poor it certainly would not be inefficient to provide some benefits to the nonpoor. Maximum efficiency would seem to imply covering all of the poor —and limiting benefits for the nonpoor to any which are necessary in connection with aiding the poor.

[5] Robert J. Lampman's proposed poverty lines are $1,500 for an unrelated individual or family head and $500 for each additional member of the family. Use of these lines for purposes of negative rates taxation seems preferable to using those of Mollie Orshansky in "Recounting the Poor—A Five-Year Review," *Social Security Bulletin*, Vol. 29 (April 1966), pp. 20-37. The lines such as $2,455 or $3,130 which she chooses seem to be unnecessarily precise. Lampman's $500 intervals add to desirable simplicity; and the Orshansky lines rise by approximately $500 intervals.

The second criterion is to assure as high a degree of horizontal equity among different family sizes as is possible. Equity implies that families in similar economic positions should be treated alike. The best measure of similarity in the position of the poor (possibly the only measure) is the percentage of their poverty lines covered by their income. The absolute number of dollars of income they receive is not the governing factor; a family of two with an income of $1,000 is better off, other things equal, than a family of six with the same dollar income of $1,000. Equity would imply that families with incomes equal to the same percentage of their respective poverty lines should receive allowances which fill the same percentage of their poverty income gaps. Provision of the same absolute amount of dollars to equally poor families of different sizes would not be equitable because a dollar of allowance can be expected to go further toward meeting the unfilled needs of a family of two than of a family of six.[6]

The third criterion is to assure that as far as possible the negative rates plan relies on the framework, concepts, and methods used in the positive tax system. This criterion—called the "carryover" criterion—implies mutual exclusion between the positive and negative tax schedules. It also implies that definitions and concepts of the present income tax system should be employed in the return filed for negative tax purposes.

Carryover Criterion versus Efficiency and Equity

It is unlikely that any one proposal for negative rates taxation could meet all three criteria outlined above. In fact, an obvious conflict exists between the efficiency objective and the desire for mutual exclusion with the present positive tax system. The reason for the conflict is that accepted poverty lines rise by approximately $500 for each increase in family size, while the value of exemptions and minimum standard deductions rises by $700 for each additional member (Table 6-1).

The only point at which a poverty line coincides with the value of EX-MSD is in the case of a family of four where the poverty line is $3,000.[7] For families with less than four members the value of EX-MSD is below the poverty line. The divergence is serious for

[6] This definition of equity assumes that income by itself is a complete measure for determining "equal poverty."

[7] This applies only to a family of four in which there is no aged member eligible for double EX-MSD.

single-member families who are allowed $900 in EX-MSD, although they need $1,500 to remain above the poverty line. In 1964, there were about 900,000 poor families with one, two, and three members whose money income exceeded the value of their EX-MSD.[8]

It turns out that in one respect the divergence between accepted poverty lines and the value of EX-MSD is not so serious. Many of

TABLE 6-2. The Aged Poor: Poverty Lines Compared to Double Tax Exemptions and Deductions[a]

Family Size	Poor Families, 1964		Poverty Lines	Value of EX-MSD Under Present Law	
	Number (Thousands)	Percent with Aged Head		Head Only Aged	Spouse Also Aged
One person	5,088	56.2	$1,500	$1,600	
Two persons	2,483	62.8	2,000	2,300	$3,000
Three persons	1,104	b	2,500	3,000	3,700

Source: Derived from U.S. Department of Commerce, Bureau of the Census, *Current Population Reports*, Series P-60, No. 47, "Income in 1964 of Families and Persons in the United States" (1965), Tables 3 and 4, pp. 24–25.
[a] The aged are those 65 or more years old. The poverty lines are described in footnote 5 of this chapter.
[b] Figures are not available for three-person households having an aged head.

the single poor persons are over 65 years of age. The present positive tax law grants double EX-MSD for taxpayers over 65 years of age, and double EX-MSD also for spouses over 65. Table 6-2 shows that if the proposal for negative rates taxation were to follow this present tax law, the problem of the treatment of poor families with only one member could be solved for the 56 percent of those who are aged. However, if aged couples (both spouses over 65 years of age) were allowed double EX-MSD, they would have ex-

[8] U. S. Department of Commerce, Bureau of the Census, *Current Population Reports*, Series P-60, No. 47, "Income in 1964 of Families and Persons in the United States" (1965), Tables 3 and 4, pp. 24–25. It is assumed that the number of family members reflects the number of dependents claimed for federal income tax purposes. Adjustment was made for double EX-MSD for the aged. It was assumed that if a Census family (two or more persons) had an aged head, the family had only two members. When interpolations were made it was assumed that families were spread evenly throughout a given income bracket. Also it should be recognized that not all of the 900,000 were taxable. Many may have had money income in excess of their adjusted gross income.

TABLE 6-3. Percentage of Poverty Income Gap Filled by a 50 Percent Negative Tax Rate Applied to Unused Exemptions and Deductions[a]

Income Before Allowance as Percentage of Poverty Line	Percentage of Poverty Gap Filled for Families of Different Sizes						
	One	Two	Three	Four	Five	Six	Seven
0	30	40	46	50	53	55	57
10	28	39	45.5	50	53	55.5	57
20	25	37.5	45	50	54	56	58
30	21	36	44	50	54	57	59.5
40	17	33	43	50	55	58	61
50	10	30	42	50	56	60	63
60	0	25	40	50	57	62.5	67
70	b	17	37	50	59.5	67	72
80	b	0	30	50	64	75	83
90	b	b	10	50	79	100	116

[a] Dollar amounts of poverty lines and EX-MSD for families of different sizes are shown in Table 6-1.
[b] No unused EX-MSD. Will pay a positive tax if adjusted gross income equals total money income.

emptions and deductions whose value exceeds the poverty line by $1,000. This would mean that many aged couples who were not poor could receive negative rates taxation allowances.

The conflict with the efficiency objectives is especially notable in the families with more than six members; they have EX-MSD substantially in excess of poverty lines. In 1964, there were about 500,000 nonpoor families with money income less than the value of their EX-MSD.[9]

The unused EX-MSD approach also conflicts with the equity criterion. Because the value of EX-MSD diverges from the poverty lines for families with more or less than four members, the unused EX-MSD approach fails to produce horizontal (or vertical) equity. This point is illustrated in Table 6-3 which indicates the percentage of the poverty income gap filled for families of different sizes with incomes equal to given percentages of their poverty lines. For example, a two-member family and a six-member family with incomes equal to 40 percent of their respective poverty lines (the incomes would be $800 and $1,600 respectively) would receive allowances of $400 and $1,400 respectively.[10] The $400 allowance would fill

[9] *Ibid.*, Table 4, p. 25

[10] The two-person family with no aged members would have $1,600 in EX-MSD. Its $800 income subtracted from $1,600 would equal $800 of unused EX-MSD. Similarly, the six-person family (with no aged members) would have $4,400 in EX-

TABLE 6-4. Negative Tax Rates Applied Against Unused Exemptions and Deductions Necessary to Fill 50 Percent of the Poverty Income Gap

Income Before Allowance as Percentage of Poverty Line	Percentage of Unused EX-MSD Equal to 50 Percent of Poverty Gap, by Family Size						
	One	Two	Three	Four	Five	Six	Seven
0	83	62.5	54	50	47	45	44
10	90	64	55	50	47	45	43.5
20	100	67	55.5	50	47	44	43
30	117	70	56.5	50	46	44	42
40	150	75	58	50	46	43	41
50	250	83	60	50	45	42	39.5
60	a	100	62.5	50	44	40	37.5
70	a	150	68	50	42	37.5	35
80	a	a	83	50	39	33	30
90	a	a	250	50	32	25	21

a Poverty line is above value of EX-MSD. Thus the tax rate goes to infinity, and for practical purposes is meaningless.

33 percent of the two-person family's $1,200 poverty income gap whereas the $1,400 would fill 58 percent of the six-member family's $2,400 poverty income gap. There seems to be little justification on either economic or social grounds for this lack of equitable treatment of two families who are similarly poor.

"Perfect" horizontal equity could be achieved if poverty lines rather than EX-MSD were used as the breakeven lines for negative rates taxation. Alternatively, the EX-MSD for the positive tax system could be revised to equal the poverty lines for all sizes of families. Such perfection is illustrated in the case of the four-member family (see Table 6-1) where the poverty line coincides with the value of EX-MSD.

Any schedule of rates that is applied to the poverty income gap can be translated into a schedule of rates based on unused EX-MSD.[11] It is quite simple to find a set of rates which, when applied against unused EX-MSD, will fill 50 percent of the individual family's poverty income gap. Table 6-4 presents such a set of rates. This table implies that the negative rates tax schedule could be translated

MSD; and $4,400 minus income of $1,600 would equal $2,800 in unused EX-MSD. At the negative tax rate of 50 percent, the allowances would come to $400 and $1,400 respectively.

[11] This assumes that a money income measure is used to determine unused EX-MSD.

into a table of allowances which could reflect whatever set of rates its designer might prefer.

If the poverty line is the approach chosen, there is the question of how to treat a unit which is both eligible to receive allowances and required to pay taxes. This is the problem of giving with one hand and taking with the other. If the negative tax rate is higher than the 14 percent positive tax rate, which applies in the cases of the taxable poor, the taxable poor will receive more than they pay in personal income taxes. For example, suppose a single person has an income of $1,100.[12] Now he is subject to a 14 percent tax on $200 ($1,100 minus $900 in EX-MSD), which comes to $28. His poverty line, however, is $1,500, so he has a poverty gap of $400. Thus, with a 50 percent negative tax rate he would receive $200. When the Internal Revenue Service received the $28 it would pay the $200, so that this person would receive $172 net from the government.[13] While such a procedure would not ensure equitable treatment of small families, it represents a means by which the taxable poor could benefit from a negative rates taxation plan. One drawback of this approach, however, is that with a 50 percent negative tax rate, the marginal tax rate on income which is also subject to the 14 percent positive tax rate will be 64 percent.

The following summary shows how the two sets of negative tax breakeven lines fare with respect to the efficiency, equity, and carryover criteria:

| Criteria | Rating in Choice of Breakeven Lines | |
	Value of EX-MSD	Poverty Lines
Efficiency	Poor	Good
Equity	Poor	Good
Carryover	Good	Poor

The poverty lines turn out to be strong where the value of EX-MSD is weak, and vice versa. Poverty lines seem to be somewhat stronger than EX-MSD on economic grounds, but politically they may be less so since they fail to use present tax concepts and fail to keep completely clear of the positive tax system.[14]

[12] Assume also that all of his income is adjusted gross income.

[13] This might be a good way to encourage low-income people to file tax returns instead of not filing and taking the chance of nonenforcement.

[14] The section in the next chapter on the appropriate tax unit for purposes of negative rates taxation notes that poverty lines establish a greater incentive for

How important are efficiency and equity? How important politically and practically is it to avoid the positive tax system? In light
of the underlying philosophy of negative rates taxation, assurance
that all of the poor are covered is probably the most important criterion in choosing negative tax breakeven lines. Negative rates
taxation has been conceived of as a general income maintenance
proposal designed to provide cash payments to all the poor, without
confining payments to special categories of the poor. Failure to
provide allowances to all the poor would mean that negative rates
taxation is not as general as its philosophical base implies. This failure would also contribute to horizontal inequity if a single negative
tax rate were adopted.

The value of EX-MSD as a basis upon which to calculate the
negative rates taxation base should not be rejected out of hand. The
present tax law is not designed to reflect accurately either the minimum amount of income necessary for a single person to avoid living in poverty, or the minimum increase in income necessary to
support an additional family member at a level just above that of
poverty. Nonetheless, it approximates to a remarkable degree the
poverty lines of families having from two to six members (and single aged persons). Moreover, the poverty lines themselves are, at
best, approximations of the income an average family requires to
meet its basic needs.

Social Dividend Tax Schedules

Social dividend taxation drops the fixation on breakeven lines
that is associated with negative rates taxation. Once the guaranteed
minimum incomes are chosen, the important issue is the choice of

---

family "fragmentation" than does the value of EX-MSD. That is, the potential increase in the poverty income gap is $1,000 if a person can file by himself rather
than as part of a family. The potential increase, due to separate filing, in the value
of unused EX-MSD is only $200 for persons below 65 years of age and $900 for
the aged—assuming the aged are allowed to claim double EX-MSD for negative
rates taxation purposes. Thus the value of EX-MSD somewhat improves its position vis-a-vis the poverty lines. The poverty lines, however, regain some lost ground
over EX-MSD with respect to the incentive to have children. The value of EX-MSD
provides a pecuniary incentive to have children equal to X percent of $700 (where
X is the negative income tax rate). Poverty lines provide a pecuniary incentive of
only X percent of $500.

the tax schedules required to raise the revenues necessary to finance the social dividend plan and other government expenditures financed by the individual income tax.

Distinctions in Three Tax Schedules

In social dividend taxation, there are three different tax schedules for which it is possible—and useful—to make distinctions. The first is the tax schedule applied against income below the breakeven income level. This defines the rate (or rates) at which the allowance guarantee is reduced. A useful name for it is the "allowance" tax schedule. Second is the tax schedule applied against income above the breakeven level of income. It raises the revenues necessary to finance the net cost of the plan. The net cost is the total amount of redistribution of income from families with incomes above breakeven levels to families with before-allowance incomes below the breakeven levels. This type hereinafter is called the "social dividend finance" tax schedule.[15] And third is the "positive" tax schedule which may be applied against the income of some or all families— the number depending on the level of exempt income, the definition of taxable income, and the actual distribution of income. Its purpose is to raise the revenues necessary to finance government expenditures other than the allowances.

Figure 6-2 illustrates the relationship of these three tax schedules. The allowance tax schedule (*AB*) is a single 50 percent rate applied against the income of those who receive net allowances. It is assumed the guaranteed minimum income is $3,000. Therefore, the breakeven level of income is $6,000. The social dividend finance tax schedule (*BC*) consists of a single 15 percent rate applied against income in excess of $6,000.[16] The present positive tax schedule (*DE*) is used to finance government expenditures other than the allowance. The dotted line (*FGH*) is what might be called a "combined" tax schedule. It is simply the total of the positive tax schedule and the allowance and finance tax schedules.

The social dividend plans devised by Lady Rhys-Williams,

---

[15] Usually, the "allowance" and "social dividend finance" tax schedules are combined to form the "social dividend tax schedule." Here, for analytical purposes, a distinction is made between the two parts of the social dividend tax schedule.

[16] It is simply assumed here that a 15 percent tax rate is necessary to raise the revenue which will cover the net cost of the plan.

FIGURE 6-2. Relationship of Different Tax Schedules for a Social Dividend Plan (Family of Four)

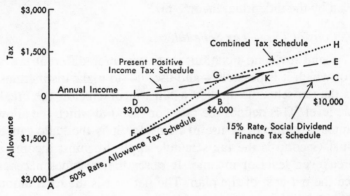

Robert R. Shutz, and D. B. Smith (described in Chapter IV) are variants of the plan illustrated in Figure 6-2.[17] Shutz and Smith develop single tax schedules which are designed to finance all government expenditures. Tobin's plan (see Chapter IV) includes only the allowance and positive tax schedules.[18] In his plan, the allowance tax schedule is extended beyond the breakeven level of income in order to tie in with the positive tax schedule. In Figure 6-2 this schedule is shown by lines *ABKE*. Figure 6-2 best illustrates the Rhys-Williams plan. It differs only in that Lady Rhys-Williams applies a single social dividend tax on all income instead of adopting different allowance and finance tax rates as in Figure 6-2. If a single social dividend tax rate were adopted it would have to be about 33⅓ percent.[19] However, a single rate would make a social dividend plan very costly. Thus it is useful to vary the rates and think in terms of two different tax schedules.

[17] Lady Juliette Rhys-Williams, *Something to Look Forward To* (London: MacDonald, 1943) and *Taxation and Incentive* (New York: Oxford University Press, 1953); Robert Rudolph Shutz, "Transfer Payments and Income Inequality" (unpublished doctoral dissertation, University of California, 1952); and D. B. Smith, "A Simplified Approach to Social Welfare," *Canadian Tax Journal*, Vol. 13 (May-June 1965), pp. 260-65.

[18] James Tobin, "Improving the Economic Status of the Negro," *Daedalus*, Vol. 94 (Fall 1965), pp. 889-95.

[19] To guarantee each family a poverty-free minimum income would cost about $155 billion. Family money income in 1964 was about $470 billion (personal income of $495 billion minus imputed income). A rate of 33⅓ percent applied against $470 billion of money income yields about $155 billion.

Gross versus Net Cost

The gross cost of a basic income guarantee equal to the poverty lines is in the neighborhood of $155 billion.[20] The net cost of such a plan—or the total redistribution of income involved—is about $30 billion if income below the breakeven line is taxed at a 50 percent rate. The net cost is about $45 billion if a flat 33⅓ percent rate is levied on all income.[21] As each individual or family is guaranteed a basic minimum income, the tax rate applied against the family's or individual's income must cover the gross cost (approximately $155 billion) of the plan. That is, in order to wipe out the $30 bil-

FIGURE 6-3. Alternative Sets of Social Dividend Tax Schedules

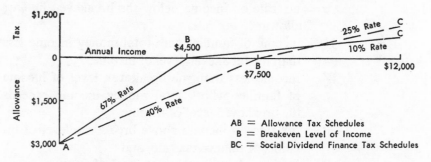

lion or $45 billion net cost, the tax rate on income must be great enough to raise $155 billion—even though $125 or $110 billion is never collected, but is simply an accounting statistic.

Given the distribution of income, the net cost of a transfer-by-taxation plan depends upon the level of the minimum income guarantee and the tax rate applied to the income of net allowance recipients.[22] Once the minimum income guarantee is decided upon, the net cost depends solely on the allowance tax rate. The higher

[20] Based on 47 million families at approximately $3,000 a family and 12 million unrelated individuals at $1,500 each.

[21] This abstracts from indirect redistributional effects produced by a transfer-by-taxation plan such as those that might arise from work disincentives.

[22] The amount of redistribution depends on the distribution of income as well as the social dividend tax rate or rates. The net cost of a negative rates taxation plan with a 50 percent negative rate is in the neighborhood of $5 billion to $7 billion. The present positive tax system could be relied on to finance such payments with small increases in existing rates or, at worst, with small deficits. (See Chapter IX.)

the allowance tax rate the lower the net cost; conversely, the lower the allowance tax rate the higher the net cost. Thus, given the guaranteed minimum income, a relatively low tax rate below the breakeven income level must be associated with a relatively high tax rate above the breakeven income level if the plan is to be fully financed through a tax on income. This is illustrated by Figure 6-3.

Selection of Social Dividend Tax Rates

A simple formula for selecting the pairs of rates which will raise revenues to finance a given social dividend plan is as follows:

(6-1) $C = \alpha(V + W) + \beta(Z)$

where: C = the gross cost of the plan,
            α = tax rate on income below the breakeven line, or allowance tax rate,
            V = income of families with total money income less than the breakeven level of income,
            W = income less than the breakeven level of income of families whose total money income exceeds the breakeven level of income,
            β = tax rate on income above breakeven level of income, or finance tax rate, and
            Z = income above breakeven level of income.

For example, assume that

            C = $150 billion,
            α = 50 percent,
            V = $80 billion,
            W = $120 billion (e.g., 20 million units with over $6,000 in money income),
            β = rate that is being solved for, and
            Z = $250 billion.

Then: $150 = .50(80 + 120) + \beta(250)$
            $150 = 100 + 250\beta$
            $50 = 250\beta$
            $20\% = \beta$

It may be desirable to add no additional tax liability to the present tax liability of middle-income units. Suppose the net cost of a social dividend plan were financed by a 40 percent tax on incomes in excess of two times a family's breakeven income level ($12,000 in the case of a family of four).[23] A 40 percent "finance" tax rate combined with the present tax rates may well be unbearable. For example, under the present tax law, a married couple with two children and a money income of $44,000 ($40,000 of which is taxable), pays $11,940 in taxes. If this is added to the tax levied in order to finance a social dividend plan with a 40 percent rate on money income over $12,000, the family would pay an additional $12,800 in taxes (.40 times $32,000). The total income tax liability of this family would be $24,740, or somewhat over 60 percent of the family's money income. Again, if a married couple with two children has a money income of $220,000 ($200,000 of which is taxable), it pays $110,780 in taxes under the present law and would pay $83,200 in additional taxes to finance the social dividend plan. This adds up to $193,980, or 88 percent of the family's money income. The total tax on the last $20,000 of income, in this case, would be $21,800, or a marginal tax rate of 109 percent.

[23] The 40 percent rate represents only a rough guess.

CHAPTER VII

Some Technical Problems

THREE TECHNICAL ISSUES require particular attention in devising a workable transfer-by-taxation plan. First is agreement on the appropriate definition of income for transfer-by-taxation purposes. In turn, this issue, which concerns the appropriate tax base, may be broken into three parts: the tax base for negative rates taxation; the tax base for financing a social dividend plan; and the positive tax base, assuming the adoption of a social dividend plan. The second issue is determination of the most equitable tax unit to be used in a transfer-by-taxation plan. And the third involves questions with an important bearing upon the administration of a transfer-by-taxation plan.

The Income Base

Because transfer-by-taxation is an income-conditioned plan, a precise definition of income naturally is important. The definition adopted by the present income tax system is "adjusted gross income" (AGI), and AGI excludes some important components of money income. However, it is difficult to exclude any type of income for purposes of transfer-by-taxation because of the welfare nature of such a plan. It is hard to justify excluding income where such exclusion increases the allowance income an individual or family is eligible to receive.

In negative rates taxation, a definition of "taxable income" is relatively unimportant; the question of the appropriate definition of income may be confined to the income measure for determining eligibility for, and the level of, allowances. There are two reasons why this is possible. First, the cost of a negative rates plan is modest enough so that it is not necessary to build into the plan a means by which it finances itself. Second, the basic minimum income guarantee is usually low enough so that it is not necessary to question the desirability in the existing income tax system of exempting given amounts of a taxpayer's income.

This neglect of the definition of taxable income is not possible in social dividend taxation. One reason is that proposals for social dividend plans have been made in terms of paying everyone, and then taxing all income. Another is that the net cost of a plan which would guarantee something like poverty-free minimum incomes is too great to neglect incorporating into the plan's mechanics a means of financing its net benefits. And, finally, a high guaranteed minimum income raises the question of whether it is legitimate to exempt any income from taxation.

The Tax Base in Negative Rates Taxation

Should any form of money income be excluded from income for the purposes of determining eligibility for negative rates taxation allowances and setting the level of such rates? Adjusted gross income is about $70 billion less than personal income because of the exclusion from the tax base of such forms of personal income as public transfer payments and interest on state and local bonds.[1]

[1] It is assumed that the definition of income should not be narrower than the present AGI definition. In fact, present taxable income is about half of AGI because of personal exemptions and deductions. There seems to be no reason to specifically exempt income for purposes of negative rates taxation, although income may effectively be exempted where the negative tax rate is zero over certain ranges of income as in Plan C of Chapter IX. A case might be made that there should be personal deductions for negative rates taxation purposes. A family with special expenses may deserve higher allowances than a similarly situated family which does not have extraordinary expense. However, it would seem to be better for some other program to subsidize heavy medical expenses or casualty losses. But it might be useful to allow deductions for expenses incurred in taking and keeping a job. This would have the effect of reducing the effective allowance tax rate.

Conceptually, the case for using total money income (TMI) instead of AGI as a measure for negative rates taxation is strong.[2] Individuals and families are judged to be poor or not poor on the basis of the level of their income. All forms of cash income are included in determining whether or not a person or family is living in poverty.[3] Use of AGI excludes sources of income available to those who are not poor as well as to the poor. This means that if AGI were used as the measure of income for transfer-by-taxation purposes, some nonpoor families or individuals (especially those who receive transfer payments) might be judged eligible to receive allowances under the negative rates plan. Thus, TMI is a more efficient measure of income for negative tax purposes.

On grounds of equity, money income clearly is superior to AGI. Consider, as an example, a family of four with $2,000—all of which is earned income. With a 50 percent negative tax rate, that family would receive $1,000 less in net allowances than a family of four with $2,000 of which all is excludable income (say, unemployment compensation) would receive. Moreover, using AGI constitutes a carryover—from the positive tax system to the negative side—of the disadvantaged position of those with earned income vis-a-vis unearned income. Whatever rationale exists in the positive tax system for this unequal treatment would not seem to exist on the negative side, where there should be less concern over the form which income takes in determining eligibility for, and the level of, allowances.[4]

[2] Total money income is the sum of factor income and transfer payments. Henry C. Simons, in his classic work *Personal Income Taxation* (Chicago: University of Chicago Press, 1938), made a strong argument for a broad definition of income for income tax purposes. Simons would define income as a person's or family's consumption plus its change in net worth. Taken literally, this would include in income not only all of realized capital gains, but also unrealized capital gains. While Simon's view has not been wholly accepted, a good many economists have recognized the deficiencies in the present adjusted gross income definition of income used for tax purposes. For example, see William Vickrey, *Agenda for Progressive Taxation* (New York: Ronald Press, 1947) and Richard Goode, *The Individual Income Tax* (Washington: Brookings Institution, 1964).

[3] Mollie Orshansky has made an adjustment for income-in-kind received by farmers. See "Counting the Poor: Another Look at the Poverty Profile," *Social Security Bulletin,* Vol. 28 (January 1965), pp. 9-10.

[4] This statement is subject to the objection that to the extent that it is desirable to reduce the public assistance programs one is concerned about the form a person's income takes. Moreover, Friedman (as noted in Chapter IV) envisaged the negative

A disturbing facet of an AGI measure of income is its potential as an incentive to substitute transfer income for earned income. In this respect, it would tend to alter the choices between work and leisure that would be made in the absence of a transfer-by-taxation plan. A negative tax rate of 50 percent, for example, would help induce some substitution of, say, unemployment compensation or old-age, survivors and disability insurance (OASDI) for earned income if an AGI measure of income were used. A person with a low earning potential might prefer to receive $1,200 a year in unemployment compensation rather than $2,000 a year in wages. Assume, for example, a 50 percent negative tax rate and a poverty line of $3,000 for the family of four. An AGI measure of income would mean that the four-member family with $1,200 in unemployment insurance (its only income) would receive $2,700 in after-allowance income ($1,200 plus $1,500 allowance). But the same sized family with $2,000 in wages would receive a $500 allowance (50 percent of the difference between $3,000 and $2,000), and therefore would have an after-allowance income of only $2,500.

The problem created by paying allowances to a person who is potentially taxable may be reduced by using AGI. For example, a single individual with a $1,200 income is rated poor; and if all that income is AGI, is also taxable. But often, especially in the case of the aged, who make up a large percentage of the poor single-member families, AGI is much less than total money income. If the individual with the $1,200 income has only $500 in AGI (with the other $700 excludable), he will not be taxable. It may be easier, politically, to justify making negative tax allowances to such persons who, in fact, are not now taxable than to those who are actually taxable.

The claim of superiority for AGI rests only on the fact that the concept is imbedded in the positive tax system. To some persons who have a stake in the present concept, total money income may

income tax as replacing all presently existing welfare programs. It made sense for him to use an AGI measure of income just because he wanted to exclude welfare payments from the public scene. The statement is strictly correct only in the sense that one is looking at existing poverty—poverty caused by a lack of income in general rather than a lack of a given type of income. The poverty program, of course, is concerned with the poor's lack of earned income or social insurance income. See Milton Friedman, *Capitalism and Freedom* (Chicago: University of Chicago Press, 1962).

be regarded as a red herring. For these persons, AGI is politically acceptable in a way that total money income is not. But on the whole, AGI is clearly inferior to money income as a measure of income for negative tax purposes. However, three forms of income might be excluded from the income base for negative tax purposes. These are public assistance, receipts which represent a drawing down of wealth, and gifts.

PUBLIC ASSISTANCE. From two points of view, a good case can be made for excluding public assistance from the measure of income. First, a technical difficulty is created by inclusion of public assistance (PA) payments in the measure of money income adopted for transfer-by-taxation purposes. This involves the posture taken by welfare agencies in deciding what payments should be made to a given family or individual. Essentially, the welfare agencies are placed in the position of raising the negative tax allowances by 50 cents for each dollar of reduction in public assistance payment.[5] Second, there is a value judgment that implicitly or explicitly must be made in deciding whether to include or exclude public assistance in the income base. This revolves around the role PA should play in a negative tax plan.[6]

The technical problem can best be analyzed by recognizing two different means of administering the negative tax allowances. On the one hand, allowances could be made in the year income is received. This would involve prediction of a family's income in order to decide whether it is eligible to receive payments, and if so, in what amounts. On the other hand, allowances could be paid after a year's lag—that is, they would be based upon the previous year's income.

If allowances are paid in the year income is received, and if public assistance is included in income, the welfare agencies are placed in a difficult position. As noted above, the amount of assistance payments they decide to make will determine the amount of negative rates taxation allowances that will be paid out. If the welfare agencies decide to minimize their own payments, then they would pay nothing at all and leave the field to the transfer-by-taxa-

[5] This assumes that the negative rates taxation plan has a flat 50 percent rate.

[6] Presumably, the public assistance programs would disappear if a social dividend plan were adopted. This, however, cannot be presumed if a negative rates plan were adopted.

tion allowances. However, it is possible that the negative tax allowance alone would not "pay" a family as much as it had been receiving in the form of public assistance.[7] If the welfare agency wants to assure that a family will not suffer because of a change to negative tax allowances it will be forced to take one of two steps.

The agency would have to make assistance payments which would be included in the family's money income. This would reduce negative tax allowances. For example, suppose a family of four had no income other than PA, from which it had been receiving $1,700. Now suppose a negative rates plan with a flat 50 percent rate is introduced. Without PA, the family would receive $1,500 (50 percent of the poverty line of $3,000)—a reduction of $200 from the $1,700 it had been paid when under public assistance. If the welfare agency felt it must help maintain the family's previous standard of living, it would plan to make payments of $200. If this $200 were included in money income of the family, negative tax allowances at the 50 percent rate would fall by $100, necessitating a further planned increase in PA. The final solution would be a $400 public assistance payment and a $1,300 negative tax allowance.[8]

The agency, as an alternative, would have to make its welfare payment completely supplemental to the negative tax allowance. That is, it would plan to make no assistance payments. This would maximize the payment under the negative rates plan—$1,500 in the example given above. Then the welfare agency could add $200 as a purely supplemental payment after it was "sure" that the maximum negative tax allowance had been, or would be, made. If this resulted from a policy of including PA in money income, it would be best to exclude PA from money income.

Suppose negative tax allowances are made the year after income is received—that is, with a year's lag. Then what the welfare

[7] This would be likely under some negative rates plans.
[8] The following equation yields a solution to the problem:

$$Y = PA + .50\ [PL - (MI + PA)] + MI$$

where

Y = income level to be achieved,
PA = public assistance
PL = poverty line, and
MI = money income not including PA.

TABLE 7-1. Hypothetical Combinations of Negative Tax Allowances[a] and Public Assistance Payments for a Family of Four

Year	Case One[b]		Total Annual Income Sought For Family	Case Two[b]	
	Negative Tax Allowance (1)	Public Assistance Payments (2)	(3)	Negative Tax Allowance (4)	Public Assistance Payments (5)
Zero	$ 0	$ 0	$ 0	$ 0	$1,700.00
First	1,500.00	200.00	1,700.00	650.00	1,050.00
Second	1,400.00	300.00	1,700.00	975.00	725.00
Third	1,350.00	350.00	1,700.00	1,137.50	562.50
Fourth	1,325.00	375.00	1,700.00	1,218.75	482.25
Fifth	1,312.50	387.50	1,700.00	1,258.87	441.13
Sixth	1,306.25	393.75	1,700.00		
Equilibrium levels[c]	$1,300.00	$400.00	$1,700.00	$1,300.00	$ 400.00

[a] Assuming a negative tax rate of 50 percent, and a poverty line of $3,000.

[b] These are hypothetical combinations of negative taxes and PA. In Case One, the family begins with no public assistance, but in each subsequent year, public assistance supplements negative taxes so that total income will equal $1,700, shown in column 3. In Case Two, negative taxes are based on the family's previous year's income which by assumption consists only of public assistance; in response to negative tax payments based on the previous year's income, PA is reduced so that total income remains at $1,700.

[c] The equilibrium levels are those for which no further adjustments in PA and negative tax payments need be made.

agencies did one year would determine what the Treasury would do the following year. An example illustrates the problem. Again assume that a family of four with no other income receives $1,700 in public assistance. If the welfare agency reduced PA to zero (which would mean the family would have no income at all in the year before negative tax allowances began), the family would receive in the following year $1,500 in negative tax allowances. The welfare agency would be forced to decide whether or not to add $200 (so that the family would receive $1,700). If it decided to add the $200, in a few years it would be forced to add $400. Columns 1, 2, and 3 of Table 7-1 illustrate the process in such a case. As the welfare agency makes assistance payments it reduces the transfer-by-taxation payments made the next year.

In another case, suppose welfare payments were $1,700 in year zero and negative allowances will not be paid until the next year. Columns 3, 4, and 5 of Table 7-1 show what would happen. The iterative process leads back to $1,300 in negative allowances and

$400 in public assistance payments. Different rate schedules and different amounts by which negative tax allowances fall short of public assistance standards produce different solutions to the equation indicating how much in allowances and how much in assistance payments will be made. But one thing is certain: inclusion of public assistance in income will not maximize negative tax allowances received by a given family unit or minimize PA payments received by the family.

If PA is excluded from the money income measure, welfare agencies would be free to choose the size of a supplement, if any, to a family's income after negative tax allowances had been added.

The preceding discussion leads to a value judgment about the role of public assistance if a negative rates plan were introduced. The philosophy of transfer-by-taxation is different from that of public assistance. A transfer-by-taxation plan is designed to make net allowance payments to all low-income families—no matter why they have low incomes. But eligibility for public assistance depends on the reasons for poverty—whether it be caused by age, lack of a male head of family, or high medical payments. If a negative rates plan is to be considered something more than just another means by which to make transfer payments to the poor, it would be best to reduce PA to as small a role (in pecuniary terms) as possible, and to allow the negative tax plan as broad a scope as possible for making cash payments to low-income families. This is possible by making public assistance, if it is needed at all, purely supplemental to the maximum negative tax allowance payable—given other income of the family. It makes little sense to be ambiguous about where negative rates taxation leaves off and PA begins. Ambiguity is exactly the effect that would be produced by inclusion of PA in the income measure for negative tax purposes.

What in fact is the quantitative relationship between present public assistance payments and a negative rates taxation plan with a 50 percent negative tax rate? In order to throw light on this question, it is necessary to assume that money income other than PA is zero. Public assistance payments vary from state to state. However, use of averages gives some idea of how well a negative rates plan compares with aid to families with dependent children (AFDC)[9] and old-age assistance.

[9] The present AFDC was aid to dependent children (ADC) before 1962.

In late 1961, the average state monthly requirement for an AFDC family of four (mother and three children) was $168.79—or $2,025.48 a year. Most states did not achieve these requirements. The state average of unmet need was 11.6 percent of requirements, or $19.58 a month for a family consisting of a mother and three children.[10] Thus, on the average, a mother and three children with no other income would have received, in 1961, $149.21 monthly— or just under $1,800 a year. The same family would have received

TABLE 7-2. Average State Aid to Families with Dependent Children Received by a Mother and Three Children with No Other Income, 1961

Average Monthly AFDC Payment	Annual Equivalent	In Number of States[a]
Less than $75	Less than $900	2
$75 – 100	$ 900 – 1,200	3
100 – 125	1,200 – 1,500	4
125 – 150	1,500 – 1,800	12
150 – 175	1,800 – 2,100	12
175 – 200	2,100 – 2,400	11
Over $200	Over $2,400	4

Source: U.S. Department of Health, Education, and Welfare, Bureau of Family Services, "Characteristics of Families Receiving Aid to Families with Dependent Children, November–December 1961," April 1963. Based on Tables 38 and 41.
[a] Excludes Massachusetts and Oregon.

$125 a month, or $1,500 annually, in negative tax allowances under a negative rates plan with a 50 percent rate. Table 7-2 shows that in 1961 the average AFDC payment to a family of this type was $1,500 or less in only nine states. Thus, in almost all states it would be necessary to supplement negative tax allowances with public assistance if AFDC recipients were not to be made worse off by adoption of a negative rates plan with a flat 50 percent rate. In

[10] "Requirements" are defined as the welfare agency's determination of the income needed to purchase what is necessary for maintaining the state's level of living established for the program. Such amounts exclude vendor payments for medical care. See Gerald Kahn and Ellen J. Perkins, "Families Receiving AFDC: What Do They Have to Live On?" in *Welfare in Review*, Vol. 2 (October 1964), pp. 10-12. It would be better if data for a more recent year were used. However, these data are, so far as I know, the most recent giving breakdowns by family size. "Unmet need" is defined as the difference between requirements and income from all sources (including assistance).

twenty-four states, this supplemental payment would have had to be less than $600 a year.[11]

How would recipients of old-age assistance (OAA) fare under the negative rates taxation plan? Here the problem is complicated somewhat by the fact that almost 40 percent of OAA recipients also receive old-age, survivors and disability insurance. Thus OASDI benefits should be included in the money income measure for negative tax purposes.[12] In 1963, OAA recipients who had neither OASDI nor any other income except public assistance received an average of $85.79 a month, but about $14 was in the form of vendor medical payments.[13] This leaves about $72, or $864 a year, for a single person. Under the negative rates plan when OAA is excluded from money income, this person would receive $750 (50 percent of $1,500) or $114 less than OAA would pay.[14] Those single persons receiving both OAA and OASDI received an average of $107 a month (or $1,284 annually) of which $47 was in OASDI and, therefore, included in the money income for negative tax purposes. The average annual total of this income (when PA is excluded) was $564. These persons would have a transfer-by-taxation allowance of $468 ($750 minus .50 times $564), giving the person a total income (plus allowance) of $1,032. This would be about $100 less than the average OAA-OASDI recipient was receiving in 1963 —after making adjustment for vendor medical payments.[15]

It seems clear that even if a negative rates plan is adopted public assistance programs cannot be eliminated without making public assistance recipients worse off in monetary terms. Instead, the adoption of a negative rates plan would mean that there would be two public transfer programs, one federal and one state, instead of one program designed primarily to assist the poor. This would re-

[11] In late 1961, the estimated average annual income, including assistance, per AFDC recipient was $431. This means that the average income of an AFDC family of four was $1,724—or $224 more than $1,500. Kahn and Perkins, *op. cit.*, p. 8.

[12] In 1963, 37.2 percent of OAA recipients also received OASDI benefits. See U. S. Department of Health, Education, and Welfare, *Welfare in Review,* March 1964, p. 20.

[13] The $14 is a rough estimate.

[14] The value of exemptions and minimum standard deductions allowed a single aged person is $1,600; the poverty line is $1,500.

[15] With Medicare, a negative tax allowance plus OASDI is even more competitive with OAA and OASDI.

quire two administrative agencies at different levels of government to coordinate cash disbursement activities.

TRANSFERS WHICH RESEMBLE CAPITAL CONSUMPTION. Some transfer payments represent a drawing down of wealth in the form of annuities. This applies to the employee's contribution to private retirement income, and it may also apply to his contribution to OASDI and railroad retirement. Opponents of taxing such transfers argue that the beneficiary, by contributing to OASDI, railroad retirement, and private retirement programs is involved in the act of saving, and that he should not be taxed on the return of this principal. Taxation of all benefits would result in a tax on wealth. Under present law, OASDI is treated more liberally than private retirement income; all OASDI benefits are excluded from taxation, even though the employer paid half of the contributions. But the private pensioner can receive only his own contributions tax free; all benefits exceeding his own contributions must be included in his adjusted gross income.

Richard Goode in *The Individual Income Tax* takes issue with those who consider OASDI and railroad retirement benefits as earned benefits, and therefore a form of annuity. Workers, he points out, "do not have property rights in social security benefits, and Congress may reduce or withdraw benefits at any time. The benefit formulas give preferential treatment to workers who were already employed when the system was adopted or extended and to low-paid workers."[16]

Taxation of retirement benefits may also involve double taxation. As the beneficiary paid taxes on the income he contributed to the public or private retirement plan, inclusion of all his benefits will subject him to double taxation. There is no simple solution to this problem. A superficial one would be to have the beneficiary include only half of his benefits in his income for negative taxation purposes, reflecting presumably the matching contributions made by the employer. Another possibility is to cease taxing the income out of which contributions are made, and tax only the benefits. The difficulty with these solutions is that there is, at least in the case of OASDI, no attempt made to create a one-to-one correlation between contributions and benefits. These "solutions" are more con-

[16] Goode, *op. cit.,* p. 106.

vincing in the case of private retirement income, where a greater attempt is made to match the insurance principle of benefits equaling contributions.

It seems preferable to accept the welfare, rather than tax equity, aspect of a negative tax plan, and thus to include all retirement benefits in the definition of income. This means that the emphasis is placed on developing an income measure which comes close to reflecting the family's consumption power without getting bogged down with the problem of wealth. It seems sensible to regard the retirement programs, public and private, as income maintenance programs designed to offer income security where there otherwise would have been little or none. Moreover, the public retirement programs, at least, represent a form of "forced saving" and do not closely resemble the drawing down of wealth built up by conscious and voluntary saving.

Other public transfer payments such as unemployment compensation and workmen's compensation should be included. But the level of such benefits should not be changed as the negative tax plan is introduced. Neither the wealth nor double taxation arguments apply here.

GIFTS AND OTHER SPECIAL TYPES OF INCOME. How should freewill gifts be treated?[17] Should they be excluded from income for purposes of negative rates taxation? Essentially, gifts pose the same sort of problem as public assistance. The giver of a gift to a poor person or family may think twice if that "giving" reduces the recipient's negative tax allowance. Where gifts are a regular source of income, the recipient would probably be unable to file a negative tax return because he would not meet the relevant support tests. It is best, then, to exclude gifts from money income.

No case can be made for excluding interest on state and local bonds, capital gains income, and dividend income. What about imputed rent on owner-occupied houses? This effectively is an exclusion from adjusted gross income, since the family which owns its home is better off than the family which rents, even though the two families have the same money income. In principle, imputed rent

---

[17] Freewill gifts are those between persons and between private charitable institutions and persons. However, scholarships should not be considered freewill gifts, and should be included in the income measure for negative tax purposes.

should be included. The same is true of home-produced food which may be a major source of real income to many farm families. However, until there is some more accurate accounting of the nonmonetary rental income received by families who own their homes and the income-in-kind of families who produce their food it may be best to treat both as exclusions.[18]

The Social Dividend Finance Tax Base

An important factor in determining the social dividend finance tax base is the heavy cost of a social dividend plan. It seems evident that the economic system cannot afford the luxury of exempting income through personal exemptions and deductions (at least, not of the present magnitude)[19] from both social dividend finance and positive taxes. Thus, it is hard to avoid the conclusion that the present concept of taxable income provides too narrow a base against which to apply the social dividend finance tax schedule. At a minimum, the tax base should be adjusted gross income. But, should any form of income be excluded from taxation for the purpose of financing the social dividend plan?[20]

A substantial portion of income excluded under the income tax is transfer income resulting from various welfare programs. If a so-

[18] Presumably the "rental income" of owner-occupied houses could be estimated by applying an appropriate rate of interest to the owner's equity in the home. Richard Goode suggests either disallowing the personal deductions for mortgage interest and property taxes or allowing tenants to deduct rental payments. He notes, however, that these are incomplete solutions (op. cit., pp. 127-29). Including as income for transfer-by-taxation purposes a figure representing imputed rental income helps solve part of the problem of dealing with assets. For many families, especially those who are likely to be recipients of net allowances, the chief asset (other than consumer durables) is a home. By including rental income in the income base of such families, it is possible to approximate the annual income from the wealth of these families. However, computing rent on owner-occupied houses may give a distorted picture of such "income" of the aged. Many aged remain in houses with far more space than they need, but inertia keeps them there.

[19] Taxable income (that is, AGI minus exemptions and deductions) was $195 billion in 1964—just about equal to the gross cost of the social dividend proposal and other government programs financed out of the federal income tax.

[20] In this chapter, the social dividend tax schedule is thought of as beginning at the first dollar of income. In Figure 6-2, the social dividend finance tax schedule is the schedule beginning at the breakeven level of income. This would allow, conceptually at least, the definition of income for determining net social dividend allowances to differ from that for determining the tax liability in financing those net allowances.

cial dividend plan were a substitute for such programs, AGI would more closely resemble before-allowance money income than at present. If the social dividend plan were a complement to some or most of the present public welfare programs, should transfer income be excluded for finance tax purposes? (Undoubtedly, the public assistance programs would be abandoned in any case.)

One can argue that adoption of a plan as far-reaching as a social dividend plan makes all other public transfer programs of secondary importance. This might imply that the income from these programs should be used to finance the basic plan. On the other hand, a 15 to 30 percent tax placed on income received under social security programs (OASDI and unemployment insurance) may undermine these programs. Workers may object to making contributions to a plan such as OASDI when its benefits may be taxed away at uncomfortably high rates. Moreover, taxing money income for social dividend finance purposes would result in double taxation of income, because a tax would already have been paid on the income used to make social security contributions. This argument has merit, and it may make sense to omit contributions to public and private retirement plans from the tax base, at least for the purpose of financing a transfer-by-taxation plan. This would make the income measure more akin to the concept of personal income used by the Office of Business Economics in the U.S. Department of Commerce than to money income.

The Positive Income Tax Base

It has been implicitly assumed that the present positive tax base under a social dividend plan would remain the same—or would undergo only minor changes. Is there any reason for maintaining the present positive tax base if a "generous" social dividend plan were adopted? The tax base can be broadened by (1) revising the definition of income for tax purposes and (2) narrowing the difference between adjusted gross income and taxable income. The first method is concerned with the concept of excludable income; the second involves reducing or eliminating personal exemptions and deductions.

EXEMPTIONS. The issues related to personal exemptions are clearer than those having to do with deductions, and will be treated first.

Richard Goode lists four major functions of personal exemptions: (1) keeping the total number of returns to a manageable minimum and, particularly, holding down the number with tax liability less than the cost of collection; (2) freeing from tax the income needed to maintain a minimum standard of living; (3) helping achieve a smooth graduation of effective tax rates at the lower end of the scale; and (4) differentiating tax liability according to family size.[21]

The first function involves administrative efficiency. As Goode notes, this is no longer a real matter of concern. Computers, the withholding process, the increase in literacy, and the reduction of farm employment have "lessened the administrative advantages of high exemptions," and the simplest procedure would be to eliminate the exemptions.[22] Goode's third point, providing a means by which effective tax rates may be smoothly graduated, is an important function of personal exemptions where marginal rates begin well above a zero level. In 1960, for example, 60 percent of the taxable returns fell within the first bracket (for which the marginal rate was 20 percent) but were subject to effective rates ranging from zero to 14 percent. The percentage rises from zero as the ratio of AGI to exemptions and standard deductions rises.[23] The Revenue Act of 1964 increased the percentage of returns subject to explicit graduation by dividing the old first bracket into four brackets, but progressivity at lower income levels still results mainly from personal exemptions. If personal exemptions were omitted from the positive tax system, progressivity at the lower income levels would be produced only if the marginal rate in the first bracket were close to zero and the brackets were narrow—as narrow as in the Revenue Act of 1964.[24]

The second and fourth functions of personal exemptions— freeing income needed to maintain a minimum standard of living and differentiating tax liability according to family size—would become unimportant if a social dividend plan were adopted. A social dividend plan can do what personal exemptions by themselves could never do; that is, it can make a minimum income a certainty

[21] Goode, *op. cit.*, pp. 224-25.
[22] *Ibid.*, p. 225.
[23] *Ibid.*, p. 228.
[24] This assumes that the minimum standard deduction or standard deduction is also discarded.

and can vary the minimum by family size.[25] By guaranteeing a socially acceptable minimum income, a social dividend system makes all income, other than the basic allowance, "clear income." Thus ability to pay extends to the first dollar other than the basic allowance. Except for their function of producing a smooth graduation in the low-income brackets, personal exemptions are made much less important by a social dividend system and modern computer technology.[26]

DEDUCTIONS. Two types of deductions can be identified. One type is the deduction for expenses incurred in earning income. There can be little dispute that, in principle, deduction of such expenses from gross income is justifiable under any tax system.[27]

The second kind is the deduction for personal expenses. Personal deductions "cover living expenses and certain costs of obtaining income that do not qualify as business expenses."[28] They include interest paid, medical expenses, philanthropic contributions, and certain taxes paid. A minimum standard deduction may be claimed by the taxpayer in lieu of itemizing personal deductions. Richard Goode has outlined four major purposes of personal deductions. They are: (1) to allow for costs of obtaining nonbusiness income; (2) to relieve hardships that would arise from strict application of a tax on economic income; (3) to encourage voluntary support of certain socially desirable activities; and (4) to promote intergovernmental comity in a federal system.[29]

Adoption of a social dividend system would not necessarily make any of these four functions irrelevant. That is to say, personal deductions, unlike personal exemptions, would be justified even if every individual and family were assured a basic allowance of relatively generous proportions. This is not to say, however, that all present personal deductions should be retained if a social dividend

[25] A social dividend system also avoids the dispute over whether personal exemptions should (a) be a percentage of income, (b) decline as income increases, or (c) be uniform as at present.

[26] However, if the social dividend tax rate on income below the breakeven income level is high (that is, 50 percent as in Figure 6-2), additional positive income taxes levied on this income may result in undesirably high marginal tax rates.

[27] For a good discussion of the issue of distinguishing cost and consumption expenses, see Goode, *op. cit.*, Chap. V.

[28] *Ibid.*, p. 153.

[29] *Ibid.*, p. 156.

system were implemented. In fact, there may be personal deductions which should be eliminated simply as a reform of the present tax system.[30] Moreover, the cost of a social dividend plan provides a degree of urgency in limiting personal deductions to a minimum consistent with good economics and the sociopolitical goals of society. Necessarily, the size of this minimum is a rather vague notion. Nevertheless, many economists would agree that Congress has been too liberal in legislating personal deductions which, in 1962, reduced taxable income by about $46 billion.[31]

In 1962, adjusted gross income was $349 billion and taxable income was $195 billion. In addition to the $46 billion of personal deductions, the total value of exemptions stood at $108 billion. If a social dividend system had been in existence in 1962 and the personal exemptions and half of personal deductions had been eliminated, taxable income would have been increased by $131 billion. This would have raised taxable income to $326 billion. Individual income tax revenues were $45 billion in 1962, which was 23 percent of taxable income. A 14 percent proportional tax rate would have raised the same amount of revenue if the tax base had been broadened in the manner just described.

EXCLUSIONS. Another method mentioned earlier for increasing taxable income is broadening the definition of adjusted gross income to include income which is excluded for tax purposes.[32] Some exclusions are justified. Goode states that the "exclusion of a particular item from taxable income . . . is justifiable when it serves an important social or economic purpose that could not be so well served by other means."[33] Excludable income which, according to Goode, could have been included in AGI came to about $20 billion in 1960. This same amount would have raised AGI in 1962 from $349 billion to $369 billion. In addition, benefits under the vet-

<hr>

[30] *Ibid.,* Chap. VII.

[31] U. S. Department of the Treasury, Internal Revenue Service, *Statistics of Income, Individual Income Tax Returns, 1962,* pp. 37-40. Of this amount, itemized deductions amounted to $41.6 billion and standard deductions about $4 billion.

[32] A broad definition of income is the Haig-Simons definition. This definition equates personal income with consumption plus the change in net worth. Simons, *op. cit.,* Chap. 2. See also Goode, *op. cit.,* pp. 13-14.

[33] *Op cit.,* pp. 99-100. Goode also notes that exclusions are justified when they obviate excessive costs of administration and compliance.

erans' and unemployment insurance programs should be included in AGI if a social dividend plan were adopted.[34] Goode justifies their exclusion on the basis that these "transfer payments generally meet needs that merit high priority."[35] It can be argued that under a generous social dividend plan the services provided by these transfer payments are no longer of such high priority that they warrant tax treatment different from that of most other income.[36]

Since a social dividend plan would increase the importance of a broad definition of income for positive tax purposes, desirable changes in the treatment of capital gains would gain in urgency.

The Unit of Taxation

The present tax unit would need some adjustments for transfer-by-taxation purposes in order to avoid inducements to separate filing under transfer-by-taxation and in order to meet the welfare purposes of such a plan. To this end, the advantages and disadvantages of a "family" tax unit to be used in filing a transfer-by-taxation return are considered in this section.

Shortcomings of the Present Tax Unit

Under the present system of income taxation, the tax unit is not always equivalent to a "family unit." For example, several family members may be represented on more than one return. Moreover, some families and individuals whose incomes are very low either are not required to file a tax return or fail to file one. Thus, there is no one-to-one correspondence between the present tax unit and the number of family units.[37] This is of consequence because the desired

[34] This assumes that a social dividend plan would not bring about the abandonment of those two programs.

[35] *Op. cit.,* p. 105.

[36] It is assumed that the public assistance program would be abandoned. If it were not completely abandoned under a social dividend plan, this would probably reflect some unmet needs of high enough priority to warrant continued exclusion for tax purposes.

[37] There is no generally accepted definition of the family for economic purposes. Different organizations which have made surveys of family income and expenditure have defined the family or basic income expenditure unit differently. For example, in the U.S. Department of Commerce, the Office of Business Economics and Bureau of the Census define families as units of two or more individuals related by blood, marriage, or adoption, and residing together. According to this definition, "unattached individuals" are persons who are not living with any relatives. The Federal

tax unit for transfer-by-taxation purposes is one which approximates a "welfare" unit. The extent of individual economic well-being is determined by totaling the income of all members of a unit who normally pool their incomes and share costs.[38]

The present tax unit does not meet the efficiency and equity tests discussed in Chapter VI. In some families, several members may earn incomes which added together would exceed the breakeven level of income for transfer-by-taxation purposes. If each—or some—of these income earners were allowed to file a separate transfer-by-taxation return, each filer might be eligible to receive an allowance. But individuals are not poor or in need simply because they earn little or no income. The relevant question is whether one or more members of the immediate family is a productive earner; or, if family members are aged, whether one or more is a recipient of substantial retirement income, public or private. In order to determine whether a person deserves an allowance, the economic resources of some reasonably well-defined socioeconomic unit should be examined.

There are two factors which may induce individual members of a family to file separate transfer-by-taxation returns. One arises because the poverty line for a four-member family is only double that for a single-member unit.[39] The other arises if the tax rate below the breakeven level of income substantially exceeds that above the breakeven level. In this case, a family whose total income exceeds the breakeven level of income would find it "pays" to have its earn-

---

Reserve Board and the Survey Research Center of the University of Michigan conduct a Survey of Consumer Finances. In that survey, the basic income expenditure unit is the spending unit, defined as all related persons living in the same dwelling who pool their income to meet major expenses. In the Bureau of Labor Statistics, U.S. Department of Labor, the basic income expenditure unit is the "reconstructed economic family" or single consumer unit; that is, persons dependent upon a pooled income for their major items of expense and usually living in the same household. T. Paul Schultz, *Statistics on the Size Distribution of Personal Income in the United States,* Joint Economic Committee, 88 Cong. 2 sess. (1964), pp. 50, 60, 74, and 85.

[38] Some poor persons may be living together and pooling income because of economic necessity—not because they want to. It would be undesirable if the transfer-by-taxation tax unit were so rigid as to maintain or reinforce this dependency. To make independence possible may be one of the more desirable qualities of a transfer-by-taxation plan.

[39] This problem can be by-passed by using, in a negative rates plan at least, the value of EX-MSD rather than poverty lines as breakeven levels of income.

ing members file separately (claiming no dependents) if one of the nonearners is also allowed to file and includes the other nonearners as dependents. Unfortunately, these two factors also establish some minor inducement to "fragment" or break the family into smaller units if a family tax unit is adopted.

Proposal of an Alternative Tax Unit

An alternative to the present tax unit is the family. In fact, the family probably is the closest approximation to an ideal unit for measuring welfare. However, using the family as the basic unit for transfer-by-taxation purposes creates certain problems. It is not always clear who should be included in the family unit for these purposes.[40] For transfer-by-taxation, it is useful to think in terms of a "basic" family unit—that is, a unit in which all the members can definitely be considered members of the family from both sociological and economic points of view—and of a criterion for deciding what other persons should be considered a part of that family. This basic family unit would pool its income and file a transfer-by-taxation return if its pooled income were less than the appropriate breakeven level of income. The definition of persons outside the basic family unit could be based on the support tests in the present tax law.[41]

A reasonable definition of the basic family unit is mother, father, or legal guardians, unmarried children and students under 22 years of age.[42] The following set of rules might be used to define

[40] However, it will become obvious that the definition of the tax unit for transfer-by-taxation purposes which is presented in this section has more in common with the more sociological definitions of the family unit used by the Census and Survey of Consumer Finances than it has with the "economic interdependence" definition used by the Bureau of Labor Statistics.

[41] Persons outside the basic family unit would be considered members of that family unit if they obtained more than half of their support from members of the basic family unit.

[42] This would effectively prohibit the great majority of undergraduate college students from filing their own transfer-by-taxation returns. However, there is some question regarding whether graduate students should be allowed to file. Graduate students can generally expect that their investment in education will pay off rather handsomely in the future. It is doubtful whether the graduate student should receive allowances because he has chosen temporarily to limit his earnings. Certainly, if students over 21 were allowed to file, they should include as income all scholarships and fellowships—including the tuition value thereof—even though these are presently excluded for income tax purposes.

eligibility to file and income to be reported on a transfer-by-taxation return.

1. Eligibility to file is limited to those who are mainly supported by themselves or their children. Spouses must file jointly unless one has deserted the family and is subject to laws regarding nonsupport. The deserting spouse is not eligible to file a transfer-by-taxation return. No unmarried minor is eligible to file.[43] Eligibility to file is further limited to students over 21 years of age. In a family whose members depend upon a child's income, one of the parents would file rather than the child.[44]

2. Those who can be claimed as dependents by each filer are limited to persons for whom the filer is the main source of support, except that a minor or a student under 22 years of age can be claimed as a dependent even if that minor or student provides more than half of his own support.

3. The provisions of the present income tax law will be used to determine who is supported by whom.[45]

4. The income reported by the filer must include all presently taxable and nontaxable money income received by himself and his dependents except for (a) public assistance and (b) free-will gifts.

The first provision is the key to the definition of the basic family unit. This provision ties in with the support tests in the tax law, except that it is designed to force the family to file as a unit irrespective of the support tests. The third provision indicates that the present support test will be used to judge whether persons other than members of the basic family unit are in fact self-supporting and therefore eligible to file a separate transfer-by-taxation return. Special cases, if any, should be spelled out in the law.

Should the present tax unit be abandoned altogether or should it be retained for positive tax purposes? Abandonment would mean

[43] However, it is not clear that a child who has left home and is completely self-supporting should not be allowed to file a negative tax return.

[44] In this particular case, there may be some rationale in allowing the child to file a separate positive tax return. The rest of the family would be allowed to file a negative tax return which would include neither the working child as a dependent nor his income.

[45] With the addition of a provision that no person can be claimed as a dependent on more than one tax return (positive or negative). Also, if the negative tax standard is to be the value of EX-MSD rather than the poverty lines, the provisions of the present tax law should be used to establish the number and value of EX-MSD in each tax return.

a major reform of the existing individual income tax system. Retention might mean that some individuals in a unit which is eligible to receive transfer-by-taxation allowances may also be taxable.

Under a negative rates taxation plan using tax exemptions and deductions as breakeven lines but a different family unit, a person with enough income to be taxable may be declared a dependent for transfer-by-taxation purposes. For example, the proposed tax unit for transfer-by-taxation makes it possible for a child with taxable income to be in a unit eligible to receive allowances. However, cases of this sort are probably not important enough to warrant abandoning the present tax unit for positive income tax purposes.

If a social dividend plan were adopted, many taxable persons might be in units receiving net allowances. It seems possible to tax one kind of unit for positive tax purposes and to determine eligibility for net social dividend allowances on the basis of a unit defined in a different way. Nevertheless, there may be real administrative problems in coping with two different definitions of the tax unit, and possibly two different definitions of income.

Problems Created by the Proposed Tax Unit

The family tax unit outlined above does not solve all the problems raised by a welfare, rather than a tax-collecting, proposal. In fact, it may create some problems, including these three:

1. Unfortunately, use of the family tax unit creates an incentive for persons to leave a family and "declare" themselves independent of that family unit. This is caused by the same factors which induce separate filing. If separate filing is effectively prohibited by adoption of a family tax unit, some families or persons may resort to explicit separation. There is some doubt whether the increased allowance received by a family if its major earner deserts or separates is enough to cover the costs created by the necessity to maintain a second household. Moreover, it is doubtful that more than a very small percentage of families would split up in order to obtain their maximum transfer-by-taxation allowances. Nevertheless, in some marginal cases the fragmentation problem may be very real.

2. Features of the family tax unit may create a disincentive for children to work. Under the present tax system, a child is allowed $900 in EX-MSD against his earned income while his parents are allowed to claim the child as a dependent (worth $700). In

a transfer-by-taxation plan with a family tax unit, the child's income would be pooled with that of his parents, but only one dependency could be claimed (worth $500 using poverty lines or $700 using the value of EX-MSD). The family tax unit with its provision for pooling of income also means that the child's income would be taxed at the allowance tax rate. If that rate were 50 percent the child would face a marginal tax rate of 50 percent, which might well reduce his incentive to work. If the present tax regulations were followed (including no pooling of income), the child's income would not reduce the family's allowance by 50 cents for each dollar earned and the child would still be counted as a dependent.

3. There is also the problem of assuring that persons who are not self-supporting, but are otherwise eligible to file for transfer-by-taxation purposes, are prevented from filing. A son who is 20 years old and is not a student might find that it "pays" to leave his parents' household and fail to report the support he receives from them in order to file a negative tax return. Or, he might have his parents reduce their support enough so that he would become his own main source of support.[46] An even more critical problem is posed by the following example. Assume a person 20 years old who is not a student, has no income, and receives $700 support from his family. In year one, he borrows $800 in order to make ends meet. In year two, he applies for a transfer-by-taxation allowance on the basis that he has no income but is the main source of his own support. He receives a transfer-by-taxation allowance of $750 under a negative rates plan (equal to 50 percent of $1,500) plus $700 from his parents. In year three, he again files a transfer-by-taxation return claiming the $750 allowance makes him the main source of his own support.[47] This could continue year after year.

The family unit represents another step away from the concepts and methods of the present tax system. It means that some present taxpayers (most of them children) may no longer pay taxes, but will become part of a family which is eligible to receive transfer-by-taxation allowances. Redefinition of the tax unit for transfer-by-taxation purposes highlights the welfare aspect of a transfer-by-taxation

---

[46] It might be a very good thing to leave the parents' household, even if his reasons for doing so are poor ones.

[47] Presumably, the negative tax allowance is regarded as a part of a person's self-support.

proposal. It is worth noting, however, that not a great deal of damage is done to present tax concepts and methods regarding eligibility to file a tax return. There is continued reliance on the present support tests for determining eligibility to file and claim dependents. Defining a family tax unit would seem to be a price that must be paid in order to have both a workable and equitable transfer-by-taxation plan.

Administrative Issues

There are at least three important administrative issues to be solved before a transfer-by-taxation plan can be put into effect. These are the determination of eligibility for allowances, the timing of allowance payments, and the choice of an agency to be responsible for making allowance payments.

Eligibility

One important problem relating to eligibility for transfer-by-taxation allowances—that of defining the allowance unit—has just been discussed. Two others are (1) how to record the income of the allowance unit and (2) how to treat fluctuating incomes.

Given agreement upon definition of income for transfer-by-taxation purposes, it is necessary to assure that all taxable income received by members of the filing unit is reported. Especially if taxable income for transfer-by-taxation purposes includes sporadic earnings and transfer payments which usually are not reported on the present positive tax return, considerable effort will be required to assure full reporting. Since many low-income families receive a large portion of their income in transfer payments (the poor receive over 40 percent of their income in the form of public transfers), it is very important that transfers as well as earned income be reported. A large portion of public transfers is made up of veterans' and social insurance payments. Thus it would be necessary for the agency administering the transfer-by-taxation plan to receive from the Veterans Administration, the Social Security Administration, and local agencies paying unemployment benefits information on benefits they had paid to a filing unit.[48]

[48] This would necessitate a change in present Social Security Administration procedures regarding availability of information about a person's social security "account.

In the past, the reporting of farm, interest, and rental income has been inadequate.[49] For transfer-by-taxation, the continued underreporting of income, especially farm income, would seriously reduce the equity and efficiency of the plan. In general, transfer-by-taxation would require systematic attempts to assure that proprietors comply with the tax law.

Some of the very poor have rarely, if ever, filed an income tax return. It may be necessary to provide assistance for such people to assure not only that they report their income accurately but that they report at all. This is a big burden to place on the Internal Revenue Service (IRS) if it is made the administering agency; the IRS is not in the business of welfare work. But it might be possible to have social workers provide assistance in filling out tax forms. Such a solution would be unfortunate, however, if a transfer-by-taxation plan necessitated that welfare workers do the kind of investigating that they are either forced or obliged to do at present.

Since a transfer-by-taxation plan is indisputably a welfare plan it may be important to incorporate some form of tax or transfer "averaging" into the proposal. That is, from the point of view of welfare, it seems justifiable to look beyond a particular year's income in determining, first, whether a family is eligible for allowances and, second, the level of net allowances it will receive.

Two examples illustrate why some form of averaging would be useful. The first assumes that a negative rates plan is added to the existing individual income tax structure. Suppose that a family's income fluctuates widely, because the family with annual earned income which usually is substantially higher than poverty lines decides to take a year's vacation during which it has little or no earnings. It seems reasonable to prohibit negative rates taxation allowances for such families. This problem could be solved by a provision preventing payment when a family's income for a given number of past years has averaged above a certain level. For example, a rule of thumb might be that a family whose average income over the past three years was two or three times its poverty line would be ineligible to receive negative rates taxation allowances. In addition, any family whose income averaged more than, say, $10,000 over

49 Harold M. Groves, "Income-Tax Administration," *National Tax Journal*, Vol. 12 (March 1959), pp. 37-39.

the past three years would be ineligible to receive allowances. This rule is a net income requirement; however, it suggests that in the case of business or property income a gross income requirement might be adopted. For example, a proprietor whose gross business or property income exceeds a given level would not be eligible to receive allowances.

The Council of Economic Advisers has found that 30 percent of families living in poverty in one year receive income in the next year in an amount which will take them out of poverty. Of that 30 percent, however, only a small percentage receives incomes which are substantially in excess of poverty line income.[50]

Another problem involves the treatment of lump-sum payments which are designed to replace a family's earnings over a period of years. Workmen's compensation is an example. Earlier it was concluded that workmen's compensation should be included in the money income measure for calculating negative rates allowances. Lump-sum workmen's compensation payments might best be spread (or averaged) over several years in calculating the negative rates allowances.

This raises the question whether there should be some sort of income-averaging arrangement in calculating negative rates allowances. A family's negative rates allowance might be based on the difference between its poverty line (or value of EX-MSD) and its average money income over several preceding years. This would not be necessary if the negative tax rate were a single flat rate. But if the negative tax schedule were progressive or regressive it would make some sense to average—although it usually would not be likely to make a great deal of difference. For example, a family of four with no income in four years and $2,500 in the fifth year would receive, under a system without averaging, $6,125 over the five years if the regressive tax schedule described in the next chapter were applied to the family's poverty income gap.[51] If, however, a five-year averaging scheme were adopted, the total payment over

[50] *Economic Report of the President, January 1965*, p. 163. The estimate is based on families with income below $3,000 for two consecutive years.

[51] The regressive tax schedule consists of three tax rates: 75, 50, and 25 percent. The 75 percent rate is applied against income up to one-third of poverty line income. The 50 percent rate is applied against the next third of poverty line income and the 25 percent rate against the final third.

five years would be $5,625. In this case, the family would gain by an absence of averaging.

The second example is based on a social dividend plan with a single 50 percent allowance tax rate and a single 15 percent finance tax rate. Assume a family of four is guaranteed $3,000 and has a breakeven level of income equal to $6,000. Suppose the total receipts (not including allowances) over a period of years had the pattern shown in line 1 of Table 7-3. Then taxes and social dividend allowances, given the assumptions above, would be those shown in lines 2 and 3 of Table 7-3. The net payment of allowances over the three years (that is, the total net allowances minus total net taxes in the three-year period) would be $1,300 ($2,500 minus $1,200). Suppose, however, an averaging plan had been adopted whereby the average of the three years' income had been the basis for calculating net taxes or net allowances. Average income over the three-year period would be $7,000 (equal to $21,000 divided by 3). Since the family's breakeven level of income is $6,000, the family would pay a tax of $150 each year on its $1,000 of income above the breakeven level of income ($1,000 times .15, the finance tax rate). Over a three-year period, the family would pay a total of $450 to finance the transfer-by-taxation plan. Thus, averaging would have the result, given the structure of the plan described above, of reducing (eliminating in this case) the family's net allowance. Without averaging, its net allowance payment over three years would total $1,300. With averaging, it would have no net allowances but instead would pay $450—a difference of $1,750 as a result of averaging.

TABLE 7-3. Payments to a Family of Four Under a Two-Rate Social Dividend Plan: No Averaging[a]

Item	Year			Total Over Three Years
	First	Second	Third	
(1) Income	$10,000	$10,000	$1,000	$21,000
(2) Annual net tax	600	600	0	1,200
(3) Annual net allowance	0	0	2,500	2,500
(4) Net allowance, (3)–(2)	600	600	2,500	1,300

[a] Based on a plan with a single 50 percent allowance tax rate and a single 15 percent finance tax rate for a family of four, guaranteed $3,000, which has a breakeven level of income equal to $6,000.

This result is produced by the regressivity in the tax structure under the plan. The effective marginal tax rate for low incomes is 50 percent while the rate on higher incomes (above the breakeven level of income) is 15 percent. The outcome is the opposite of the one produced by a fluctuating income under the present progressive individual income tax system. The example illustrates why averaging with respect to calculating net allowances or net taxes under a social dividend plan would be justified, in principle, although it would undoubtedly add greatly to administrative burdens.

Timing of Allowance Payments

Under the present system, income taxes are due by April 15 of the year following the one in which the tax is incurred. That is to say, a taxpayer's account with the government is settled after the year in which he earned his income, even though a portion of his income may have been withheld on each payday. It is questionable, however, whether a welfare plan can have a single settlement date in the year following that in which the need for the allowance exists. Clearly, a good welfare plan should provide income at regular intervals during the year in which it is needed. This is certainly true where the potential recipient's income is so low he would be defined as poor. Under a negative rates plan, almost all recipients of net allowances would be considered poor. Many recipients of net allowances under a social dividend plan would not be defined as poor, however, and supposedly could wait until the end of the year to receive the allowance without undue hardship. Even so, the largest net allowance payments made under a social dividend plan would go to poor families. It would be undesirable either to make these payments at one time or to make them a year after they are needed.

It can be argued justifiably that many of the poor are poor year in and year out, so that they would receive substantial allowances each year. But if there is a year's lag in paying allowances, fluctuating incomes would tend to raise allowances when a family's income rose and to lower allowances when the family's income fell and the family was in greater need.

Whether allowance payments are lagged or not, it seems clear that they should be paid at several regular intervals during the year, not all at one time. At the least, the payments should be made each quarter; monthly payments would be better.[52] If payment were made more often than once a month the burden on the Internal Revenue Service would be excessive.

There are, however, two important administrative problems in a plan for payment during the month or quarter in which the income used in calculating the payments is earned. One problem is how to estimate in advance the "income deficit" upon which the level of net payment is based. The second is how to treat overpayments made as a result of faulty estimates of a family's annual income.[53]

Annual income could be estimated in the same way that the Social Security Administration adjusts required social security contributions to earnings or the Internal Revenue Service determines the amount of income to be withheld. Furthermore, payments might be made periodically at an annual rate which equaled the basic guarantee, and income up to the breakeven level of income at the allowance tax rate would be withheld. The income in excess of the allowance tax rate would be withheld at a rate equal to the finance tax rate.[54] However, this would be a cumbersome method for the relatively small negative rates taxation plan under which net payments would go mainly to the poor. The social dividend plans involve net allowances to a much larger portion of the population. Thus for the latter plans, it would not be unreasonable to pay the gross rather than the net allowance. Still many persons might object to making periodic payments to a large number of families who would not need them and who on a net basis would receive no allowances. Another approach would be to make gross payments only to families who are likely to be eligible for net allowances but to credit allowances against the taxes of families with higher incomes. That is, the credit would be subtracted from the family's gross tax liability (tax rate times income received) in determining its net tax liability (tax rate times income received minus the basic allowance due the family).

Another problem is encountered when a person is not employed

[52] The Office of Tax Analysis, U. S. Department of the Treasury, has estimated the increased administrative cost of monthly, rather than quarterly, payments to be $3.8 million. However, this is for a plan which would provide negative rate allowances to poor families with children, not for a social dividend plan.

[53] The problem would be lessened if eligibility for net allowances were not based on annual income, but on income received in some shorter period.

[54] This abstracts from withholding for positive tax purposes.

in the first half of a year but gets a job in the second half of the year. This is the problem of collecting overpayments of allowances. Since the person may have almost no earnings in the first half year, he may receive substantial net allowances. With employment in the second half, his earnings may be so high that he becomes ineligible on a yearly income basis either for net allowances or for allowances as large as he had received earlier in the year. This problem can be avoided where the gross allowance is paid to the family and where gross taxes are withheld, as in some social dividend plans. But such a solution is not a practical alternative under a negative rates plan.

The overpayment problem in transfer-by-taxation is not unique. Presently the treatment of beneficiaries of old-age, survivors, disability, and health insurance (OASDHI) who are under 72 years of age creates a similar problem. The law reads that a potential beneficiary of OASDHI who is under 72 loses benefits if annual income is over $1,500. Although the law also provides that a beneficiary does not lose any benefits for any month in which he earns from work $125 or less, it is possible to conceive of situations in which the OASDHI recipient earns enough late in the year to force the Social Security Administration to reclaim benefits provided early in the year. The OASDHI officials now recoup overpayments in one of two ways: (1) ask the beneficiary to make a money refund; (2) withhold benefits in the following year equal to the overpayment.

Agency Responsible for Making Payments

By definition, a transfer-by-taxation plan is related to the tax system. Thus, it seems reasonable to assume that the Internal Revenue Service would be responsible for collecting the revenues destined to finance the plan.[55] But who should be responsible for making allowance payments?

If allowance payments were made once a year—at the time income tax returns were filed—and if administering a transfer-by-taxation plan were limited to determining whether a unit was eligible for an end-of-the-year allowance, it would be clear that the IRS would be the most appropriate administering agency. But suppose the plan necessitated a monthly payment to a large part of the pop-

---

[55] The Internal Revenue Service now collects social security contributions even though the federal social security program is generally administered by the Social Security Administration.

ulation—a payment which at a yearly rate would equal the guaranteed minimum. Then it might be well for the IRS simply to collect revenues and leave the responsibility for payments to an independent agency. The coverage of the plan would seem to make a major difference. At one extreme, there would be a need for adding only a few lines to the short tax form. At the other extreme, periodic payments adding in a year to the guaranteed minimum would have to be made to millions of families. In the former case, the IRS would need to make only a small change in procedure. It would be doing little more than expanding the concept of the tax refund to include transfer-by-taxation allowances. In the latter case, the IRS would be taking on a whole new function which could be so burdensome it might well be left to another agency.

Choice of the administrative agency for a transfer-by-taxation plan may depend, in part, on the relationship of transfer-by-taxation to two other programs:—to social insurance on the one hand, and to public assistance on the other. If a transfer-by-taxation plan is not supposed to replace the social insurance system, but is nonetheless felt to endanger that system, a good strategy might be to administer the social insurance system in conjunction with the transfer-by-taxation plan. The assumption here is that transfer-by-taxation allowances would supplement social insurance, and that social insurance benefits for which workers have helped to pay are just as important a part of the income maintenance system in the United States as the transfer-by-taxation plan.

If the transfer-by-taxation plan takes the form of a negative rates plan, public assistance would still be necessary for some families.[56] The relationship of the two programs may depend on whether or not public assistance is considered supplemental to negative rates allowances. Continuation of public assistance would mean two administrative setups. At the very least, this would require a degree of interagency coordination which is not now necessary.

[56] Presumably public assistance would be ended under a social dividend plan.

CHAPTER VIII

The Incentives Question

THE QUESTION OF INCENTIVES inevitably arises when discussion turns to a proposal for a guaranteed minimum income. Would guaranteeing a minimum income and taxing it away at high rates as before-allowance income rises reduce work effort? Would it create an incentive among some demographic groups to have more children?

Work Incentives

It is useful to begin a discussion of how transfer-by-taxation affects work incentives by distinguishing between marginal tax rates and average tax rates. Under the present progressive income tax system, the marginal and average rates are positive and rise as taxable income rises. The picture is somewhat different on the "negative" side of the system. There the marginal rates are positive and they may be high—in fact, a good deal higher than the present marginal tax rates on the taxable income of low-income groups. However, the average tax rate is a negative rate which approaches minus infinity as income approaches zero. This is shown in Table 8-1. Note that the average tax rate is negative because transfer-by-taxation allowances are treated as negative taxes. This is a useful way in which to treat allowances because it helps clarify the analysis of how negative tax rates might affect work incentives.

It is common to divide the effect of income taxes into two parts: a "substitution effect" and an "income effect." Income taxation produces a substitution effect by reducing the price of leisure relative to the price of work. The substitution effect is usually associated with the marginal tax rate since that rate indicates the amount of the after-tax return from another hour of work. Income taxation

TABLE 8-1. Marginal and Average Tax Rates on the Income of a Family of Four Under Two Negative Rates Taxation Plans[a]

Income Before Allowance (Dollars)	Plan with 50 Percent Allowance Tax Rate				Plan with Regressive Allowance Tax Rate Schedule			
	Allowance (Dollars)	Positive Tax (Dollars)	Average Tax Rate[b] (Percent)	Marginal Tax Rate (Percent)	Allowance (Dollars)	Positive Tax (Dollars)	Average Tax Rate[b] (Percent)	Marginal Tax Rate (Percent)
0	1,500	0	$-\infty$	50	1,500	0	$-\infty$	75
500	1,250	0	-250.0	50	1,125	0	-225.0	75
1,000	1,000	0	-100.0	50	750	0	-75.0	50
1,500	750	0	-50.0	50	500	0	-33.0	50
2,000	500	0	-25.0	50	250	0	-12.5	25
2,500	250	0	-10.0	50	125	0	-5.0	25
3,000	0	0	0	0	0	0	0	0
4,000	0	140	$+3.5$[c]	14	0	140	$+3.5$[c]	14
5,000	0	290	$+5.8$[c]	15	0	290	$+5.8$[c]	15
6,000	0	450	$+7.5$[c]	16	0	450	$+7.5$[c]	16

[a] Both plans use tax exemptions and minimum standard deductions (EX-MSD) for breakeven lines.
Average tax rate equals tax minus allowance divided by income.
[c] Assumes money income equals adjusted gross income (AGI). Thus for a family of four which does not itemize deductions any income in excess of $3,000 is taxable.

produces an income effect by reducing the net compensation from work. This reduction in net compensation is reflected in the average tax rate. It is usually assumed that the income effect produced by taxation will induce the taxpayer to work more in order to offset the losses due to taxation. Thus, the positive income tax system tends to produce substitution and income effects which work in opposite directions, although they may not be completely offsetting.

What happens when a transfer-by-taxation plan is adopted? Clearly the marginal tax rate will create a substitution effect in which leisure would be substituted for work. But what about the income effect? In which direction will it operate? Because the average tax rate of those persons and families eligible for transfer-by-taxation allowances is less than zero, the effect of negative taxation is to raise incomes, not reduce them. Those eligible for allowances will find that it takes less work in order to maintain the same income position they had before the introduction of the allowances. It is likely, then, that the income effect will be reduced work effort, especially when earned income is below the minimum income guarantee. Thus it seems likely that both the substitution and income effects produced by a transfer-by-taxation plan will operate in the direction of reducing work effort.[1]

Empirical Evidence on the Effects of High Tax Rates

The little evidence available on the effect of high income tax rates on effort, or work incentives, is drawn mainly from studies of upper income groups. Thus at the outset caution is necessary, because the effect of high marginal tax rates on low-income classes may be quite different from their effect on upper income groups. The two groups may react differently because their attitudes toward work are not the same, or the levels of the average tax rates do not seem equally burdensome. Much of this evidence is based on three studies.[2] Sanders studied the effect of taxes on 160 executives in the United States; in 1956, Break studied the influence of the income tax in England upon 306 solicitors and accountants; and more recently Barlow, Brazer, and Morgan have reported on the effect of taxes on work and investment decisions of 957 members of upper income (over $10,000) groups.

Sanders found that taxation had not materially reduced the services of corporation executives. Nor did taxes seem to have an unambiguous effect on the decision to retire. Most of the executives found one or another reason to rationalize their work effort in the face of high marginal tax rates. Among the reasons for not reducing

[1] This view is Richard Musgrave's as described in *The Theory of Public Finance* (New York: McGraw-Hill, 1959), p. 252.

[2] Thomas Sanders, *Effects of Taxation on Executives* (Boston: Graduate School of Business Administration, Harvard University, 1951). George F. Break, "Income Taxes and Incentives to Work: An Empirical Study," *American Economic Review*, Vol. 47 (September 1957), pp. 529-49. Robin Barlow, Harvey E. Brazer, and James N. Morgan, *Economic Behavior of the Affluent* (Washington: Brookings Institution, 1966). Also see by the same authors, "A Survey of Investment Management and Working Behavior Among High-Income Individuals," *American Economic Review, Papers and Proceedings*, Vol. 55 (May 1965), pp. 252-64.

work effort were nonfinancial incentives to work and the "compulsions of administrative organization and disciplines."[3] Sanders did find some executives who limited their work for tax reasons. These tended to be owners of businesses, who were their own bosses, and not responsible to superiors. He also found that, in some cases, taxes played an important part in causing an executive to refuse additional business for his company. In addition, taxes were cited as a reason for refusing a promotion or an advantageous offer from another company when the change would have little effect on net compensation.

Break's study of the English scene does not yield any clear indication that high tax rates reduce work effort. About half of the 306 solicitors and accountants he interviewed said the hours they worked were not at all influenced by taxes. Among the other half, 40 said taxes definitely reduced work effort; 31 said taxes definitely increased work effort; and 79 left in doubt whether, in fact, high marginal tax rates had an effect on work decisions.[4] Overall, there was no clear preponderance either way. Break's conclusion is that the "net effect, be it disincentive or incentive, is not large enough to be of great economic or sociological significance."[5]

The Morgan, Barlow, and Brazer study, conducted by the University of Michigan Survey Research Center, failed to turn up evidence that income taxes substantially reduce work effort. They found that only 6 percent of the total income of earners of high incomes accrues to persons who really do less work because of the income tax. Moreover, of this group who did "less work," three-fourths worked at least thirty-four hours a week, forty-seven weeks a year.[6] Among the groups with the strongest tax-created disincentives to work were the self-employed professionals, those with large asset holdings, and older age groups.[7] Morgan and his associates conclude that "the economic activities of most of the [high-income]

---

[3] Sanders, *op. cit.,* pp. 12-13.

[4] Break, *op. cit.,* pp. 236-41.

[5] *Ibid.,* p. 543.

[6] Morgan, Barlow, Brazer, *American Economic Review, op. cit.,* p. 262. In order to deal with the possibility that those affected received a high proportion of the income of upper income groups, each of the 957 individuals was weighted in accordance with his "economic importance." Income was used as the measure of such importance (p. 253).

[7] *Ibid.,* p. 261.

group were not dominated by precise calculations of monetary gain."[8] They found that demands of business associates and clients, inertia, and, in some cases, altruism, help explain why high marginal tax rates did not prevent long hours of work. Thus "it would appear that the loss of work effort in the economy due to the existence of the federal income tax instead of some feasible alternative has been small in the extreme."[9] *Only refers to upper income*

Richard Goode recently summarized the literature on the effects of income taxation on incentives, and concluded that the effect of taxation on incentives is unclear and "may be weaker than popular discussions imply."[10] However, Goode notes that the movement of labor between occupations may be more sensitive to taxation than the total labor supply seems to be. A reduction in the real wage caused by taxation may not reduce work, he says, but it may add an incentive to change jobs in order to raise the real wage.

It may be difficult, however, for low-income groups to find jobs which raise the real wage. And, as Sanders found, the fact that the increase in net compensation may be small (owing to a high marginal tax rate) is a reason why executives, at least, were less mobile than they might have been if marginal tax rates had been lower.

Some experience with a high marginal tax rate among low-income workers has occurred under the social security system. The old-age, survivors and disability insurance (OASDI) retirement test until 1966 provided that a worker 65 through 71 years of age[11] could earn up to $1,200 a year without losing any benefits. However, earnings between $1,201 and $1,700 reduced benefits $1 for each $2 earned—that is, earnings were "taxed" at a 50 percent rate; and earnings in excess of $1,700 reduced benefits dollar for dollar—that is, a 100 percent "tax" rate was applied to earnings, starting at $1,700 and continuing to the point at which benefits were reduced to zero.[12] Lowell Gallaway has examined the effect of the OASDI retirement test upon participation in the labor force and

[8] *Ibid.*, p. 263.

[9] *Ibid.*, p. 262.

[10] Richard Goode, *The Individual Income Tax* (Washington: Brookings Institution, 1964), p. 57.

[11] The provisions still do not apply to workers over 71 years of age.

[12] Beginning in 1966, a beneficiary can earn up to $1,500 a year before he begins to lose benefits. Dollar-for-dollar reductions only begin when earnings exceed $2,700 a year.

earnings of the elderly.[13] He concluded that there is no observable impact upon labor force participation. But he also concluded that the retirement test reduces by 15 percent median earnings of male participants in the labor force who are 65 to 71 years old.[14] This indicates the retirement test does provide an actual disincentive to earning.

In his study, Gallaway used 1957 data from the Continuous Work History Sample. The data indicate that there were fewer workers aged 65 to 71 in the $1,200 to $2,400 earnings class than there would have been without a retirement test. (The $1,200 to $2,400 earnings class is the one in which the trade-off between earnings and benefits takes place. Gallaway assumes most persons with earnings over $2,400 have lost all their benefits.)[15] This reduction is reflected in the smaller percentages of workers aged 65 to 71 in the $1,200 to $2,400 class compared with the percentages of workers aged 62 to 64 and over 71 years of age in this class. The two latter age groups were not subjected to the retirement test. The effect of what can be termed "high marginal tax rates" is also reflected in the fact that the percentage of male workers aged 72 who in 1959 were earning from $1,200 to $2,400 is considerably larger than the percentage of male workers aged 71 who a year earlier were earning similar amounts. The conclusion is that when some of the workers become 72 years old—and are no longer subject to the retirement test with its high marginal tax rates—they begin to earn more than $1,200.[16]

Evidence on the Effects of a Guaranteed Minimum Income

A high marginal tax rate is not the only reason why a transfer-by-taxation plan may adversely affect incentives. Another is the

---

[13] Lowell E. Gallaway, *The Retirement Decision: An Exploratory Essay*, Department of Health, Education, and Welfare, Research Report No. 9 (1965), pp. 18-23.

[14] *Ibid.*, p. 47.

[15] *Ibid.*, pp. 19-20.

[16] *Ibid.*, pp. 22-23. In 1961, the percentage of employed workers aged 72 entitled to OASDI benefits was 27.2 percent, somewhat higher than the comparable figure of 25.4 percent for persons aged 71. There was also an increase in the number of entitled workers resulting, according to Gallaway, from removal of the retirement test. Since there was a greater than average percentage of the newly entitled persons who were employed, and did not previously apply for OASDI benefits because they were steadily employed, the effect is to increase the overall percentage of employed workers aged 72 who were entitled to benefits that year.

level of the guaranteed minimum income. The level may be high enough that some families might be so satisfied with what they receive through the transfer system that they would substantially, or completely, reduce their work effort. Unfortunately, there is little available evidence in this respect, although the public assistance programs may provide some clues. But any findings must be placed against two sets of facts: the type of person receiving public assistance and the existence of an implicit 100 percent marginal tax rate. As noted earlier, most welfare recipients receive public assistance under programs of aid to families with dependent children (AFDC)[17] and old-age assistance (OAA). It is not likely that full-time work is a feasible alternative to public assistance for many of these recipients. Moreover, the fact that assistance payments are reduced dollar for dollar means that someone who is earning a very low income and is eligible for assistance—and who has few prospects for earning more than he or she would receive in assistance—may view public assistance as a real alternative to working. This would seem true of many dependent mothers who are eligible for assistance under the AFDC program. One estimate indicates that approximately 70 percent of the female recipients of AFDC are unlikely to improve their money income if they go to work on a full-time basis.[18] The comparable figure for families headed by a male receiving AFDC-UP is about 40 percent.[19]

These figures are interesting because they illustrate the economic irrationality of a plan which effectively entails a 100 percent marginal tax rate. There is no financial gain for many AFDC recipients if they refuse assistance and go to work. In fact, they may lose certain benefits in kind, such as those covering hospital and dental costs. Also costs, such as travel and child care expenses, are incurred in going to work.

---

[17] Prior to 1962 this program was known as aid to dependent children (ADC). For convenience throughout this discussion it will be referred to as AFDC.

[18] Leonard Hausman, "Incentive Budgeting for Welfare Recipients" (unpublished paper, University of Wisconsin, January 1965). The earnings data on which this estimate is based take into consideration involuntary unemployment and part-time employment that welfare recipients are likely to experience if they go to work.

[19] Aid to families with dependent children with an unemployed parent is known as AFDC-UP. Over twenty states have such programs making AFDC payments to families with an able-bodied male head who is unemployed.

To what extent do families move out of public assistance programs by earning income or, at least, provide for some of their needs out of earnings? One scrap of evidence regarding the earning decisions of AFDC recipients comes from a study on incentive budgeting carried out by the Denver Department of Welfare. The Denver plan allowed some AFDC recipients to "keep" the first $25 of monthly earnings and 25 percent of monthly earnings in excess of $25. Thus for each earned dollar (per month) above $25 the marginal tax rate was 75 percent until the public assistance grant was reduced to zero.[20] The Denver study then compared the results for those receiving the special incentives with those receiving no special incentives.

The findings are as follows: Cases in existence in July 1959, but discontinued for any reason by September 1961, amounted to 29.3 percent of the special incentive budgeting group and 29.6 percent for the other group.[21] Of those who discontinued, 34 percent of the incentive budgeting group did so because of earnings; the comparable figure for the nonincentive budgeting group was 33.2 percent. Thus only about 10 percent (34 percent of 29.3 percent) of the original study group was discontinued because of earnings. Of the 70 percent of the cases which had not discontinued in August 1961, only 2.7 percent had earnings. However, among the incentive budgeting group, the percentage was 3.5 percent compared with only 1.9 percent for the other group.[22]

The Denver study gave evidence that the incentive budgeting principle "may be effective for a specific and selected segment of the caseload." Under it, an earner was more likely to retain his job. However, the study showed that this principle could not be "adopted without reservation for the total caseload." Unfortunately, the incentive budgeting formula "failed to recognize that, although desire, motivation and concern is held by recipients (as brought out in this study), physical, social and mental problems faced by these re-

[20] *The Incentive Budgeting Demonstration Project,* Final Report, prepared by the Colorado State Department of Public Welfare and the Denver Department of Welfare (December 1961), p. II.

[21] *Ibid.,* Table 1, p. 10. However, it took more earnings to get completely off assistance under the incentive budgeting plan. For example, the breakeven point for a family receiving $150 a month in assistance would be $225 in the Denver incentive budgeting plan.

[22] *Ibid.,* p. 10.

cipients are, in fact, the reasons for their inability to be self-sustaining."[23]

The recognition by the Denver study that many AFDC recipients have important social, physical, and mental handicaps adds evidence that some persons or families have little or no earning potential. Undoubtedly such persons or families would rely heavily on a guaranteed minimum income. They may represent the main justification for a guaranteed minimum income because they illustrate so well that some consumer units simply cannot rely on work as a source of income. However, it would be misleading to use the behavior of such persons or families as a basis for predicting how other potential earners will act.

Brehm and Saving have recently made an empirical study of the demand for general assistance payments.[24] Since they were mainly interested in the effect of assistance upon work incentives, they did not investigate the categorical assistance programs (old-age assistance, aid to families with dependent children, aid to the blind, and aid to the permanently and totally disabled).[25] Recipients of relief payments under these programs usually are not in a position to make a decision between earnings and relief payments. The model used by Brehm and Saving is a "special case" of the demand for leisure in which the demand for general assistance payments depends upon: (1) the consumer's earned income; (2) the minimum income which society deems desirable; and (3) the discount factor which the consumer applies to relief doles.[26]

The empirical results of the Brehm and Saving study show that the percentage of a state's population receiving general assistance payments is directly related to the level of the average monthly general assistance payment and to the ease in meeting the qualifications for receipt of general assistance. They also found "that nearly one-half of all assistance recipients are not on assistance due to zero wage alternatives."[27]

---

[23] *Ibid.*, pp. 16-18. Of thirty-nine cases in June 1961 who were earning under the incentive budgeting plan, all but nine had incomes in excess of $25 and thus were subject to high marginal "tax" rates.

[24] C. T. Brehm and T. R. Saving, "The Demand for General Assistance Payments," *American Economic Review*, Vol. 54 (December 1964), pp. 1002-18.

[25] *Ibid.*, p. 1007.

[26] *Ibid.*, p. 1017.

[27] *Ibid.*, pp. 1017-18.

The Brehm and Saving findings seem to imply that transfer-by-taxation payments to which little stigma is applied might materially reduce the work effort of many low-income households, and that the number so affected would be positively related to the level of the guaranteed minimum. However, their empirical results do not separate the effect of an implicit 100 percent tax rate from the effect of being able to rely on a guaranteed minimum.[28] Many of those who could have worked, but were content to receive assistance, might have acted differently if they could have retained something like 50 percent of their earnings.

Additional evidence on the effect of transfer payments upon work incentives comes from Lowell E. Gallaway.[29] Having employed data from the Continuous Work History Sample to examine the response of the aged to the high marginal tax rates in the OASDI retirement test (as described above), Gallaway turned to the labor market response of the aged to the receipt of additional transfer income such as that due to negative income taxation. Gallaway's model is similar to the Brehm and Saving model, and it leads him to question whether negative income taxation will improve the income position of poor families with members in the labor force. Instead of raising the income levels of the working poor, a negative income tax might cause a substitution of leisure for work great enough to offset the additional income due to receiving negative income tax payments.

Gallaway calculates that a 10 percent negative tax rate (certainly a low rate compared to the rates adopted by proponents of negative taxation) applied to the unused portion of the exemptions of the aged would reduce work effort enough so as to actually reduce the total income of elderly males presently in the labor force. This estimate, however, seems to depend critically upon an earlier estimate by Gallaway that an increase of one percentage point in OASDI benefits relative to the median earnings of all men would produce a decrease of 1.4 percentage points in the extent of labor force participation by elderly males.[30] It might be argued that those who

---

[28] Of course, the general assistance program does not really guarantee a minimum income. A person or family is "assured" some level of income only if the person or family qualifies for entry onto the relief rolls.

[29] Gallaway, "Negative Income Tax Rates and the Elimination of Poverty," *National Tax Journal*, Vol. 19 (September 1966), pp. 298-307.

[30] *Ibid.*, pp. 303-05. This estimate also depends on a calculation that the elasticity

are not aged are less likely than the aged to leave the labor force in response to the receipt of transfer income. Labor force participants who are not aged are less likely to have relatives able to help support them if they stop work and more likely to have important obligations to children. Gallaway, however, seems to hold a different view. Although he is not certain whether his results can be generalized to apply to persons under 65, he notes that "there is evidence to suggest that there are similarities in labor market responses

TABLE 8-2. Characteristics of the Heads of Poor Families Affecting Participation in the Labor Force[a]

Families	1947	1963
With aged head[b] (in thousands)	2,472	3,052
Headed by a female (in thousands)	1,927	2,299
Total with aged or female head	4,399	5,351
With head not in labor force as percentage of all poor families	30[c]	48[d]

Source: U.S. Department of Commerce, Bureau of the Census, *Current Population Reports*, Series P-60, No. 45 "Low-Income Families and Unrelated Individuals in the United States: 1963" (1965), pp. 10–11.
[a] Measurement of poor families is for those with income less than $3,000 (in 1963 dollars).
[b] Does not include unrelated individuals over 65 years old. In 1963, 2.65 million of these aged unrelated individuals had incomes under $1,500.
[c] Figure is for 1950.
[d] The 48 percent somewhat overstates the case because the poverty line used for all families was $3,000. This would tend to overstate the number of aged poor and underestimate the number of families with children. The latter are likely to have heads of working age.

among all groups in the population." He concludes that his empirical findings strongly suggest that the labor force response of the aged "is sufficient to negate the effects of the negative income tax proposal upon the money income levels of those in the labor force at the time the proposal might be enacted."[31]

The poor, like those who are not poor, may put a high value on leisure. But now, more than in earlier days, leisure tends to involve expenditure, and this increases the incentive to earn. In a society so consumption-oriented as that of the United States it does not seem likely that a transfer-by-taxation plan with a 50 percent rate over

of earnings with respect to wage reductions is .2. *Ibid.*, p. 300. This calculation is derived from the response of the aged to the 50 and 100 percent marginal tax rates implicit in the OASDI retirement test. However, the magnitude of the earnings response to wage reductions might be smaller when the negative tax rate is 10 percent or some other rate well below 50 percent.
[31] *Ibid.*, p. 307.

the long run would create a substantial reduction in the work done by the poor. It is also important that the heads of between 40 and 50 percent of the poor families are not in the labor force. (See Table 8-2, especially note d.) Moreover, a large number of poor families have no logical income earner. If the past trend continues, the percentage of poor families who are aged, have no male head, or have a disabled head, is likely to grow. Therefore, increasingly, the poor are those for whom good reasons can be given for not working. If this percentage were to approach 100 percent, it might be possible to have an allowance tax rate that is 100 percent, or close to it, without substantially reducing the amount of work effort.[32]

Real costs

What would be the real cost of a negative rates plan if high marginal tax rates on low incomes actually damage work incentives? Even if the poor stopped all work, before-allowance income

[32] One way to avoid, at least in part, the potential effects of high marginal tax rates in the allowance tax schedule is to use something other than income as a basis for determining the level of net allowances. It has been suggested elsewhere that the rate at which allowances are reduced be based on the level of a family's consumption expenditure. See Joseph Farber, "The Individual Subsidy Plan," *Feedback* (publication of The Institute for Cybernetic Research), Vol. 4 (January-February 1966). Thus a family which is willing to limit consumption and amass savings will be able to continue to earn with a minimum disincentive to work.

A plan using consumption as a basis for calculating allowances would be structured in a manner similar to one using income. There would be a guaranteed minimum income and a tax rate on consumption expenditure which would together determine a breakeven level of expenditure. The drawbacks of such a plan—which probably more than offset its advantage with respect to work incentives—are: (1) It would place undue emphasis upon saving. It may be good Calvinist doctrine for the poor to save; but it is not likely that the poor will be able to save, and it is possible that the family's "health" will be harmed by strenuous saving accompanied by very low levels of expenditure. This plan also would penalize the family which borrowed in order to consume more than its income. (2) Such a plan would be much more difficult to administer than one which uses income as a basis for calculating net allowances. Very few persons are likely to be able to enumerate their level of expenditures over any lengthy period. For a good discussion of administrative problems connected with taxing consumption expenditures, see Goode, *op. cit.*, pp. 28-33. There Goode discussed the problems involved in administering the expenditure tax proposed by Nicholas Kaldor. (3) Such a plan might result in some persons paying income taxes while receiving allowances. This would occur when a person's income is high enough to be taxable, but his expenditure is low enough to make him (and his family) eligible for allowances.

would not be reduced to zero. It is estimated that about one-half of the income of the poor is labor income, which includes entrepreneurial earnings as well as wages and salaries.[33] In 1964, the money income of the poor totaled $16.8 billion, of which income from labor was about $8.3 billion. Assuming that families above the poverty line are not affected by high marginal tax rates below the poverty line, the maximum real cost of a negative income tax in terms of output lost would have been $8 billion in 1964.[34] Undoubtedly, a negative tax rate of 50 percent would not cause labor income to fall to zero, so the real cost of a negative rates plan would be substantially less than $8 billion.

Employer Incentives

The potential disincentives to work created by a transfer-by-taxation plan are compounded if the plan also creates an incentive for employers to reduce wages. This was one of the major objections to the Speenhamland system of relief adopted in England in the early nineteenth century (as described in Chapter IV). The Speenhamland system, like the present public assistance programs, had an implicit 100 percent tax rate on income. That is, by simply bringing wages up to a subsistence level, the Speenhamland system left little incentive to work on the part of many laborers. It also created an incentive for employers to reduce wages and let the state (or local government) pay part of the laborers' wages.

Under a transfer-by-taxation plan with a 50 percent allowance tax rate, each dollar of reduction in wages would be replaced by only 50 cents of allowances. It seems unlikely that employers in industries having an annual wage[35] higher than the guaranteed minimum income would be any better able to reduce wages if a transfer-

[33] This estimate is derived from data of the U. S. Department of the Treasury, Office of Tax Analysis, based on special tabulations of the Survey of Consumer Expenditures, 1960-61, of the Bureau of Labor Statistics, U. S. Department of Labor. That Survey indicates that 42 percent of the money income of the poor is transfer income. Another 49 percent is labor income; the remaining 9 percent is profit, interest, rent, and other forms of money income such as alimony, dependency allotments, and military pay.

[34] If the negative tax rate were very close to 100 percent, families with income above the poverty line undoubtedly would be affected. Some might cease work altogether, preferring a guaranteed income at or near a poverty line to a hard-won income not much above a poverty line.

[35] The number of hours worked in a year times the wage rate.

by-taxation plan were adopted than they are now. In industries where the annual wage is less than the guaranteed minimum income, resistance to wage cuts may be weakened because the guaranteed minimum assures that the worker's income would be higher than before. Offsetting this effect is the possibility that a guaranteed minimum income would reduce the supply of low-paid labor (since some persons would no longer be willing to work for the low wages) thus creating a tendency to push wages up.

A transfer-by-taxation plan may also create an incentive for employers and employees to enter into wage agreements which would benefit both the employer and the employee at the expense of the general taxpayer. For example, an employer might defer wages so that an employee would be eligible to receive transfer-by-taxation allowances. Later, something less than 100 percent of the deferred wages would be paid to the employee. Both the employer and employee could gain if the positive tax rate were substantially less than the negative tax rate.

Work Incentives and the Shape of the Allowance Tax Schedule

The allowance tax schedule need not consist of a single tax rate. It could take on various shapes designed so as to produce different potential effects on work incentives, different levels of net allowances for given levels of family income, and different overall net costs of a transfer-by-taxation plan. The effects on incentives of each variant presumably would differ. Consider a negative rates taxation plan and the effects produced by such schedules as the following:

1. A progressive tax schedule with a marginal tax rate of 25 percent on the first third of poverty line income, 50 percent on the next third, and 75 percent on the last third.[36]

2. A regressive tax schedule with marginal tax rates on income of 75 percent on the first third of poverty line income, 50 percent on the next third, and 25 percent on the last third.

[36] Another way to put it is that this schedule fills the poverty income gap at 75, 50, and 25 percent marginal rates. That is, until the gap reaches one-third of the poverty line level of income the income gap is filled at a 75 percent rate. If the gap exceeds one-third of the poverty line level but is less than two-thirds of the poverty line level, this "marginal" portion of the gap is filled at a 50 percent rate. If the gap exceeds two-thirds of the poverty line income level, then that part in excess of the two-thirds level is filled at a 25 percent rate.

FIGURE 8-1. Alternative Negative Rate Schedules (Family of Four with Poverty Line Income of $3,000)

Part 1-a. Progressive Allowance

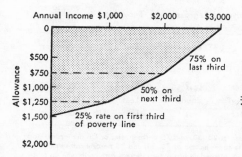

Part 1-b. Regressive Allowance

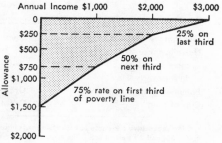

Part 1-c. Set-Aside Allowance

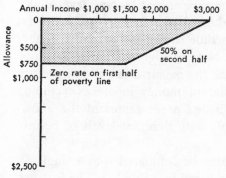

Part 1-d. Conditioned-Incentive

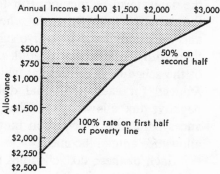

3. A set-aside schedule in which there is no tax on income up to a level equal to 50 percent of the poverty line, but in which, thereafter, a tax rate of 50 percent is applied.

4. A conditioned-incentive schedule which uses a 100 percent marginal rate on income up to 50 percent of the poverty line and a 50 percent rate thereafter.[37]

Figure 8-1 illustrates each of these alternative allowance tax

[37] This schedule was suggested by George Hildebrand in "The Negative Income Tax and the Problem of Poverty" (unpublished paper, U. S. Department of Labor, Winter 1965).

TABLE 8-3. Alternative Allowance Tax Schedules Compared with a Single 50 Percent Rate Schedule[a]

Item	Schedules Compared with a Single 50 Percent Rate			
	Progressive	Regressive	Set-Aside	Conditioned-Incentive
Guaranteed minimum income level	Equal	Equal	Less	Greater
Net allowance to families with income equal to 50 percent of their poverty line	Greater	Less	Equal	Equal
Potential disincentives to work	Greater?	Equal?	Less	Greater
Cost of plan	Greater	Less	Less	Greater

[a] The progressive allowance tax schedule taxes income at 25, 50, and 75 percent rates or fills the income gap at 75, 50, and 25 percent rates. The regressive schedule taxes income at 75, 50, and 25 percent rates or fills the income gap at 25, 50, and 75 percent rates. The set-aside schedule has a zero percent rate on income up to 50 percent of the breakeven level of income and a 50 percent rate thereafter. And the conditioned-incentive schedule uses a 100 percent rate on income up to 50 percent of the breakeven level of income and a 50 percent rate hereafter.

schedules. The progressive allowance tax schedule and the regressive allowance tax schedule, shown in Parts 1-a and 1-b, guarantee the same level of income. But the guaranteed income level under the negative rates set-aside schedule shown in Part 1-c is lower; and the conditioned-incentive schedule shown in Part 1-d is higher than with the first two schedules. Note in Figure 8-1 that the slope of the schedule is the rate at which the negative tax allowances are reduced for each additional dollar of money income (excluding negative tax allowances). The shaded areas represent the allowances paid to a four-person family with different levels of before-allowance annual income.

Each of these tax schedules may be compared with a single 50 percent flat rate schedule as summarized in Table 8-3. The first two schedules—the progressive and regressive allowance schedules—provide a good comparison with the flat 50 percent rate schedule because in each case the guaranteed minimum level of income is the same. However, for families with any income at all the net allowance would vary depending upon which rate schedule is adopted. Table 8-4 illustrates these differences. The progressive schedule would be easiest on the first dollars of income. For example, a family of four with a $3,000 poverty line would lose only $250 of its guaranteed basic allowance if its income were $1,000. The regressive schedule, on the other hand, would reduce the allowance paid to a family by $750 if the family's income were $1,000. Thus, a plan with the progressive schedule would cost considerably more than one with a regressive schedule. The potential incentive to earn more income, at least up to the breakeven level of income, is thought to be lower under the progressive schedule than under the regressive schedule because the effective marginal rate rises as earnings rise. For a family of four with $2,500, an extra dollar earned means a 75 cent reduction in allowance under a plan with the pro-

TABLE 8-4. Amounts of Allowances Paid by a Negative Rates Plan with Progressive and Regressive Negative Tax Schedules

Income as Percentage of Poverty Line	Allowance by Number of Members in Family						
	One	Two	Three	Four	Five	Six	Seven
Progressive Schedule:[a]							
0	$750	$1,000	$1,250	$1,500	$1,750	$2,000	$2,250
10	712	950	1,118	1,425	1,662	1,900	2,137
20	675	900	1,125	1,350	1,575	1,800	2,025
30	637	850	1,062	1,275	1,488	1,700	1,912
40	575	766	958	1,150	1,342	1,533	1,725
50	500	667	833	1,000	1,167	1,333	1,500
60	425	567	709	850	992	1,133	1,275
70	316[b]	450	562	675	788	900	1,012
80	182[b]	300	375	450	525	600	675
90	49[b]	122[b]	188	225	262	300	337
Regressive Schedule:[c]							
0	750	1,000	1,250	1,500	1,750	2,000	2,250
10	631	850	1,062	1,275	1,488	1,700	1,912
20	525	700	875	1,050	1,226	1,400	1,575
30	412	550	688	825	963	1,100	1,237
40	325	433	542	650	758	867	975
50	250	333	417	500	583	667	750
60	175	233	292	350	408	467	525
70	92[b]	150	187	225	263	300	337
80	33[b]	100	125	150	175	200	225
90	−26[b]	22[b]	63	75	88	100	113

[a] Under the progressive allowance tax schedule income is taxed at 25, 50, and 75 percent rates; or the income gap is filled at 75, 50, and 25 percent rates.

[b] Adjusted for present positive tax payment on assumption that adjusted gross income equals total money income.

[c] Under the regressive allowance tax schedule income is taxed at 75, 50, and 25 percent rates or the income gap is filled at 25, 50, and 75 percent rates.

gressive schedule but only a 25 cent reduction under a plan with the regressive schedule.

The regressive schedule and the single 50 percent schedule are thought to be nearly equal in the potential disincentive to work (see Table 8-3). On the one hand, the falling marginal rates in the regressive schedule make increased earning more worthwhile; on the other hand, the high 75 percent rate tends to induce those who earn very low incomes to rely solely on the guaranteed minimum. That is, if a family cannot raise its earnings much above one-third of the breakeven level of income (in the cases illustrated here, the poverty line) it gains little by working.

The set-aside schedule is in some sense a progressive schedule in that it moves from a zero to a 50 percent rate. The zero rate in this schedule is designed to provide an inducement—or at least a minimum disincentive—to earn some income. At the same time, the schedule would provide such a low guarantee that few families would be likely to rely solely on the guaranteed minimum as their source of income.

The conditioned-incentive schedule, which in a sense is the converse of the set-aside schedule, is designed to provide a high guaranteed minimum, but its combination of 100 percent with 50 percent marginal tax rates creates significant potential work disincentive effects—especially for families with income amounting to less than 50 percent of their poverty lines. Interestingly, both this schedule and the set-aside schedule would provide the same net allowance as a flat 50 percent schedule to a family with half its poverty line income. However, the conditioned-incentive schedule, by providing a much higher guaranteed minimum, would make a transfer-by-taxation plan much more expensive than would the set-aside or the flat 50 percent schedule.

Incentives to Enlarge Families

How would a transfer-by-taxation plan affect the birth rate? Would an income guarantee which varies with the size of the family create an incentive for some families to have more children than they would otherwise desire by making children a "cash crop"?[38]

[38] A somewhat related question is the relationship between decisions made at various stages of family development and the level of the family's income. For

The answers to these questions are as elusive—and almost as worrisome—as those regarding the plan's effect on work incentives. On this subject, it is useful to identify two questions. One is whether a transfer-by-taxation plan would raise the overall birth rate. The other is whether a transfer-by-taxation plan would raise the birth rate among poor families. It is perfectly possible that a transfer-by-taxation plan might not materially affect the overall birth rate, but might induce increased births among families with very low incomes. Clearly, it may not be desirable to implement a plan designed to raise the income of the poor which also adds to the dimension of poverty by creating undue incentives to add to the size of poor families.

Relationship Between Income and Family Size

What is the relationship between income and family size? This question can be answered on either a historical or a cross-section basis. During the past century in the Western world, the birth rate and size of families have experienced a long-term decline, although there has been something of a reversal, or halting, of this secular trend in the years since World War II.[39] The long-run decline, however, has been subject to cyclical variations; rises in the birth rate have been associated with periods of prosperity and declines with periods of depression.[40] The long-run fall in the birth rate and family size is relevant to the present discussion only if it can be assumed that the rise in income by itself is an inducement to having smaller families. If this were the case, providing increased income to the poor might well be a useful means by which to reduce the size of poor families—a development which, by itself, would reduce the dimension of the poverty problem. However, the fall in the birth rate and family size seems to have resulted more from factors associated with the rise in per capita income—for example, industrial-

---

an examination of this question see Alvin Schorr, "The Family Cycle and Income Development," *Social Security Bulletin*, Vol. 29 (February 1966), pp. 14-25.

[39] Ronald Freedman, Pascal K. Whelpton, and Arthur A. Campbell, *Family Planning, Sterility and Population Growth* (New York: McGraw-Hill, 1959), p. 2.

[40] Hope T. Eldridge, *Population Policies: A Survey of Recent Developments* (Washington: The International Union for the Scientific Study of Population, 1954), p. 121.

ization, urbanization, increased education, and changing religious views—than from the rise in per capita income itself.[41]

A study of the relationship between income and fertility, or income and family size, on a cross-section basis may provide a more useful gauge of the possible effect of a transfer-by-taxation plan upon the birth rate. There is a good deal of evidence indicating an inverse relationship between family income and number of children in the family, although in the United States the fertility differentials between different socioeconomic groups seem to have narrowed. This narrowing of fertility differentials is credited both to greater knowledge of contraceptive methods achieved by a more universally educated and urbanized society and to a decline in the economic utility of children on farms.[42] Further, it may make a difference whether the husband's income or the family income is related to fertility. A working wife adds to family income, thereby making possible adequate support of more children. However, the working wife may also have less time to bear and bring up additional children, although an extensive work history by the wife is more likely to affect the spacing of children than total family size.[43] There is also evidence that fertility is dependent upon the husband's relative income —that is, the relation between the husband's income and the income of other men in the same socioeconomic class. Deborah Freedman has found that a husband's income which is above the average of those in the status groups to which he compares himself is associated with more children. But having an average income in the status group with the absolutely higher income bracket means fewer children.[44]

[41] George J. Stolnitz, "The Demographic Transition: From High to Low Birth Rates and Death Rates," *Population: The Vital Revolution,* ed. Ronald Freedman (New York: Anchor Books, 1964), Chap. 2, pp. 30-34.

[42] Deborah S. Freedman, "The Relation of Economic Status to Fertility," *American Economic Review,* Vol. 53 (June 1963), p. 415.

[43] *Ibid.,* p. 422. Also see Ronald Freedman, Whelpton, and Campbell, *op. cit.,* p. 302.

[44] Deborah Freedman, *op. cit.,* p. 422. Her study was confined to a sample of nonfarm, white, married women, aged 18 to 39, who planned to use some form of family limitation because they are fecund (p. 416). In 1963, the average size of poor families in the United States was 4.1 members. The figure for nonpoor families was 3.6 members. See Mollie Orshansky, "Who's Who Among the Poor: A Demographic View of Poverty," *Social Security Bulletin,* Vol. 28 (July 1965), p. 14. Families exclude unrelated individuals.

Neither historical nor cross-section data indicate that an income maintenance plan would substantially raise the nation's birth rate. Historically, increases of income have not raised the birth rate, at least not over the long pull. A transfer-by-taxation plan would redistribute income from upper income to lower income groups, and would tend to increase the disposable income of families whose size is larger, on the average, than the size of the families whose disposable income is reduced by the plan. Nevertheless, it is not clear what effect such redistribution would have on the overall birth rate. Although Deborah Freedman found economic variables as important as other social and demographic variables such as religion, education, and age in explaining variations in family size, neither the economic nor the social and demographic variables were especially important in determining the size of the family.[45] Moreover, there is no proof, as noted in an earlier chapter, that family allowance plans have caused the postwar rise in birth rates occurring in many European countries and in Canada.

These comments by no means erase all concern that some recipients of substantial net transfer-by-taxation allowances would respond to such a plan by having more children. For, although the evidence indicates that family size falls as family income rises, the cause and effect relationship (if there is one) would be reversed by a plan which would provide, for a given level of family income, higher benefits if the family added to its number. A plan which would provide an additional $500 annually for each additional child is not likely to induce a family whose income is $10,000 to have another child. But for a family living on a pittance, $500 might be enticing. True, the family might rationalize that it wanted the child anyway—and it may be true that the child would have been born with or without the additional income—but it is not easy to avoid the implication that without the allowance the child might not have been born.

Table 8-5 shows what an additional family member means in added allowances under alternative transfer-by-taxation plans. It is

[45] Deborah Freedman, *op. cit.* Among the members of the group interviewed there was a general desire to have from two to four children. However, this group contained only couples who desired to plan the size of their families. The social and demographic variables employed included education, religion, farm background, and age.

TABLE 8-5. Increase in Transfer-by-Taxation Allowances Resulting from Adding a Member to the Family[a]

Income as Percentage of Poverty Line[b]	Negative Rates Plans, Alternative Allowance Tax Schedules[c]				Social Dividend Plans, Alternative Guarantees	
	Flat Rate of 50%	Regressive Rate[d]	Set-Aside Rate[e]	Conditioned-Incentive Rate[f]	Poverty Line and 50% Rate[g]	Flat Minimum for Family[h]
0	$250	$250	$125	$375	$500	0
10	250	250	125	375	500	0
20	250	250	125	375	500	0
30	250	250	125	375	500	0
40	250	209	125	375	500	0
50	250	209	125	375	500	0
60	250	209	250	250	500	0
70	250	183	250	250	500	0
80	250	125	250	250	500	0
90	250	125	250	250	500	0

[a] Family income is assumed to remain constant.
[b] Poverty line is based on original size of family.
[c] The negative rates plans utilize the Lampman poverty lines (that is, $1,500 for an unrelated individual or family head and $500 for each additional member of the family) as breakeven levels of income.
[d] Regressive schedule uses 75, 50, and 25 percent marginal rates over intervals equal to one-third of poverty line income.
[e] Set-aside schedule has a zero percent rate on income up to 50 percent of the breakeven leve lof income and a 50 percent rate thereafter.
[f] Conditioned-incentive schedule has a 100 percent rate on income up to 50 percent of the breakeven level of income and a 50 percent rate thereafter.
[g] Assumes at least two members in family before adding the new member. Provides a guarantee equal to the Lampman poverty lines and uses a 50 percent allowance tax rate.
[h] Provides $3,000 for a family and $1,500 for an unrelated individual.

interesting that the negative rates plans with allowance tax schedules designed to reduce the potential discouragement to work (the regressive schedule and set-aside plans) are also those in which the potential incentives to have more children are relatively low.

The fertility problem could be limited by a social dividend plan such as that which provides a flat guaranteed minimum income for families of two or more members and avoids the problem of childbirth incentives by providing no additional allowances for additional family members. However, the guaranteed minimum in such a plan incorporates a bias against large families and a bias in favor of small ones. It is one thing to draw up a plan which will reduce the incentives for larger families, but another thing to build in a penalty for families that are larger than the present average size of three to four members. A preferable plan might vary the basic allowance according to family size up to some point, and then gradually or abruptly reduce the additional allowance to zero. In the Tobin plan, which provides $400 for each family member, the upper limit on a family's basic allowance is $2,700. For each person up to six members, the guarantee is $400; the seventh and eighth members add an additional $150 apiece; nothing is added for family members in excess of eight.[46] A structuring of allowances in this manner would seem a more reasonable way in which to limit the fertility incentives of a plan.

The Fertility Relief Controversy of the 1930's

The fear that maintenance of income will raise the birth rate among recipients is not new. In the mid-1930's, at the height of the Great Depression, a spate of articles claimed that the birth rate of relief recipients was higher than that for low-income persons not on relief. The implication often was that public support was an inducement to have children. Several of the more professional studies have been analyzed and criticized by the demographer, Frank Notestein.[47] His general conclusion is that although relief families were more fertile than those not on relief, they were also more fertile before their dependency on relief. Thus the higher fertility of relief families in the early 1930's, in contrast with the fertility of comparable families not on relief, can be explained by factors other than receipt of public support.[48] Further, the suggestion "that dependency does not increase fertility, is supported by a priori considerations." Sudden loss of income is not likely to shift established

[46] James Tobin, "Memorandum on Basic Income Allowances" (unpublished paper, Yale University, Summer 1965), p. 2. A declining per capita basic allowance after the fourth child is suggested, but not specified, by Tobin in "Improving the Economic Status of the Negro," *Daedalus*, Vol. 94 (Fall 1965), p. 891.

[47] Notestein, "The Fertility of Populations Supported by Relief," *The Milbank Memorial Fund Quarterly*, Vol. 14 (January 1936), pp. 37-49. Notestein cites articles, purportedly showing a relationship between fertility and public support, by Paul Popenoe and Ellen Morton Williams, "Fecundity of Families Dependent on Public Charity," *The American Journal of Sociology*, Vol. 40 (September 1934), pp. 214-20; Edgar Sydenstricker and G. St. J. Perrott, "Sickness, Unemployment and Differential Fertility," *Milbank Memorial Fund Quarterly*, Vol. 12 (April 1934), pp. 126-33; and Samuel A. Stuffer, "Fertility of Families on Relief," *Journal of the American Statistical Association*, Vol. 29 (September 1934), pp. 295-300.

[48] Notestein, *op. cit.*, p. 48. Notestein also cites the experience with the birth rate in the state of New York. He found that the rise of the birth rate there in 1934, which reversed an earlier trend, did not come primarily from the relief groups (p. 47).

attitudes toward childbearing in the direction of the general attitudes of persons who have grown up in lower income groups.[49] If
Notestein's conclusion is correct, the loss of income should reduce
childbearing because to support new children would be more of a
burden than before.

The controversy of the 1930's is interesting not only because it
illustrates that the relationship of income maintenance to fertility
has been debated before. It also illustrates the importance of making appropriate comparisons. According to Notestein, those who
saw a connection between fertility and relief were misled by comparing families on relief with those not on relief. The proper comparison would have been the experience of a single group before
dependency on relief and its experience after becoming dependent
upon relief. The same applies to the effect of a transfer-by-taxation
plan upon the fertility of the poor. It would not do to compare the
fertility of recipients of net allowances with families who pay net
taxes. Rather, the appropriate question is whether recipients of net
allowances would increase the size of their families above what it
would have been had the transfer-by-taxation plan not been implemented.

Unfortunately, Notestein's conclusions cannot assuage all
doubts. His examination of the problem was not extensive. Even if
it had been, there is still the question whether moving onto relief as
a result of a loss of family income is the same as becoming a recipient of transfer-by-taxation allowances without any change in the
family's before-allowance economic status. Notestein could claim
that it was to be expected that "decline" into dependency status
would not increase the family's size because the family would be
governed by the presumably higher living standards it maintained
before dependency on relief. But what happens when a family, by
having another child, can raise its income level above what it has
been? The answer to this question does not seem to be helped by
the hypothesis concerning relative status which was advanced by
Deborah Freedman. Presumably, under a transfer-by-taxation plan,
there would be a rise in the income of all the members of a socioeconomic group with which a low-income family would compare
itself. Thus, a given family's relative position vis-a-vis its own status
group would remain more or less the same.

[49] *Ibid.,* p. 49.

Perhaps Alvin Schorr has made the most apt statement on this question:

A rigorous scientific demonstration has not been provided that income maintenance will lead to a higher birth rate or that it will not. A new income-maintenance program would in all probability lead some people, including some people who are poor, to have additional children. But this effect would probably be trivial in relation to concurrent developments and not discernible in subsequent population figures. Balancing any small effect, a substantial income-maintenance program should significantly improve the circumstances of many families. In their children's generation, at least, it may provide the competence and climate to achieve the family size that that generation genuinely wants.[50]

[50] Schorr, "Income Maintenance and the Birth Rate," *Social Security Bulletin,* Vol. 28 (December 1965), p. 30.

CHAPTER IX

Costs, Benefits, and Financing

HYPOTHETICAL PLANS for transfer-by-taxation, outlined in this chapter, are used as a basis for estimating costs and benefits of different types of programs. They also serve as a springboard for investigating different methods of financing negative taxes. Because of their similarities and differences, the nine plans could be grouped in various ways. For example, five are negative rates plans, two are social dividend plans, and two have features somewhat different from either of these types of negative taxation. Again, the family's poverty line in all except three of the plans is used as the break-even level of income—that is, the net allowance is reduced to zero at the poverty line—or is used as the level of the minimum income guarantee. Another difference among the plans is the nature of the schedule of rates. Of the five negative rates plans, three employ the poverty lines; but one, the set-aside plan, is grouped separately because of its unique schedule of rates. The fill-the-gap plan, which essentially is a negative rates plan with a 100 percent negative tax rate, is given separate treatment because—unlike the negative rates plans—it ignores the incentives issue. Thus, the plans outlined below are grouped roughly to indicate, where possible, those with comparable types of benefits or tax schedules.

138

Plans A-1 and A-2. Both of these are examples of a negative rates plan. Each would provide a guaranteed minimum income equal to 50 percent of a family's poverty line, which is the breakeven level of income. The allowance tax schedule, however, would take different forms for each. For Plan A-1, a 50 percent flat rate would fill 50 percent of the family's poverty income gap. For Plan A-2, a regressive tax schedule would levy a 75 percent tax rate on the first third of poverty line income, and marginal rates of 50 and 25 percent, respectively, on the remaining thirds.

Plans B-1 and B-2. These also are examples of a negative rates plan. However, they would use the value of present tax exemptions and minimum standard deductions (EX-MSD) as breakeven lines, and they would guarantee a minimum income equal to 50 percent of the value of EX-MSD. In both plans, the negative tax rate would be a flat 50 percent applied to unused exemptions and deductions. The difference in these two plans lies in their treatment of the aged. In Plan B-1, each member of the tax unit would be allowed a single exemption and minimum standard deduction. Plan B-2, as in the case of the present tax system, would double the allowance for EX-MSD for the aged—that is, for the filer and spouses who were 65 years old or more.

Plan C. This set-aside plan is a special form of a negative rates plan which, as a variant of plans A-1 and A-2, merits separate attention. A zero percent rate would be applied on the first half of income up to the family's poverty line and a 50 percent tax rate on the second half.

Plans D-1 and D-2. Two examples of social dividend plans would guarantee a minimum income designed to "assure" that the family would not live in poverty. The guarantee under both would be equal to the poverty line, but the tax schedules would take different forms. Plan D-1 would levy a flat 50 percent allowance tax rate; this would require a 15 percent finance tax rate. Plan D-2 would depend on a single social dividend tax rate of 33⅓ percent, with no distinction between the allowance and finance tax schedules.[1]

[1] The $155 billion gross cost of a plan such as D-2 (see Chapter VI) was approximately 33⅓ percent of $470 billion in 1964. The $470 billion amount is based on estimates that the money income figure of the Office of Business Economics (OBE) of the U. S. Department of Commerce is about 95 percent of its personal income figure. The Bureau of the Census reported about $400 billion of money income

Plan E. This fill-the-gap plan is a variant of the negative rates or social dividend types of plan, but is treated separately because of the implications posed by its negative tax rate. Using the poverty line as the breakeven level, it would guarantee an allowance to make up the difference between the family's money income and its poverty line, with an effective negative tax rate of 100 percent on the allowance.

Plan F. In this example, the Tobin plan described in Chapter IV is adjusted to include coverage for aged members of the family. It is a cross between negative rates and social dividend taxation. Under the plan, $400 would be allowed for each of six family members; $150 would go to the seventh and eighth members, and no further allowances would be made for additional members of the family. The tax unit would be subject to a 33⅓ percent tax on income up to the level where the net tax liability under the Tobin plan equaled the tax liability of the present positive tax system.

Costs and Benefits

What would be the approximate net cost of these representative transfer-by-taxation plans? Cost estimates, presented in Appendix D, are based on 1964 Census data. No adjustment has been made in the appendix tables for (1) any reduction in public assistance (PA) and (2) the possibility that public assistance income would be excluded from the definition of income for transfer-by-taxation purposes. However, Table 9-1 not only summarizes the findings in the appendix tables, but it also presents other estimates based on certain assumptions about the treatment of public assistance payments.

A few of the assumptions on which the cost estimates for the hypothetical plans are based should be made explicit. The nature of the income distribution data of the Bureau of the Census which were used in making the estimates governs the following assumptions:

Assumption 1. The Census family is assumed to be a reasonably close approximation of the unit eligible to file a transfer-by-taxation return.

---

in 1964. It is estimated that underreporting in the Census Bureau's Current Population Survey amounts to about 15 percent of the OBE's total money income figure.

TABLE 9-1. Summary of Cost Estimates for Hypothetical Transfer-by-Taxation Plans, 1964[a]

(In billions of dollars)

Hypothetical Plans	Cost: Public Assistance Included in Income Measure[b] (1)	Cost: Public Assistance Excluded from Income Measure[b]		
		Total[c] (2)	Less Reduced PA in All Governments[d] (3)	Less Reduced Federal Contribution to PA[e] (4)
Plan A-1	$ 6.1	$ 8.0	$ 4.6	$ 6.3
Plan A-2	4.4	6.8[f]	3.4	5.1
Plan B-1	5.2	7.1	3.7	5.4
Plan B-2	6.9	8.8	5.4	7.1
Plan C	4.9	5.4[g]	3.9	4.7
Plan D-1: Unadjusted[h]	31.2	33.1	28.5	30.5
Plan D-1: Adjusted[i]	24.2	26.1	21.5	23.8
Plan D-2: Unadjusted[h]	51.3	53.2	48.6	50.9
Plan D-2: Adjusted[i]	41.4	43.3	38.7	41.0
Plan E: Earnings not reduced	12.3	16.1[j]	11.5	13.8
Plan E: Earnings reduced 25%[k]	14.4	18.2	13.6	15.9
Plan E: Earnings reduced 50%[k]	16.5	20.3	15.7	18.0
Plan E: Earnings reduced 75%[k]	18.6	22.4	17.8	20.1
Plan E: Earnings reduced 100%[k]	20.7	24.5	19.9	22.2
Plan F[l]	11.3	12.6	9.2	10.9

[a] The hypothetical plans are described in the text; more detailed cost estimates for families of different sizes are given in Appendix Tables D-1 through D-5.

[b] In calculating net allowances.

[c] The level of public assistance (PA) does not affect the cost of the plan. However, with a 50 percent allowance tax rate, the cost of a plan will rise 50 cents over that cost shown in column 1 for each $1 of PA excluded. Note that in 1964, only $3.8 billion of the $5.1 billion in public assistance expenditures was in the form of money payments. It is only this portion of PA which is excluded from money income.

[d] Public assistance programs, in 1964, cost $5.1 billion. This includes vendor medical payments and medical assistance to the aged. It is assumed that there is no reduction in the $450 million of medical assistance for the aged. The remaining $4.6 billion is assumed to have constituted expenditures incurred in making payments to families who would be eligible for transfer-by-taxation allowances. The following reductions in the $ 4.6 billion of public expenditures are assumed. Under Plans A-1, A-2, B-1, B-2, and F, public assistance expenditures are reduced 75 percent—from $4.6 billion to $1.2 billion. This is a reduction of $3.4 billion. Under Plan C—with a guaranteed income of only 25 percent of the poverty line level of income—public assistance is reduced by one-third, or by $1.5 billion to $3.1 billion. Under Plans D-1, D-2, and E, public assistance payments are eliminated. The reduction in public assistance payments is $4.6 billion. There is no consideration given to the possible reduction in administrative costs under any of these assumptions.

[e] It is assumed that the federal government's share in all government reductions in public assistance payments is 50 percent.

[f] This reflects an increase in transfer-by-taxation payments over those in column 1 equal to 62.5 percent (rather than 50 percent) of the $3.8 billion in public assistance excluded from the measure of money income for transfer-by-taxation purposes. The 62.5 percent is midway between the 75 and 50 percent marginal rates on the first two-thirds of poverty line income. These would be the income levels affected by reducing public assistance or by simply not including it in calculating transfer-by-taxation allowances.

[g] Assumes that only $1 billion of the $3.8 billion public assistance money payments is subjected to the 50 percent portion of the set-aside plan's tax schedule. Since the rate on income below 50 percent of the poverty line level of income is zero, only the public assistance payments in excess of 50 percent of the family's poverty line affect the level of transfer-by-taxation allowances. That is, when public assistance is excluded from income for transfer-by-taxation purposes, the total amount of allowances rises by only 50 percent of the assumed $1 billion in public payments which represents public assistance income in excess of 50 percent of a family's poverty line.

[h] Unadjusted for underreporting of income in the Current Population Survey for 1964 of the U.S. Bureau of the Census. See footnote d to Appendix Table D-4.

[i] Adjusted for underreporting of income in the Census Bureau's Current Population Survey for 1964. See footnote e to Appendix Table D-4.

[j] Rise is by full amount of the $3.8 billion in public assistance payments. This is because Plan E simply fills the gap between the poverty line and some measure of a poor family's income.

[k] It is assumed that 50 percent of the total money income (TMI) of the poor is labor income. Bureau of Labor Statistics (BLS) data for 1961 indicate that public and private transfers provided 42 percent of the income of the poor in 1961. See line 7 of Table 2-4. It is also assumed that families with income above the poverty line do not reduce their income to levels below the poverty line level.

[l] There is a 33⅓ percent tax rate on income up to the level when net tax liability equals that under the present positive tax system. For comparison of total cost given in column 2 with Tobin's own estimate, see discussion in Appendix D.

Assumption 2. Except in the case of public assistance, the definition of income for transfer-by-taxation purposes is assumed to approximate the money income measure used by the Census Bureau.

Assumption 3. Under almost any assumption about public assistance, there would be some reduction in the public assistance payments made to a given family. With an allowance tax rate of 50 percent, for each reduction of $1 in public assistance, transfer-by-taxation allowances would rise by 50 cents. Thus, the federal government might expect some saving to the extent that reductions in public assistance payments would not be associated with equivalent increases in transfer-by-taxation allowances. However, there might not be any saving—in fact, there might be an increase in the combined cost of the federal share of the public assistance and transfer-by-taxation programs—if state and local public welfare officials reacted so as to spread the present public assistance payments more thinly over a larger portion of the poor population.[2] Since the lower the average assistance payment the higher the share paid by the federal government, a policy of maintaining total public assistance payments at the present level, but spread over a larger part of the population, would increase the total amount of public assistance payments made by the federal government.[3]

Assumption 4. It is assumed that, except for Plan E, the transfer-by-taxation plans will not reduce the amount of work done. In the case of Plan E—the plan which fills the poverty income gap—the 100 percent allowance tax rate is very likely to have more than a negligible influence upon the amount of work done by members of low-income families. Therefore, Table 9-1 presents alternative cost estimates for Plan E on the assumption that earnings are reduced by 25, 50, 75, and 100 percent. Note that the cost of the plan, if there were a reduction of 100 percent in work effort, would

[2] This possibility was pointed out to me by James Lyday and Walter Williams of the Office of Economic Opportunity.

[3] In 1961, the formula for federal contributions to old-age assistance programs was 80 percent of the first $31 monthly payment and 50-65 percent of the next $35, depending upon per capita income in the particular state. The formula for federal contributions to aid to dependent children programs was, in 1958, 14/17 of the first $17 of monthly payments and 50-65 percent of the next $13, depending on state per capita income. John Turnbull, C. Arthur Williams, Earl Cheit, *Economic and Social Security* (2nd ed.; New York: Ronald Press, 1963), pp. 72-74.

be less than the total income of $29 billion needed by the poor in order not to be poor. Almost 50 percent of the income of the poor is in the form of transfer payments or earnings which cannot be attributed to their current labor effort. Presumably this income would not be lost if the poor ceased to work. However, the cost would be greater than that shown in Table 9-1 if there were a reduction in work effort of persons and families whose income is just above the breakeven levels of income. Also, it should be noted that the cost of Plan E would be in excess of the figures shown in column 2 of Table 9-1 if poor families did not bother to collect their social security benefits and other transfer income. Robert J. Lampman has calculated that the cost of a plan similar to Plan E, for these reasons, might rise to $32 billion.[4]

Assumption 5. It is assumed that the transfer-by-taxation plan produces no change in the before-allowance distribution of income other than that produced by a reduction in, or elimination of, public assistance. If it did produce such a change, the cost estimates might be thrown out of line.

Assumption 6. The mechanical aspect of making the estimates is based on assumptions that: (a) The best measure of the average income of families in a given income bracket is the midpoint of the income bracket. (b) Where interpolation is necessary, a linear interpolation provides good approximations of the actual conditions. Thus, for example, it is assumed that within a $500 income bracket the number of families falling within each $100 interval of that bracket is equal to one-fifth of the total number of families in the $500 bracket.

Assumption 7. It is assumed that no public transfer program except public assistance is affected by the adoption of a transfer-by-taxation plan. Hence, the cost estimates do not take into consideration the possibility that a transfer-by-taxation plan (especially a social dividend plan) might allow a reduction in, or an elimination of, additional public transfer programs. A reduction in public transfer payments made to persons and families whose income is below the breakeven levels of income, for example, would increase the allow-

---

[4] Lampman, "The Guaranteed Minimum Income: Is it Worth What it Would Cost?" (unpublished paper prepared for delivery at the Conference on the Guaranteed Minimum Income, School of Social Service Administration, University of Chicago, Jan. 14-15, 1966), pp. 8-9

ances made under Plan D-1 by only 50 cents for each $1 of reduction in transfer income. There would be no increase in allowances in response to a reduction in public transfers received by households with income above the breakeven lines. An elimination of old-age, survivors and disability insurance (OASDI), unemployment insurance, and veterans' pensions and compensation programs would have raised the cost of social dividend Plan D-1 by only a fraction of the $24 billion[5] paid out by these programs in fiscal year 1964-65. If 75 percent of the $24 billion (or $18 billion) went to families whose total income was below the breakeven levels, then social dividend payments would have risen by only $9 billion if the $24 billion in public transfers had not been paid. The difference of $15 billion ($24 billion minus $9 billion) would have reduced the overall cost of social dividend Plan D-1 from $31 billion to $16 billion. However, the reduction or elimination of these public transfer programs would have the effect of reducing many recipients' incomes to levels near or at the poverty line. This would happen to those families who presently rely almost solely upon transfer income received under the OASDI, unemployment insurance, and veterans' programs.

Column 1 of Table 9-1 shows that the costs of the transfer-by-taxation plans range from $4.4 billion for the negative rates Plan A-2, with a regressive rate schedule applied against the poverty income gap, to either $41.4 billion or $51.3 billion for the social dividend Plan D-2. These estimates are based on the assumption that public assistance (PA) payments do not change, and that public assistance is included in the measure of income for transfer-by-taxation purposes. Column 2 gives estimates of the cost of the plans if the $3.8 billion of PA money payments made in 1964 were excluded from the measure of income.[6] Exclusion of public assistance payments makes the set-aside Plan C, at $5.4 billion, cost less than any other plan presented here. This is because the allowances under Plan C do not rise with reductions in income below 50 percent of

[5] Ida C. Merriam, "Social Welfare Expenditures, 1964-65," *Social Security Bulletin*, Vol. 28 (October 1965), Table 1, p. 4.

[6] Total public assistance programs cost approximately $5.1 billion in 1964. This figure does not include administrative costs. It does include expenditures on medical assistance for the aged and vendor medical payments as well as money payments under the categorical and general assistance programs.

the poverty line level of income. When public assistance payments are excluded, the cost of the social dividend Plan D-2 rises to either $43.3 billion or $53.2 billion, depending upon whether figures are adjusted for underreporting of Census data. Column 3 shows what would be added to costs at all levels of government by a transfer-by-taxation plan. The figures in column 3 show the effects of assumed reductions in all types of public assistance expenditures (which include vendor medical payments and medical assistance to the aged) as a result of the adoption of a transfer-by-taxation plan. Column 4 shows the added cost to the federal government of the transfer-by-taxation plans on the assumption that the reduced cost to the federal government is 50 percent of the reduction in total public assistance expenditures.

It is interesting that the negative rates Plan A-1, with a flat 50 percent rate applied against the poverty income gap, is more expensive than negative rates Plan B-1, with a 50 percent rate applied against unused EX-MSD if the aged and blind are allowed only single EX-MSD. However, if the aged are allowed double EX-MSD, as in Plan B-2, the cost of the plan exceeds that of Plan A-1 based on the poverty gap.

Plan F, the Tobin plan, provides guaranteed minimums similar to those in Plan A and Plan B (see Appendix Table D-5). However, it costs considerably more because of the lower allowance tax rate and the tax reductions given to taxpayers with incomes below the level at which the Tobin tax schedule ties in with the present positive tax schedule.

Table 9-2 shows how the net allowances paid under each of the transfer-by-taxation plans are distributed by size of family. Under the negative rates plans utilizing the poverty gap approach—Plans A-1 and A-2—about 45 percent of the allowances would go to families with one and two members. The figure is somewhat less than 40 percent in the case of the social dividend Plan D-1 and under 35 percent for D-2. And it amounts only to 23 and 19 percent in the cases of Plan B-1 and Plan F which do not allow double the amount of EX-MSD for the aged. The very large families (six or more members) receive a larger proportion of the allowances under the negative rates plans utilizing the EX-MSD approach—Plans B-1 and B-2—than they do under plans utilizing the

TABLE 9-2. Distribution of Allowances, Transfer-by-Taxation Plans, by Family Size, 1964

Plan[a]	Allowances as Percent of Total to Families with Different Number of Members							Total from Plan
	One	Two	Three	Four	Five	Six	Seven or More[b]	
A-1	29.5	15.8	9.4	9.1	8.8	7.4	19.9	100.0
A-2	29.2	16.1	9.6	9.2	8.7	7.6	19.6	100.0
B-1	12.3	10.6	9.1	10.8	12.1	11.1	33.9	100.0
B-2	20.3	22.0	6.8	8.1	9.1	8.3	25.4	100.0
C	28.1	16.2	9.4	9.2	9.0	7.4	20.6	100.0
D-1	21.3	17.4	10.2	10.7	11.2	9.0	20.1	100.0
D-2	16.8	17.1	11.5	13.5	13.4	9.8	18.0	100.0
E	29.5	15.8	9.4	9.1	8.8	7.4	19.9	100.0
F	7.9	10.8	9.9	12.8	16.0	14.8	27.7	100.0

[a] See descriptions of the plans in the text.
[b] Computed on the assumption of an eight-member family.

poverty line approach. These differences reflect the fact that, compared with the poverty lines, the value of EX-MSD favors large families rather than small ones.

One of the more interesting facets of transfer-by-taxation is found in estimates of the proportion of total allowances that would be received by various socioeconomic groups. Table 9-3 provides some estimates of what certain Census groups—the aged, the nonwhite population, the farm population, families with children, heads of families with little education, and heads of families who did not work at all—would have received under one of the negative rates plans based on the poverty gap. Unfortunately, except in the case of families with children, the figures are for unrelated individuals and all families. There is no breakdown by family size. The assumption made, except in the case of aged families,[7] is that the average family has four members and, therefore, a $3,000 poverty line. Unrelated individuals have the usual $1,500 poverty line. Thus, the estimates also apply roughly to the EX-MSD approach, since a family of four has $3,000 in EX-MSD.

[7] Aged families (not including aged unrelated individuals who are listed separately in the Census data) are assumed to have two members and, therefore, a $2,000 poverty line.

TABLE 9-3. The Share of Total Allowances Which Would Be Received by Certain Demographic Groups Under a Hypothetical Negative Rates Plan, 1964[a]

Group	Number Eligible for Allowances (Thousands) (1)	Total for Group (Millions) Income Needed Not to be Poor (2)	Actual Money Income (3)	Poverty Gap (2)–(3) (4)	Share Poverty of Gap Equals Share of Allowances[b] (Percent) (5)	Average Allowance at 50% Rate .50×(4)÷(1) (6)
Families with head 65 years and over	4,376	$ 7,345	$ 4,361	$ 2,984	24.3	$340
Families with children	4,500[c]			6,750– 7,290[c]	55– 60[c]	750– 810[c]
Families whose head had no more than an 8th grade education	7,614	18,922	10,754	8,168	66.6	536
Farm families	1,559	4,323	3,022	1,301	10.6	417
Nonwhite families	2,779	6,802	3,647	3,155	25.7	567
Families whose head did not work in 1964	6,077	11,914	6,846	5,068	41.3	417
Families whose head worked full time for 40 weeks or more in 1964	3,170	8,448	5,198	3,250	26.5	513
Totals[d]	12,139	29,106	16,835	12,271	—	505

Source: Estimates based on U.S. Bureau of the Census, *Current Population Reports*, Series P-60, No. 47, "Income in 1964 of Families and Persons in the United States" (1965), Tables 1, 3, 4, 7, and 11.

[a] The Census data do not permit breakdowns by family size for the demographic groups presented here. Thus the assumption used here is that all families have four members and a $3,000 poverty line, except aged families composed of two members with a $2,000 poverty line. A $1,500 poverty line is used for unrelated individuals, who are shown separately in the Census income distributions. This means that the results roughly apply to the unused EX-MSD approach as well as to the poverty gap approach. It is assumed that the tax schedule consists of a single 50 percent rate.

[b] The poverty gap of $12.3 billion was derived earlier by using poverty lines that vary with family size. Note that with a flat rate the share of allowances will be the same as the share of the poverty gap.

[c] The figure is based on poverty lines which vary with the number of children. Since there are some families with only one parent, it is impossible to be more precise. The 4,500 figure is from Mollie Orshansky, "Who's Who Among the Poor: A Demographic View of Poverty," *Social Security Bulletin*, Vol. 28 (July 1965), p. 4.

[d] Columns do not add to totals. Also totals are based on poverty lines which vary with family size.

Table 9-3 shows that two-thirds of the allowances would be received by families in which the formal education of the head did not go beyond the eighth grade. Between 55 and 60 percent of the allowances would be received by families with children.[8] The estimates also indicate that almost a quarter of the allowances would be received by the aged, slightly over a quarter by the nonwhite population, slightly over 10 percent by farm families, and over 40 percent by families whose head did not work at all (many of whom were aged). Only a little over a quarter of the allowances would go to families whose head worked full time for forty weeks or more.

[8] A more accurate figure is not possible since the breakdown by number of children in the family does not include the size of the family. In some families there is only a single head or parent. However, assuming 25 percent of the families with children who were eligible for allowances had only a single head or parent, the figure for 1963 was 57 percent. This assumption is based on Mollie Orshansky, "Children of the Poor," *Social Security Bulletin*, Vol. 26 (July 1963), p. 8.

Financing a Negative Rates Plan

How might a negative rates plan or a type like the Tobin plan be financed? The estimated cost to the federal government of these plans is between $5.1 billion for Plan A-2 and $10.9 billion for Plan F, the Tobin plan (see Table 9-1). These costs are small enough so that they would not require a major reorganization of the tax system such as that which would probably be necessary if social dividend Plan D-1 or Plan D-2 were adopted. However, the estimated costs are great enough to necessitate some consideration of how they would be paid for year in and year out.

The negative rates allowances could be financed by deficit financing—that is, by increasing the national debt—or by increasing tax revenues. Tax revenues can be increased either by raising tax rates or, if a more dynamic view is taken, by a rise in revenues as national income rises. In some recent years, the economy has been shackled to an extent by what economists call a "full employment surplus." This, defined briefly, is the amount by which federal revenues would exceed federal government expenditures if the economy were at full employment. From 1960 until very recently, there was a substantial full employment surplus, although there was an actual deficit (expenditures exceeded revenues) in the budget over most of the period. The full employment surplus averaged about $10 billion between 1960 and the end of 1963, and then fell to about $3 billion in 1964 as a result of the major cut in income taxes that year.[9] In 1965, the full employment surplus was reduced to very low levels.[10]

Interestingly, the rapid economic growth from 1961-63 took place without a reduction in the full employment surplus, although the surplus fell somewhat in 1962 before rising again in 1963.[11] Either a cut in taxes or an increase in expenditures seems to have been required for a substantial reduction of the surplus. There is a tendency for income tax revenues to rise at a faster rate than the rate at which per capita national income rises—largely because the marginal tax rate is higher than the average income tax rate and

[9] *Economic Report of the President, January 1965,* Chart 9, p. 64.
[10] *Economic Report of the President, January 1966,* Chart 4, p. 43.
[11] *Economic Report of the President, January 1965,* p. 64.

stays higher. In addition, the corporate income tax is elastic with respect to income. This means—assuming that (1) rapid economic growth continues and (2) the individual income tax is an important means of raising federal revenues—that the economy may find itself with recurrent full employment surpluses. Of course, if government expenditures for military or other needs are forced to rise at a rapid rate most of the potential full employment surplus may be offset. However, the full employment surplus might also be the means of financing negative rates taxation allowances. In this way, negative rates taxation would represent tax cuts for the poor designed not only to meet the needs of the poor but also to avoid the dampening effect of full employment surpluses.

If negative rates allowances were financed by floating additional national debt or by the full employment surplus, they would tend to have the same kind of stimulating effect on the economy as any tax cut or increase in government expenditures. Moreover, negative rates allowances might be presumed to produce countercyclical effects. Both the size of the poverty income gap and the value of unused EX-MSD might be expected to increase in periods of recession and to fall in periods of boom. Given the negative rates tax schedule, allowances would then tend to rise in recession and to fall in prosperity. Of course, looked at from the secular point of view, the poverty income gap and unused EX-MSD can be expected to fall as a result of economic growth and other programs to eliminate poverty.

Using a full employment surplus to finance a negative rates plan has one drawback. It is a good thing to have a full employment surplus when it is needed. Thus fiscal policy requires that the full employment surplus be adjusted to the needs of the economy. Using it to finance a particular plan would tend to reduce its availability as a tool of fiscal policy.

Financing a Social Dividend Plan

Since the cost of a social dividend plan would be from $25 to $50 billion, its financing would present greater problems than financing a negative rates plan. It seems necessary to think in terms of a special tax schedule which would be used to raise the revenue required to finance the social dividend plan (as discussed in Chapter

VI). It does not seem possible to finance such a plan with the present tax system.

One of the first steps is to determine what tax rate levied against money income in excess of breakeven income levels, in 1964, would have raised revenues sufficient to finance the social dividend plans.[12] The estimated unadjusted cost for 1964 is $31 billion for Plan D-1 (under which public assistance programs are abandoned and a flat 50 percent allowance tax schedule is used). Money income above breakeven levels amounted to $210 billion in 1964.[13] A flat rate of 14.8 percent on this income would have raised the necessary revenues.

Next is the question: Should the finance tax schedule be proportional, regressive, or progressive in its structure? There seems little justification for a regressive finance tax schedule. It would conflict with ability-to-pay principles. It would also conflict with an effort to keep taxation of upper-middle income groups ($8,000 to $12,000) —which already are subject to substantial positive tax rates—at levels which would not hinder work incentives. A progressive tax schedule is objectionable because to add high marginal finance tax rates to the present marginal positive tax rates on upper income groups might mean marginal tax rates near, or even in excess of,

[12] For Plan D-2 the required rate for all income has been given as 33⅓ percent (see Table 9-1).

[13] The figure represents an adjustment of Census data for underreporting. Personal income in 1964 was $495 billion, about $470 billion of which is money income. (About 5 percent of the Office of Business Economics personal income figure is imputed income.) An estimate of the money income of families, based on the Census income distribution data, yields $400 billion—$154 billion of which was income above the breakeven level of income. How should the remaining $70 billion of money income be treated? If any of it "belonged" to net allowance recipients (that is, families whose money income was less than the breakeven level of income), the net cost of Plan D-1 would be reduced 50 cents for $1 of unreported income. For the purpose of the present discussion, it is simply assumed that the net cost of Plan D-1 really is $31 billion, but that income above the line was $154 billion plus 80 percent of $70 billion or $56 billion, bringing the total to $210 billion. The 80 percent is based on the fact that families with income above the breakeven level of income had 80 percent of Census money income. Those with incomes below the breakeven level of income had $81 billion, or 20 percent of the total. If the remaining $14 billion of the $70 billion belonged to net allowance recipients, the cost of Plan D-1 would be reduced by $7 billion to approximately $24 billion. In this case, the tax rate on $210 billion necessary to raise $24 billion would be 11.4 percent. No account has been taken of a possible reduction in work effort as a result of adopting Plan D-1.

100 percent. Of course, the objectionable features of regressivity and progressivity can be limited by keeping the degree of each relatively slight, but there probably is little sense in bothering with either slightly regressive or slightly progressive tax schedules.

Another question is whether there should be a single tax schedule or two separate schedules. It is possible to lump together all government expenditures, including the net allowances made under a transfer-by-taxation plan, and finance them by a single tax schedule applied against an agreed upon income base. This combined tax schedule would consist of the allowance, finance, and positive tax schedules. (See Figure 6-2.) The amount of revenue that would have to be raised is the sum of the net allowances plus other government expenditures now financed by the individual income tax. This would have amounted to $79 billion in 1964 if social dividend Plan D-1 had been adopted.[14] What rate of tax on $470 billion of money income would have financed the $155 billion gross cost[15] of the social dividend plan and raised an additional $45 billion to finance other government expenditures? To raise $200 billion in revenues ($155 billion plus $45 billion) would require a 42.6 percent tax rate ($200 billion divided by $470 billion equals 42.6 percent). The total redistribution (net cost) that results from income guarantees equal to the poverty lines and a 42.6 percent tax rate is $38.3 billion.[16]

A reason for having two separate tax schedules is the possible difficulty of agreeing on a common income measure if the finance and the positive tax schedules were combined to form a single tax schedule. If there were a single combined tax schedule, it probably would be necessary to eliminate most, or all, exclusions and personal deductions and all personal exemptions also would have to be dropped. If this were not done it would not be possible to have a broad enough tax base to finance a social dividend plan in addition to present expenditures financed by the income tax. However, as noted in Chapter VII, for positive tax purposes some personal deductions and some exclusions may be useful.

[14] The 1964 cost of Plan D-1, unadjusted for underreporting of income, of $31 billion plus individual income tax revenues of $48 billion.

[15] For an explanation of why the gross cost is used rather than the net cost, see pp. 79-80 in Chapter VI.

[16] The estimate adjusted for underreporting of income is $29.8 billion.

Alternative Financing Arrangements

Up to this point, it has been assumed that the cost of a transfer-by-taxation plan would be borne by a tax on income. It has been suggested that no special tax would be needed to finance a negative rates plan; but, if increased revenues had to be raised, a slight upward adjustment of the positive tax schedule would be sufficient. Such a relatively minor increase in rates is not likely to affect work incentives. However, the additional income taxes necessary to finance a social dividend plan may well have objectionable effects on incentives. Or it may simply be considered undesirable to add any more burdens to the individual income tax system.

Two alternatives to an income tax for social dividend taxation purposes are (1) a federal sales tax or value added tax and (2) an employer payroll tax. Consumption expenditures or payrolls would provide the base for raising the required revenues. Allowances could be administered in two ways. Income could remain the basis for determining who gets net allowances. Or the basic allowance could simply be paid out annually to every family. The choice of one or the other of these two ways for administering the social dividend plan will affect the income after taxes and after allowances received by families. An example will make this clear. Suppose the plan would make annual payments to all units equal to the basic allowance guaranteed the family. This would have cost $155 billion in 1964. To finance this level of allowances by a sales tax, it would have been necessary to levy a tax rate of 38.5 percent on the $400 billion of consumption that took place in 1964.[17] If a payroll tax had been levied on the $414 billion in 1964 payrolls (this figure is based on a rather liberal definition of payrolls),[18] the necessary tax rate would have been about 37 percent.

Suppose the sales tax is adopted.[19] Further suppose that a low-income family with four members consumes its entire income, and

[17] This abstracts temporarily from the effect of sales taxes on prices and, therefore, their effect on the nominal tax rate.

[18] This totals compensation to employees, income of unincorporated enterprises, and income of farm proprietors. *Economic Report of the President, January 1965,* p. 203.

[19] I owe this suggestion to Walter Morton, Professor of Economics of the University of Wisconsin.

that its income is composed of $2,000 in earnings and $3,000 in social dividend allowances. The family's real consumption (after taking into consideration the 38.5 percent sales tax) would be 61.5 percent of $5,000 or $3,075. The family's net allowance—that is, the basic allowance minus the $1,925 paid in sales taxes—is $1,075. This can be compared to $2,000 in net allowances that the family would have received under Plan D-1.[20] Now suppose that the administering agency either pays out net allowances at the end of the year, or pays during the year after estimating what a family's income deficit, if any, will be. Net allowances under social dividend Plan D-1 would have amounted to $31 billion in 1964. This would have necessitated a sales tax of 7.8 percent on all consumption expenditures in 1964. The family of four with $2,000 in earnings and $2,000 in net allowances (or $4,000 in income including allowances) pays $312 in sales taxes if it consumes all of its income. Its net position, after taking sales taxes into consideration, is $3,688 ($4,000 minus $312). This is $613 higher than if the plan were administered by paying out gross allowances.

Now suppose that allowances are financed by a 37 percent tax on $414 billion in payrolls. Again, suppose the family of four has $2,000 in labor earnings and that gross allowance payments totaling $3,000 in a year are received by the family. Suppose, finally, that this family consumes all of its income. The tax on payrolls—assuming it falls completely on the employee—reduces earnings by 37 percent (or by $740 on $2,000 of earnings). Net earnings are $1,260. Disposable income is $4,260 ($1,260 plus $3,000). However, if the program is administered by paying out net allowances totaling $31 billion, the payroll tax on the family's earnings would be 7.5 percent, or $150 out of $2,000. The family of four would receive $2,000 in net allowances.[21] Together with net earnings of $1,850, the family would have disposable income of $3,850 ($1,850 plus $2,000).

In the case of the sales tax, the low-income family which consumes all of its income is worse off under a plan administered by

---

[20] A family of four receives $3,000 basic allowance under Plan D-1. Its tax on income below the breakeven level is 50 percent. Income before allowance was $2,000. Thus the tax is $1,000 and net allowances equal $2,000.

[21] It is assumed here that the basis for calculating net allowances is gross income, not net income, before allowances.

paying out gross allowances than under one paying out only net allowances. Conversely, when the tax is on earnings, this family is better off with gross allowances. In general, the sales tax would fall more heavily on allowance recipients than would the income or payroll tax when they were used to finance a social dividend plan. Whether the payroll tax would bear more heavily or less so on allowance recipients than an income tax would depend on how the plan was administered. This is illustrated in the following summary of the example just discussed.

Method of Financing Plan D-1	Total Income in Earnings	Income After Tax and Allowance with:	
		Gross Allowance	Net Allowance
Income tax (50% allowance tax rate)	$2,000	$4,000	$4,000
Sales tax	2,000	3,075	3,688
Payroll tax	2,000	4,260	3,850

It should be noted that to pay out only net allowances is to maintain an effective income tax rate on income below the breakeven level. Under social dividend Plan D-1 this rate is 50 percent. In addition to the 50 percent tax, there would be the 7.8 percent sales tax or 7.5 percent payroll tax—the taxes which are designed to finance the transfer-by-taxation plan. Moreover, paying the net allowance would mean that it still would be necessary to determine the level of a family's income in order to determine eligibility for allowances.

Sales and payroll tax rates close to 40 percent are not welcome substitutions in paying for a transfer-by-taxation plan. A 38.5 percent sales tax would undermine the real value of the allowances. A 37 percent payroll tax, the incidence of which falls upon the earners of income, may produce effects on work incentives similar to, or worse than, those produced by a 50 percent tax on money income.[22] In fact, the economic effects of a payroll tax are likely to be similar to those of a proportional income tax to the extent that the weight of the tax falls on income earners, while the social dividend guarantee itself goes largely, if not wholly, untaxed. Also the

[22] France levies a 16¾% payroll tax, mainly to pay for its system of family allowances. There are some who feel this tax has been injurious to work incentives. James Vadakin, *Family Allowances* (Miami: University of Miami Press, 1958), p. 134.

payroll tax is an inferior method if it is desirable to tax income other than earnings—as Chapter VII suggests it would be.

It should be noted that some or most of the incidence of a sales tax may be passed on to consumers through higher prices. The effect of a price increase—given the nominal level of basic allowances—probably would be a reduction in the nominal tax rate. Suppose, for example, that prices rose by the full amount of the sales tax. Then the $400 billion worth of consumption goods in 1964 would have cost over $500 billion (400 plus $b155$ billion dollar gross cost of the social dividend plan).[23] Another way to look at this is that the nominal gross income of families would be $155 billion greater than it is now. Given the marginal propensity to consume, the increase in the dollar value (contrasted with the real value) of consumption easily can be calculated. If the dollar value of consumption were $524 billion, the nominal sales tax rate would have to be about 30 percent. But the consumer would be no better off if, instead of prices rising, the tax had been passed backward upon the income earner through a 38.5 percent reduction in earnings. The rise in prices would simply reduce the consumption power of the guarantee as well as that of other income. The same amount of goods and services would be produced in either case, and another $155 billion in one way or another would still have to be raised to pay for the plan.

Consideration of the effect of a federal sales tax on prices suggests one other issue. Should the basic social dividend guarantee or the breakeven lines for negative rates taxation be adjusted as the price level rises? The real relevance of this question lies in the way poverty lines themselves are affected by price changes. The poverty lines are based on the cost (price) of a basic budget; for example, if the price of food rises, the poverty lines should rise. The difficulty is that Congress is not likely to change the tax system each time prices rise.

This same difficulty has arisen with respect to the value of personal exemptions presently allowed each dependent. Since 1948, the exemption for each dependent has remained at $600,[24] while for

---

[23] Where b = marginal propensity to consume out of the allowances. If $b = .8$, then consumption would total $524 billion. $[400 + .8 (155)] = 400 + 124 = 524$.

[24] Effectively, the personal exemption for low incomes was raised to $700 in 1965 by the addition of a minimum standard deduction.

the same period consumer prices, on the average, have risen 29 percent. For those who view the personal exemption primarily as a means of protecting a minimum standard of living, the price increase without an increase in the value of personal exemptions must be disturbing. In December 1964, Richard Goode suggested a restructuring of personal exemptions to take account of the price increase of the past fifteen years.[25]

The price problem may represent one real drawback of a plan which ties welfare to the tax system, but it may be a smaller problem under social dividend taxation than under negative rates taxation. The basic allowances under a social dividend plan could be raised step for step with the rise in prices. The problem is less easily solved for negative rates taxation, under which allowances are tied to the requirement that families have income below the value of their tax exemptions and deductions or below their poverty line. If unused EX-MSD is the base, price increases might considerably raise the dollar value of the poverty line, while no change would be made in the value of personal exemptions set forth in the tax law. This would mean an increasing percentage of the poor would not be eligible for allowances because many families would have no unused EX-MSD although their income might be below their poverty line. It would also mean that, with a given negative rates tax schedule, those eligible for allowances would have an increasingly smaller percentage of their poverty income gap filled by the negative rates allowances.

If, instead, allowances were based on the poverty income gap, the price rise might increase the number of taxpayers eligible for allowances. This would occur if the dollar value of EX-MSD remained the same while the dollar value of the poverty line rose as prices rose. At present, only families with three or fewer persons have poverty lines which exceed the value of their EX-MSD.[26] If a negative rates plan were adopted and prices rose by 30 percent over a fifteen-year period, with no change in the dollar value of EX-MSD, the poverty lines of families of all sizes would exceed the value of

---

[25] Richard Goode, *The Individual Income Tax* (Washington: Brookings Institution, 1964), pp. 232-33.

[26] Assumes no aged taxpayer or spouse in the family.

EX-MSD.[27] It seems clear, then, that some sort of mechanism for adjusting to the price level should be included in the tax system's computation of allowable dollar values of EX-MSD under a negative rates plan.[28] Substantial price changes over time should be taken into consideration in any welfare program.

Should changes in what society deems to be the minimum acceptable standard of living be taken into consideration in the transfer-by-taxation plans? The answer would seem to be "yes." Presumably the plans are devised to assure either an income necessary to maintain a minimum decent living standard or an income at least equal to some percentage of that standard.

The problem of an acceptable standard of living is similar to the price problem, but probably easier to solve because a change in standards takes place more slowly and is only recognized after a relatively long time. Congress would probably be more willing to alter the transfer-by-taxation system to adjust for secular changes in living standards than to adjust for changes in prices—if for no other reason than that the former change would be likely to take place much less often than the latter.

[27] The total value allowed for minimum standard deductions (MSD) is $1,000 per family.

[28] Such a mechanism might well be introduced whether or not a negative rates plan is adopted. Also, although secular deflation has been ignored, in principle a mechanism to cope with such an eventuality should also be devised.

CHAPTER X

Summary of Discussion at the Conference of Experts

PROPOSALS FOR NEGATIVE TAXES have been attracting increasing interest and support in universities, research organizations, and government circles. Because of variations among the plans—differences not only in content and cost, but also in purpose—it seems important that the crucial issues relating to negative taxes be singled out and investigated. This was the purpose of the two-day conference of experts which is summarized below.

Several points about the scope and meaning of the summary should be noted at the outset. First, the conferees seemed to prefer the more popular term "negative income taxation" to "negative rates taxation" which generally is used in my background paper. To the participants, the meaning of "negative income" was "negative taxable income" and not negative income as such. In any case, it is not likely that any acceptable negative income tax program would adopt the definition of taxable income now used by the Internal Revenue Service. Second, no formal effort was made to determine a consensus. Thus when I say there was "general agreement" on a particular issue, this statement is based on my own assessment of the discussion. Third, the proponents of particular views are not identified, and no attempt has been made to summarize every statement made by participants.

While the primary focus of the conference was on negative income taxation, the participants necessarily discussed related subjects. For convenience, the discussion is summarized under six broad topics. They are: (1) objectives of negative income taxation; (2) attractive features of a negative income tax; (3) basic problems in negative income taxation; (4) relation of negative income taxation to existing social welfare programs; (5) alternatives to negative income taxation; and (6) choice of specific transfer-by-taxation plans.

Objectives of Negative Income Taxation

Because the purpose of negative income taxation is to help fill the poverty income gap, the implication is that any negative tax plan is a welfare proposal with the main attention paid to raising the income of the poor. In general, the conference participants viewed negative income taxation primarily as a device to meet the needs of the poor rather than as a means of improving upon the distribution of income. The point was made that, since World War II, Americans have not been agitated about the distribution of income but they have recently become concerned with the problem of poverty. Thus the focus of negative income taxation should be to get more income into the hands of the lowest fifth in the income distribution, not to redistribute generally from the upper fifths to the lower ones. (In fact, negative income taxation would tend to flatten the Lorenz curve by raising low incomes relative to high incomes.)

One participant took strong exception to the view that negative income taxation should be set up and sold simply as an antipoverty weapon. He saw good grounds for reducing inequality in the distribution of income. He thought that a negative tax plan should help the poor, but should be designed also to include those who are not poor. Admitting that measures which systematically redistribute income have not been popular, he argued that it is still a mistake to single out the poor for special treatment. In fact, some wealthy persons might receive allowances, even under a plan aimed solely at the poor, because of important deficiencies in defining poverty on the basis of annual income. Moreover, a plan confined to the poor might not overcome the feeling of stigma presently associated with "relief."

Some participants replied that while income was not an altogether satisfactory measure of poverty it was the best available. One suggested that the averaging of income would solve problems created by using annual income as the definition of poverty. Others agreed that the negative income tax should be so structured as to reduce the possibility of stigma associated with a plan designed to help only the poor.

Only two participants specifically stated that an objective of negative income taxation should be eventually to replace many or all of the existing public programs. Even these two qualified their position by saying that while replacement of existing programs would be desirable, it perhaps would not be possible. There was general agreement that most present public transfer and service programs—notably social insurance and social services now associated with the war on poverty—would and should be maintained. However, some participants expressed the hope that a negative income tax would simplify and streamline the U.S. system for income maintenance. Many participants thought that the income maintenance function of public assistance programs should be reduced, and perhaps eventually eliminated. However, it was noted that some of the social services associated with public assistance would continue to be necessary.

There was mention, but no discussion, of the adoption of negative income taxation to achieve greater vertical equity in the tax system. Negative tax rates would allow the poor to share in tax cuts and would partially offset the growth of regressive taxes.

Attractive Features of Negative Income Taxation

Proponents of a negative income tax argue that it is attractive on several grounds: (1) It is universal rather than categorical, applying to all low-income units. (2) The rate at which benefits are reduced as income rises can be held well below 100 percent, thereby reducing adverse effects on incentives to work. (3) Considerably less stigma would be involved than with the present public assistance programs. (4) The rules of the income tax would be substituted for the discretion of welfare workers. Not all participants agreed that each of these features is desirable or that an operative negative income tax would, in fact, include each of these features.

Universal Coverage

One of the conferees stated that the negative income tax may be understood as a universalization of income maintenance for which he believed U.S. society is ready. Another said that the nation needs a program which sticks to a single simple definition of poverty so that the program can reach the large number of persons who are missed by more closely defined programs. At any given time, many poor persons receive neither public assistance nor social insurance benefits. As one participant put it: "The poor are generally employed people with low wages or with relatively large families against that low wage, and that is the category . . . that is not now being reached even minimally with transfers."

Some participants did not agree that the categorical approach to income maintenance should be dropped. One participant believed that by separating the poor into categories it would be easier to deal with the problem of incentives. For example, 100 percent of the poverty income gap of the aged could be filled without creating an important work incentive problem. Another view was that instead of "rocking the boat," public assistance categories might be broadened or increased. A participant who found universalization of income maintenance attractive also noted that there is some reason for the categories. The categories, he thought, essentially represent persons who are not in the labor force and who, therefore, rest more heavily upon the social conscience than do persons who could be attached to the labor force. Prevailing ethical standards seem to suggest income maintenance at higher levels for the aged, disabled, and families with dependent children than for persons who can work but choose not to do so.

High Marginal Tax Rate

There was wide agreement that an attractive feature of a negative tax proposal is that, unlike many other forms of assistance, it would allow beneficiaries to increase their disposable income by earning more—that is, an implicit marginal tax rate of 100 percent would be avoided. A number of participants noted that a tax rate of less than 100 percent is not an inherently unique feature of a negative income tax plan, nor is a 100 percent rate a feature inherent in public assistance and social insurance programs.

Stigma Effect

Several participants said that a negative income tax administered in a manner similar to the present individual income tax could reduce, perhaps eliminate, the stigma presently associated with being on relief. One said that the concern over stigma was one reason why many families in his city who were eligible for public assistance were not receiving it. Another member said he thought public assistance was demoralizing a good part of the poor population. But he was worried that the negative income tax, if it were confined to the poor, might not avoid the stigma problem. In this fear, he was joined by a participant who thought that in a few years the present image of public assistance could apply to a negative income tax.

Rules versus Discretion

A conferee suggested that it might be useful to think of the negative income tax in terms of emphasizing the use of rules, whereas discretion plays a much more important role in public assistance. But this, it was noted, is not an inherent distinction—there is no lack of rules in public assistance. Nevertheless, a high degree of objectivity is identified with the administration of the income tax law. Some participants felt, however, that discretion is needed. They warned that some people have above-average needs which will not be met by a program which makes payments attuned to average need. Many variables, assessed by the social worker, go into determining a given public assistance payment, thus making public assistance particularly useful in meeting special needs. In this respect, public assistance might win more support if it were added to the top of a program that provides some sort of income floor.

One participant stated that an important aspect of a negative income tax is that it would transfer power to make decisions on welfare operations from the states and localities to the federal government. But it was noted that taxpayers may object to unsupervised transfers to the poor.

Basic Problems in Negative Income Taxation

Having discussed the objectives and attractive features of a negative income tax, the conferees turned to three more thorny problems in negative taxation. They are: (1) the trade-offs involved in choosing the income guarantee, the negative tax rate (or rates), and the breakeven level of income; (2) the definition of income and the tax unit; and (3) the administration of a negative tax plan. Each is taken up separately.

Trade-offs

As indicated in Chapter V, a negative tax plan—in fact, any plan that would provide an income floor—involves some inescapable arithmetic. Any two of the three basic variables (the guarantee, tax rate, and breakeven level of income) determine the third in an uncomfortable manner. For example, the arithmetic indicates that the objective of a high guaranteed minimum income combined with a tax rate that keeps disincentives to work low is not compatible with the objective of confining allowances to the poor. Conversely, a low breakeven level of income and a reasonably low negative tax rate is not compatible with a high guaranteed minimum. As one participant said, "something has to give." Since the conferees generally agreed that a schedule of rates averaging much above 50 percent would not be acceptable, either the guarantee would be too low or the breakeven level of income would be too high. There was no general agreement, however, as to which objective—a high guarantee or a low breakeven level of income—is more expendable.

A number of participants thought that at very low levels of income the marginal tax rate might, without a great deal of harm, be allowed to go well above 50 percent. Income lost by dulling the incentives of working members of families whose income is below, say, $1,000 would not amount to much. However, they felt that it is very important to keep marginal rates at or below 50 percent as income approaches the poverty line. Thus, if the tax schedule is to include more than one rate it should take on a regressive form: high marginal rates on the first several hundred dollars, declining to considerably lower rates as before-allowance income reaches more substantial levels.

One participant believed that rates much in excess of 50 percent would not be enforceable. He thought that the Internal Revenue Service would collect more revenue with a 60 percent rate than with an 80 percent rate. He was inclined to favor a per capita tax credit plan, with a single tax rate for all income levels—a rate in the neighborhood of 25 or 30 percent. This would mean paying net allowances to many families which are not poor, but he did not consider this objectionable. Some participants were concerned that low rates would push the breakeven levels of income to politically unacceptable levels. One participant noted that Congress has been opposed to granting a zero tax, in the form of higher personal exemptions, to present taxpayers. He noted that the minimum standard deduction (which is effectively an increase in personal exemptions) was passed by Congress in the belief that it would not cost much money. If Congress has been unwilling to increase the number of low-income units who are exempt from income taxation, it is unrealistic to believe that Congress would now grant a negative tax to these presently taxable low-income units.

However, some participants registered support for the idea of paying allowances to families whose income is above the present level of their exemptions and deductions. One conferee said that he is convinced by the arithmetic of the negative income tax. He concluded that in the context of using transfer payments for eliminating poverty it is reasonable to provide a floor at or near the poverty line and still provide for work incentives. This means, even with a 50 percent negative tax rate, breakeven levels of income well above poverty lines, and probably close to the median income.

A somewhat different view was taken by a participant who suggested that the function of the negative tax plan might be limited to supplementing low incomes. The function of guaranteeing a high minimum income would be dispensed with, and it should be made clear to the public that the allowances would not do much for families with little or no income. Under such a plan, both tax rates and breakeven levels of income could be kept at acceptably low levels.

Some participants wondered—possibly in reaction to the hard facts of the inevitable trade-off—how significant the incentive problem really is. As one participant put it: "I have always been struck by the fact that most people worry about incentives for other people and never for themselves." He noted, however, that a group of disabled public assistance recipients stopped work when they no longer could keep what they earned and began to face an effective 100 percent tax rate. He did not know whether or not this experience could be generalized. Another participant asked what would be the quantitative effect of a 100 percent rate. It was estimated that in money terms the net cost of a plan that simply brings incomes up to poverty line levels would have been, in 1964, about $24 billion (when increases in negative tax allowances due to substitution of the allowances for other transfer income received by the poor are excluded). Approximately $12 billion of this cost is accounted for by the 1964 poverty gap. The maximum real cost in terms of output lost is the remaining $12 billion—a very rough guess—representing elimination of all the earnings of the poor, plus a small amount of earnings of some families with incomes close to, but above, the poverty lines.

One participant said that it is probably politically and ethically intolerable to do nothing for a family earning $3,001 while giving $3,000 to another family whose members are unwilling to do any work. Another said it is important from the standpoint of incentives to avoid a sharp discontinuity between negative and positive rates.

Definitions of Income and Tax Unit

Relatively little discussion was devoted to the question of how income and the tax unit should be defined for purposes of the negative income tax. Both efficiency (confining payments to poor families) and equity (similar treatment of equally poor families) demand a broad definition of money income and a tax unit resembling the consumer unit which pools its income for major items of expense (discussed in Chapter VII). As noted earlier in this volume, the present income tax unit and definition of income do not meet these specifications. Thus, if a negative income tax were not tied to reform of the existing individual income tax system, two different definitions of income and the tax unit would be needed in a system with both positive and negative rates. An additional question is whether dual definitions or concepts would create important administrative problems.

Those conferees who commented on the definition of income seemed to agree that a broad definition is necessary. No one disputed, however, the position taken in Chapter VII that payments made under the public assistance programs should be excluded from the income concept used in calculating negative tax allowances. One participant said that imputed rent should be included unless it is quantitatively insignificant—which he doubted. Others asked whether special treatment could be given to earned income. An earned income credit might reduce the incentive problems created by high marginal negative income tax rates.

Some participants expressed the view that Congress would not adopt a system under which income maintenance payments would depend on the same rules as those applied to the present positive tax system. One said he dislikes this double standard, but believes it is necessary politically. However, no one seemed to feel that two definitions of income would create important administrative problems. One participant thought that two different definitions of income might allow tax filers to transfer income to their children in order to benefit from the negative income tax. However, it was noted that this eventuality could be met by carefully defining the tax unit for negative income tax purposes.

A definition of the basic tax unit as spouses, children under 19 years of age, and students under 22, drew some criticism. One participant thought it rather arbitrary. Another felt that it would be a mistake to define a family unit and suggested, instead, a per capita tax credit. Such a definition of a family tax unit might create incentives to split the family.

Administration

The participants were sharply divided over whether the Treasury Department and its Internal Revenue Service could or should administer negative tax allowances. They were also divided over whether negative income taxation requires stricter enforcement and guidance than does present positive income taxation.

Several lines of thought developed on the question of who should be responsible for administration of a negative income tax plan. One participant thought that technical problems and the need for discretionary powers to prevent any wealthy persons from receiving allowances would prevent the Treasury from administering negative and positive taxation as a single system. He believed that the Treasury would not be able to administer a welfare system and a tax system at the same time. Another participant thought that even if the Treasury administered the plan it might still be identified as a welfare program with a means test. A contrasting view was taken by those who suggested that it would be necessary for the Treasury to administer negative taxation in order that the public would not view the plan as just another form of welfare. Proponents of this view felt that an important asset of negative income taxation is its relation to the tax system. Since almost all families have some dealings with the Internal Revenue Service, any stigma attached to receipt of allowances might be reduced. Still other participants believed that tying the negative tax to the tax structure is not important so long as the administering authority is a federal agency, and not the state and locally controlled welfare apparatus.

ENFORCEMENT. There was some concern that the satisfactory level of self-assessment and enforcement now attained in the positive income tax system might not be attainable under a negative tax system using existing approaches to enforcement. Two other related ideas were also expressed. One conferee could not visualize the Treasury transferring large amounts of money without making "validations and certifications" of the income claims of potential allowance recipients. He also thought that there would have to be adjustment for regional differences in the cost of living. Others felt that there would be difficulties in getting allowances to the families who were eligible for them. One participant noted that, at present, numerous potential public assistance recipients receive no assistance because they do not know about the public assistance program. Another said that it would be important to see that the allowances are usefully spent—at least where children are concerned.

A conferee asked whether it is a greater crime to cheat the government out of a dollar by not paying tax or by collecting a dollar that is not deserved. He argued for symmetry and less worry about enforcement. Most of the participants rejected the idea of a special welfare-type apparatus for administering a negative income tax. Aside from safeguards against fraud, the negative income tax can be administered through a set of rules applying universally, both in demographic and geographic terms.

LENGTH OF ACCOUNTING PERIOD. There was some concern over how to collect overpayments of negative income tax allowances. Chapter VII suggests that payments would have to be current, instead of at the end of the year. This could mean overpayments because of a miscalculation of the recipient's yearly earnings. Some participants thought overpayments could be repaid directly or similar amounts withheld from payments in the following year. However, others were concerned that these solutions would create a real hardship for families with few resources. One participant thought that the accounting period for determining eligibility for allowances and the level of payments would have to be very short—much shorter than a year—unless a system can be found that is sensitive to weekly or monthly changes in annual rates of earnings.

Relation to Existing Social Welfare Programs

The view prevailed at the conference that a negative tax would supplement, rather than substitute for, present public transfer and service programs. To some participants, this was "not a matter of despair." They believed that a negative tax would usefully complement the present income transfer and income-in-kind programs as well as the war on poverty programs. Others somewhat unhappily indicated that a politically feasible negative income tax would not provide payments high enough to relieve the need for some public assistance and the continuation of public housing, medical, counseling, and legal aid programs. One participant suggested that there is a qualitative, as well as a quantitative, difference between a small negative income tax plan and a "sufficient" program. The latter would alleviate, to a great extent, the need for many of the existing programs.

The before-transfer poor receive about half of total public transfer payments, and the after-transfer poor receive about a quarter of the total (see figures in Chapter II). In addition, one participant noted that available evidence indicates that, for the most part, the payments-in-kind programs—for example, medical, educational, and counseling—do not channel their funds only to the poor. He suggested that a negative income tax could be thought of as an income-conditioned family allowance which would, by fitting into a whole battery of programs, mainly benefit those elements of the poor population, especially the working poor, who receive the least benefit from the present transfer programs. Several participants thought it is important that the negative income tax be visualized against a background of progress in the fields of services and payments-in-kind.

Social Insurance and Public Assistance

Those participants who addressed themselves to the subject said that negative income tax allowances should supplement old-age, survivors and disability insurance (OASDI) and unemployment compensation. That is, OASDI and unemployment compensation would be included in the definition of income, and negative income taxes would fill—partially or wholly—whatever gap was left after an individual's or family's social insurance benefits had been accounted for. In contrast, public assistance would be excluded from the definition of income and would be treated as a supplement to negative income tax payments. Some participants visualized a negative income tax of modest size in the near future supplemented as necessary by public assistance, but eventually growing to a level at which the need for public assistance would be eliminated in all but the most unusual cases. While public assistance is gradually being eliminated, OASDI could be developing to the point at which it would assure a poverty-free income to the aged.

War on Poverty

Some participants said that under no circumstances should a negative income tax plan be considered a substitute for the so-called opportunity programs—the education and training programs which are such basic parts of the current war on poverty. One participant noted, however, that while programs of the Office of Economic Opportunity are for the long run, the poor have not accepted this premise. The poor would like to get money directly from Washington, and now. Thus a negative income tax could be regarded as an additional front in the war on poverty. Another believed that transfer programs and opportunity programs are cooperative approaches to the same problem, and that what is most attractive about the negative tax type of transfer is that it does support incentives to work.

Minimum Wage Legislation

There was spirited discussion of the question whether a negative income tax would allow a reduction in the minimum wage or an elimination of minimum wage legislation. In Chapter I the view is expressed that a negative income tax could provide all low-paid workers with a minimum income without jeopardizing the employment opportunities of any of them. Minimum wages, on the other hand, effectively apply only to workers actually employed and can —potentially, at least—create unemployment. Some participants were distressed by the implication that minimum wages should be reduced or eliminated. One participant said a negative income tax would not eliminate the need for a floor under wages. Another stated that the minimum wage issue is entirely unrelated to the negative income tax issue.

Several participants expressed concern that a negative income tax might compete for financing with other social welfare programs. One said that if it came to a question of financing a negative income tax or raising social security benefits many groups, probably including organized labor, would prefer to have larger social security payments than the negative tax.

Alternatives to Negative Income Taxation

At various points during the conference, participants touched on alternatives to negative income taxation. Since most agreed that the main object of negative income taxation is to close the poverty income gap, it seemed important to judge other income maintenance proposals on the basis of how well they would close that gap. Public assistance gained the most attention in this respect, despite criticisms leveled at it during the conference. The attention paid to public assistance as an alternative to negative income taxation can be explained by the fact that public assistance, of all existing transfer payment programs, is most directly concerned with poor people —even though it deals only with special categories of poor people. The social insurances and family allowances were perhaps given less attention because, for reasons explained below, they are not efficient means of closing the poverty income gap.

Public Assistance

At least three lines of thought were evident with regard to the reform of public assistance. One view was that there is nothing in the public assistance statute that makes adequate care of the poor impossible other than the distribution of power among national, state, and local governments. It was noted that in the late 1940's there were proposals to make public assistance a comprehensive noncategorical program with federal standards. Although the proposals did not receive much political attention then, real efforts in the same direction today might achieve the same results that a negative income tax is supposed to achieve. In addition, public assistance is more flexible than a negative tax because it can quickly meet special needs and it can account for regional differences in the cost of living.

Some proponents of this new line of thought advocated broadening the categories, adding new ones, or both. The rate at which benefits are reduced as income increases could be lowered. In this regard it was noted that there were amendments in 1962 to the public assistance section of the Social Security Act which were designed to provide public assistance recipients with greater work incentives. In 1965, there was a further increase in the amount of monthly earned income which may be exempted in determining public assistance payments (see Chapter III for details). The real problem is that very few states have taken advantage of these amendments to the federal statute. One participant summed up the view that "public assistance can be reformed" by stating that if one is trying to hit a target population with a fair degree of efficiency and keep resource outlays low and the benefits high, there is nothing —in spite of two days of hostile remarks—inherent in the present welfare system preventing the attainment of these goals.

A contrasting view was taken by other conferees. They thought that public assistance is currently inadequate, that in practice it will not be reformed, and that even a broadening of coverage and a lowering of the penalty rate (marginal tax rate) on earnings would not relieve recipients of the stigma presently associated with being on relief. Even some supporters of reform of public assistance admitted reform might no longer be politically feasible. One participant who has been close to the public assistance programs believed that refinements could be made in public assistance, but he suspected that the present public assistance programs will never provide adequate coverage and adequate payments. He noted that public assistance is basically unpopular, and carries a stigma in the United

States. In addition, it is wasteful because welfare workers spend a very high percentage of their time on investigations. He thought that a net decrease in cost could be achieved by eliminating investigations. Furthermore, he believed it would be helpful to separate the services and the income maintenance functions, and to recognize that many persons will need some form of monetary assistance no matter what levels of services they receive. Another participant noted that one objective of a negative income tax is to get away from the tradition in public assistance of close supervision of the manner in which the money is spent. A conferee said that although a 100 percent penalty on increases in income is not inherent in public assistance, a negative income tax is a more likely route to getting rid of the 100 percent rate than would be a beefed-up public assistance program. Eliminating the 100 percent rate would, he thought, necessitate a reconsideration of the basic ideas about how public assistance ought to work.

A third view—more implicit than explicit in the discussions of public assistance—was that the necessary reforms of public assistance would make it identical in form to a negative income tax. If public assistance were made universal, conditioned only on the basis of a family's income and size, the penalty rate substantially reduced, national minimum standards of assistance payments introduced, and residence requirements eliminated, then public assistance would differ from a negative income tax only with respect to who administers the program. However, this route gives less assurance than does a negative income tax that the stigma now associated with receipt of assistance payments will be reduced or eliminated.

Social Insurance

The present social insurance system, with its wage-related system of benefits, has important limitations as a general approach to reducing and eventually eliminating the poverty gap. It helps, at present, only a fraction of the after-transfer poor—and these are mainly the aged poor. It keeps out of poverty a somewhat larger number of aged persons who would be poor were it not for their benefits. However, it is not designed to deal with the problem of inadequate earnings of persons who are still employed. Since social insurance replaces earned income for persons at all income levels (although in larger proportion at lower earnings levels) an increase in benefits to bring the aged or unemployed poor out of poverty necessitates 'an increase also in benefits to the aged and unemployed who are not poor. Hence, it is an inefficient approach if the aim is to direct redistribution of income to the poor. This fact was illustrated by a participant who said that it would cost 'an additional $10 billion to $11 billion to bring about a half of the aged poor out of poverty by way of the OASDI route. Only about a third of this sum would be received by those who had been, or who remained, poor.

Family Allowances

There was almost no discussion of family allowances, even though this approach to income maintenance is quite popular in most other Western nations. One participant noted that family allowances paid to all families with children is an expensive way in which to aid poor children, since most of the benefits would be received by children who are members of nonpoor families. Presumably, this problem could be surmounted by having income-conditioned family allowances. Such an approach, however, would not differ from a negative income tax plan which confined its allowances to families with children.

Specific Transfer-by-Taxation Plans

In the final session of the conference, the participants examined four specific types of transfer-by-taxation plans. Three of the four were hypothetical plans used as a basis for estimating costs, benefits, and financing in Chapter IX; the fourth was put forward by one of the conference participants. This fourth plan, though not different in principle from either social dividend or negative rates taxation, has certain features which tie it more closely to the existing federal income tax system and to federal income tax reform. The four types of plans discussed by the conferees were defined briefly as follows:

1. A negative rates taxation plan would use poverty lines as breakeven levels of income and 'a single 50 percent negative tax rate applied against the poverty income gap. In 1964, a plan of this type (as noted in Chapter IX for Plan A-1) would have cost the federal government $6.3 billion.

2. A set-aside plan also would use poverty lines as breakeven levels of income, but it would exempt from tax all income below 50 percent of the poverty line income. Thereafter the negative tax rate would be 50 percent. This plan, in 1964 (as estimated for Plan C in Chapter IX), would have cost $4.7 billion.

3. A social dividend plan would guarantee income equal to the poverty line and would tax income below this breakeven level of income at a 50 percent rate. The gross cost, in 1964, of this plan would be $155 billion with a redistribution, or net cost, of $31 billion (as estimated for the comparable Plan D-1 in Chapter IX), which could be financed by a 15 percent tax rate on income above the breakeven income levels.

4. A tax credit plan—that suggested by one of the conferees —would have two basic features: a proportional income tax with no exemptions, and a flat-sum credit per capita. For purposes of comparison with the plans outlined above, this plan's author suggested a $400 tax credit per capita. In order to finance the tax credit plan plus other expenditures normally financed by the federal personal income tax, it would be necessary to levy a 25 percent income tax rate against an income base which would no longer be reduced by personal exemptions and which would be broadened still further through tax reform in the area of personal deductions and tax exempt income. This plan is similar to the social dividend plan described above, but its guaranteed minimum income is only about half as great. Also the tax credit plan discussed by the conferees adopts a single flat-rate income tax schedule rather than distinguishing between the social dividend tax schedule and the existing positive tax schedule. The breakeven levels of income of both of these plans, however, are similar. For example, the breakeven level of income for a family of four is $6,000 ($3,000 divided by .50) under the social dividend plan above and $6,400 ($400 times 4 divided by .25) under this tax credit plan. It is estimated that, in 1964, the gross cost of the tax credit plan would have been $76 billion ($400 times a population of approximately 190 million), with a redistribution, or net cost, of about $16 billion.

Several participants expressed concern that the proposals for the negative rates plans did not include an indication as to how they would grow over time. Some of them were willing to begin with a small program—one which filled only half of the poverty gap—but they wanted it to grow so that it would provide an income floor at or near poverty line levels of income. Thus they suggested still another plan. This one would begin as a negative rates plan (such as the first plan summarized above) and would grow to proportions similar to the social dividend plan described above. One participant said that the first two plans—the negative rates and set-aside plans—were pragmatically sound from a political point of view compared with the social dividend and tax credit plans. But he thought their attractiveness was reduced by the need for continuing to provide substantial amounts of supplementary public assistance payments. Another participant was concerned that Congress would not give a plan which started on a relatively moderate basis a chance to expand. He noted that it is hard to get Congress to change the tax laws. He also wondered whether the $5 billion to $6 billion set-aside and negative rates plans would be big enough to prevent real disappointment with respect to their effectiveness as a means for improving income maintenance.

One participant suggested a variant on the negative rates plan which would increase incentives to work. The variant would provide allowances equal to some fraction of the poverty gap plus some fraction of the change in a family's earnings. It was noted, however, that this would create a "notch" problem by making allowance payments to a family whose income had risen above the poverty line—though this would happen for only one year. (For a discussion of notch problems, see Chapter II.) Another participant questioned the need for further reduction of the allowance when a family's earnings fell.

Of the participants who said they favored a particular plan, a majority chose the negative rates plan with a 50 percent rate. This plan was favored because its target is the poor; it fills 50 percent of the poverty income gap in the most efficient manner; and because it holds out the greatest likelihood politically of getting a "foot in the door." However, some participants supported the negative rates plan only on condition that it would grow beyond its initial modest proportions. A number said it would be a mistake to undersell a plan which began by providing $5 billion to $6 billion to the poor. In this connection, some said that the cost figures given for both the negative rates plan and the set-aside plan included estimates that overstated the initial reduction in public assistance expenditures. One participant said that he would prefer that the breakeven levels of income be the value of personal exemptions and minimum standard deductions rather than the calculated poverty lines. A few supporters of the negative rates plan favored separating it from the tax system and treating it as an income-conditioned family allowance.

Support for the tax credit proposal came from the participant who thought an objective of negative income taxation is to reduce inequality in the distribution of income. Further support came from participants who liked the way in which a tax credit fits into the existing personal income tax system and the way it avoids distinguishing between the poor and nonpoor. One participant noted that the Tobin plan described in the background paper very nicely integrated the negative and positive tax schedules, and suggested that there were similarities between the Tobin and tax credit plans. Some interest in the tax credit plan was indicated by a participant who wanted a plan tied to the tax structure. However, he was concerned that the negative rates and set-aside plans have little relation to the positive income tax system, and therefore might well be administered apart from it.

In Conclusion

The two days of discussion were useful in eliciting the participants' views on where the important problems involved in the adoption of a negative income tax lie. The discussion indicated that a negative income tax is neither a simple, nor a wholly satisfactory, device for improving the current income maintenance system. It also indicated that the alternatives to negative taxation have very serious limitations. The participants, to nobody's surprise, failed to achieve a consensus either in support of or in opposition to negative income taxation. Despite this lack of consensus, it is significant that few conference members were willing to stand behind any other single income maintenance program as the primary means of better meeting the income needs of the poor. There was widespread agreement that some form of income-conditioned grant which would not be restricted to special categories of the poor is desirable.

List of Conference Participants

Gerard M. Brannon
U. S. Treasury Department

John A. Brittain
The Brookings Institution

Jesse Burkhead
The Maxwell School
Syracuse University

Robert D. Calkins
The Brookings Institution

William M. Capron
The Brookings Institution

Otto Eckstein
Harvard University

Rashi Fein
The Brookings Institution

Mitchell Ginsberg
New York City Welfare
Department

Richard Goode
International Monetary Fund

Kermit Gordon
The Brookings Institution

Christopher Green
North Carolina State University

Peter Henle
U. S. Department of Labor

Joseph A. Kershaw
Williams College

William A. Klein
School of Law
University of Wisconsin

Robert J. Lampman
University of Wisconsin

Robert A. Levine
U. S. Office of Economic
Opportunity

James M. Lyday
U. S. Office of Economic
Opportunity

Ida C. Merriam
U. S. Department of Health,
Education, and Welfare

Helen O. Nicol
U. S. Department of Health,
Education, and Welfare

Benjamin A. Okner
Ohio State University

Mollie Orshansky
U. S. Department of Health,
Education, and Welfare

Joseph A. Pechman
The Brookings Institution

William Pendleton
The Ford Foundation

Michael Reagan
University of California
(Riverside)

Alice Rivlin
U. S. Department of Health,
Education, and Welfare

Earl Rolph
University of California
(Berkeley)

177

Conference Participants *(Continued)*

Gabriel G. Rudney
U. S. Treasury Department

Mary Smelker
U. S. Department of Labor

Gilbert Steiner
The Brookings Institution

Lawrence M. Stone
School of Law
University of California
(Berkeley)

Stanley S. Surrey
U. S. Treasury Department

Harold W. Watts
U. S. Office of Economic
Opportunity

Burton A. Weisbrod
University of Wisconsin

Melvin White
U. S. Treasury Department

Walter Williams
U. S. Office of Economic
Opportunity

Louis Winnick
The Ford Foundation

APPENDIXES

APPENDIX A

Definitions of the Family Unit

DIFFERENT DEFINITIONS of the family unit which are used by federal agencies cause some confusion in estimating both the extent of poverty and the types of poor persons in the United States. The definitions used most often are those of the Bureau of the Census, U. S. Department of Commerce, and the Bureau of Labor Statistics, U. S. Department of Labor. The Census Bureau's data, based on its definition of the family, are used by the Social Security Administration of the Department of Health, Education, and Welfare.

The Current Population Survey of the Census Bureau defines the family as two or more persons living together (including children living away from home) and related by blood, marriage, or adoption. In addition, there are "unrelated individuals."

The Bureau of Labor Statistics (BLS) Survey of Consumer Expenditures defines the family as persons *usually* related and *usually* living together who pool their income and draw from a common fund for their major items of expense. The BLS economic definition of the family means that the number of single consumer units, as counted by the BLS, is much lower than the number of unrelated individuals reported by Census.[1] Since the poverty line for single-member units is 75 percent of the poverty line of two-member units, two of the Census Bureau's poor unrelated individuals may represent one nonpoor two-member family according to the BLS definition.

[1] In 1961, there were 5.1 million poor unrelated individuals by the Census count, but only 2.6 million poor single consumer units as reported by BLS.

181

Census defines the family as of a point in time and records its income for the previous years. Thus the income earned in the preceding year by a person who died before the date of the interview is not included in the family's income. In contrast, the BLS reconstructs the family unit so as to reflect the average family size throughout the year. The BLS thus allows for variations in the length of time which each member spent in the family.

The Incidence of Indirect Taxes

ECONOMISTS DO NOT AGREE on the incidence of indirect taxes. On the one hand, Richard A. Musgrave believes that indirect taxes raise prices and are borne, at least partly, by the consumers who pay for the goods.[1] If low-income families consume a higher percentage of their income than upper income families, taxes that raise consumer goods prices will produce regressivity in the tax structure.[2] On the other hand, Earl Rolph has argued that the incidence of the sales and excise taxes falls upon factor incomes. He concludes from this that the burden of sales and excise taxes does not fall upon consumers and that the burden of these taxes can be considered as similar to that of a general factor income tax with a proportional rate.[3] An examination of Rolph's argument is useful because it bears on the question of the percentage of money income paid by the poor through direct and indirect taxes.

Rolph assumes a competitive system, although he shows that other market structures (which are more realistic) make little difference to his argument. He also assumes that the imposition of a sales or excise tax

[1] Richard A. Musgrave, "The Incidence of the Tax Structure and Its Effects on Consumption," Joint Committee on the Economic Report, *Federal Tax Policy for Economic Growth and Stability,* papers submitted by panelists appearing before the Subcommittee on Tax Policy, 84 Cong. 1 sess. (1955), p. 101.

[2] If Milton Friedman's "permanent income" hypothesis holds, there would not be regressivity under a *general* sales tax if one adopts the average incidence of the tax over a period of years as a basis for determining the existence of regressivity. For his hypothesis, see *A Theory of the Consumption Function* (New York: National Bureau of Economic Research, 1965).

[3] Earl Rolph, *The Theory of Fiscal Economics* (Berkeley: University of California Press, 1954), pp. 123-47.

183

leaves aggregate money expenditure and total real output unchanged.[4] When a tax is imposed on a good, it raises the price of the good and its output is reduced. This frees factors of production which, in competition with the factors producing tax-exempt goods, lower the unit price of the employed factors, lower the price of the untaxed goods, and increase the output of these goods. Thus the net effect of the sales tax upon the price level is to raise some prices, lower others, and leave an overall index of prices where it was before the tax. This follows from the assumption that total expenditure and total output are not changed by imposition of the tax.[5]

What, then, has the sales tax done? It has lowered total factor income and unit factor income. The government receives in revenue from the sales tax an amount equal to the amount by which factor incomes fell. And the consumer has to pay more per unit for the taxed products which are now in shorter supply, but pays less per unit for the untaxed goods which are now in greater supply. Thus, says Rolph, there is no reason to presume that the consumer is any worse off than before the imposition of the tax.[6]

Rolph readily admits that the imposition of a sales tax affects relative prices. In fact, it is obvious that he could not show how the tax burdens factor incomes without first showing that the tax produces a rise in price, a fall in output, and a reduction in the demand for factors of production in the taxed industry. There is no disputing the fact that a dollar's worth of income spent on the newly *taxed* goods has less purchasing power than it had before the tax was imposed. It may well be true that the prices of tax-exempt goods and services have fallen. But unless the goods and services which are taxed and those which are not taxed are specified, there is no way to be certain that all income classes equally bear the final burden of the sales or excise tax.[7] If the tax is on goods and services for which the lower income groups spend a pro-

---

[4] *Ibid.*, p. 133. This seems to be based on the assumption of unitary elasticity of demand.

[5] Rolph fails to explain the possible effects of a sales or excise tax on a price index for private consumer goods. See Daniel C. Morgan, *The Retail Sales Tax* (Madison: University of Wisconsin Press, 1964), pp. 115-16.

[6] Rolph must assume that the sales tax revenues are expended upon goods and services which yield at least as much satisfaction as the income lost through taxes would have yielded if no sales tax had been levied. If government expenditures are not included in the analysis, then clearly consumers must be worse off after the imposition of the tax.

[7] Morgan, *op. cit.*, pp. 117-18. According to Morgan, Challis Hall and Richard A. Musgrave have emphasized the importance of examining the *uses* of income as well as the *sources* of income in determining where the real burden of a tax lies.

portionally greater percentage of their income than do higher income groups, the sales tax will be regressive. In other words, even though the initial incidence of the sales tax is upon factor incomes in general, the burden of the tax will be upon those who are heavy consumers of the taxed item. This is implicit in the admission that the imposition of the sales or excise tax affects relative prices.

It is not possible to resolve the question of whether indirect taxes should be considered as proportional income taxes with no effect on the general price level, or as (regressive?) taxes with the incidence borne in part by the consumer through an increase in prices of some goods not matched by a fall in the prices of other goods. It is possible, however, to maintain that indirect taxes in one way or another lower the incomes of poor families, even if they lower proportionately the incomes of families that are not poor. Now suppose the government were to compensate poor families, through a tax credit, for the taxes they paid. From the Musgrave point of view, the compensation would cover the reduction in disposable income due to personal taxes plus the rise in prices or the reduction in factor incomes caused by the shifting of indirect taxes. From the Rolph point of view, the compensation would cover the reduction in disposable income due to personal taxes plus the reduction in potential disposable income due to the reduction in factor incomes caused by indirect taxes.

APPENDIX C

Similarity of the Allowance Formulas

THE BASIC SIMILARITY between negative rates taxation and social dividend taxation is illustrated in algebraic terms by comparing the formulas for determining the allowance, if any, a family receives, given the family's income.

The negative tax allowance equation could be written as:

(C-1) $$(R - Q)t = A$$

and the social dividend allowance equation could be:

(C-2) $$Y_g - Qt = A$$

where Q = family income of families whose income is below the breakeven level,

A = the allowance,

and where, as in equations 5-1, 5-2, and 5-3 of Chapter V,

R = the breakeven level of income — or the level of income at which the net allowance is reduced to zero,

t = tax rate,

Y_g = guaranteed minimum income.

$R - Q$ is the negative tax base against which a rate (or rates) t is applied; Q (family income) is the social dividend base. The gross social dividend allowance minus the tax liability is $Y_g - Qt$, which equals the net allowance A. However, $Y_g - Qt$ can be converted to a form

186

which is equivalent to the negative tax formula by a simple algebraic substitution:

(C-2) $$Y_g - Qt = A.$$

But $$Y_g/t = R, \text{ or } Y_g = Rt \text{ (see equation 1,}$$
$$\text{Chapter V).}$$

Substituting for Y_g gives:

(C-1 and C-2) $$(R - Q)t = A.$$

APPENDIX D

Cost Estimates

THE DETAILS ON COST ESTIMATES for the hypothetical plans described in Chapter IX are presented in Table D-1 through Table D-5. These tables also support findings or illustrate points made in other parts of the book. For example, lines at the end of Table D-2 show the percentage of the poverty gap filled by the plans using a 50 percent negative rate applied against unused tax exemptions and deductions (EX-MSD). The percentages rise with family size, thereby illustrating, with actual figures, the results in Table 6-3, Chapter VI. Note how "poorly" one-member and two-member families are treated by Plan B-1. In contrast, lines 11 through 14 in Table D-1 show that Plan A-2 and Plan C, while filling less than 50 percent of the poverty gap, do not favor large families at the expense of smaller ones.

My cost estimates for Plan F—the Tobin plan—are based on inclusion of the aged, whereas Tobin's own estimate does not include the aged. In addition, I have made two cost estimates. In Table 9-1 and Table D-5, the estimated cost, based on inclusion of public assistance, is given as $11.3 billion. In Table 9-1, I estimate the cost when public assistance is excluded at $12.6 billion. This is somewhat below the $13.9 billion estimate, excluding the aged, made by Tobin himself.[1] There are various reasons for the differences—including, in addition to those having to do with the aged, the fact that Tobin's estimate is based

[1] James Tobin's estimate is in "Memorandum on Basic Income Allowances" (unpublished paper, Yale University, Summer 1965). His general proposal is made in "Improving the Economic Status of the Negro," *Daedalus*, Vol. 94 (Fall 1965), pp. 878-98.

on 1962 income tax data whereas my estimates are based on 1964 Census data. In addition, the tax unit and the Census Bureau's family unit are not the same—nor are the respective definitions of income. Moreover, children who work and file an income tax return may also be declared dependents on their parent's tax return. This overstates the number of persons eligible for net allowances in Tobin's calculations.

Each of the tables in Appendix D is based on data from the U. S. Bureau of the Census, *Current Population Reports,* Series P-60, No. 47, "Income in 1964 of Families and Persons in the United States" (1965); hereinafter referred to as Census, CPS for 1964.

TABLE D-1. Cost Estimates for Hypothetical Transfer-by-Taxation Plans A-1, A-2, C, and E, 1964[a]

Item	Number of Members in Family							Totals
	One	Two	Three	Four	Five	Six	Seven or More[b]	
Number of Families (by size):								
(1) All families in population (thousands)	12,057	15,713	10,045	9,137	6,224	3,284	3,432	59,892
(2) Eligible for allowances (thousands)	5,088	2,483	1,104	904	810	549	1,201	12,139
(3) Eligible families as percentage of all families, (2)÷(1)	42.2	15.8	11.0	9.9	13.0	16.7	35.0	20.3
Income of Families ($ millions):								
(4) Total needed so as not to be poor[c]	7,632	4,966	2,760	2,712	2,835	2,196	6,005	29,106
(5) Money income of eligible families	4,008	3,024	1,607	1,590	1,753	1,289	3,564	16,835
(6) Poverty income gap, (4)−(5)	3,624	1,942	1,153	1,122	1,082	907	2,441	12,271
Allowance Payments ($ millions):								
(7) Plan A-1	1,812	971	576	561	541	453	1,221	6,135
(8) Plan A-2[d]	1,297	715	425	410	389	337	869	4,442
(9) Plan C	1,371	789	459	449	438	363	1,006	4,876
(10) Plan E	3,624	1,942	1,153	1,222	1,082	907	2,441	12,271
Percentage of Poverty Income Gap Filled:								
(11) Plan A-1	50.0	50.0	50.0	50.0	50.0	50.0	50.0	50.0
(12) Plan A-2	35.8	36.8	36.9	36.5	35.9	37.1	35.6	36.2
(13) Plan C	37.8	40.6	39.8	40.0	40.5	40.0	41.2	39.7
(14) Plan E	100.0	100.0	100.0	100.0	100.0	100.0	100.0	100.0

Source: Census, CPS for 1964, Table 4, p. 25.

a Since Plans A-1, A-2, C, and E use the poverty lines for breakeven lines, they can be grouped together for statistical purposes. See definition of plans and discussion in Chapter IX.

b Computed on the assumption of an eight-member family.

c Poverty line times the number of poor families. (Lampman poverty lines of $1,500 for unrelated individual or family head and $500 for each additional member of the family.)

d Based on what families at the midpoint of an income bracket would receive in net allowances.

TABLE D-2. Cost Estimates for Hypothetical Negative Rates Plans B-1 and B-2, 1964[a]

Item	One	Two	Three	Four	Five	Six	Seven or More[b]	Totals
Families (by size)								
(1) Number all families in population (thousands)	12,057	15,713	10,045	9,137	6,224	3,284	3,432	59,892
(2) Eligible for allowances: Plan B-1 (thousands)	2,821	1,741	972	904	902	655	1,481	9,476
(3) Eligible for allowances: Plan B-2 (thousands)	4,333	3,190	972	904	902	655	1,481	12,437
(4) Eligible as percentage all families: Plan B-1, (2)÷(1)	23.4	11.1	9.7	9.9	14.5	19.9	43.1	15.8
(5) Eligible as percentage all families: Plan B-2, (3)÷(1)	35.9	20.3	9.7	9.9	14.5	19.9	43.1	20.8
Income and Allowances ($ millions)								
(6) Total income needed to have no unused EX-MSD: Plan B-1, value EX-MSD×(2)	2,539	2,786	2,236	2,712	3,337	2,882	8,590	25,082
(7) Total income needed to have no unused EX-MSD: Plan B-2, value EX-MSD×(3)	5,946	7,875	2,236	2,712	3,337	2,882	8,590	33,578
(8) Total income of families with unused EX-MSD: Plan B-1	1,269	1,689	1,290	1,590	2,084	1,734	5,076	14,732
(9) Total income of families with unused EX-MSD: Plan B-2	3,144	4,840	1,290	1,590	2,084	1,734	5,076	19,758
(10) Unused EX-MSD: Plan B-1	1,270	1,097	946	1,122	1,253	1,148	3,514	10,350
(11) Unused EX-MSD: Plan B-2	2,802	3,035	946	1,122	1,253	1,148	3,514	13,820
(12) Allowance payments: Plan B-1	635	548	473	561	627	574	1,757	5,175
(13) Allowance payments: Plan B-2	1,401	1,517	473	561	627	574	1,757	6,910
Poverty Income Gap								
(14) Size of poverty income gap ($ millions)[c]	3,624	1,942	1,153	1,122	1,082	907	2,441	12,271
(15) Percentage of poverty gap filled: Plan B-1, (12)÷(14)	17.5	28.2	41.0	50.0	57.9	63.3	72.0	42.2
(16) Percentage of poverty gap filled: Plan B-2, (13)÷(14)	38.7	78.1	41.0	50.0	57.9	63.3	72.0	56.3

Source: Census, CPS for 1964, Tables 3 and 4, pp. 24–25.
[a] As noted in Chapter IX where the hypothetical plans are described, Plan B-2 differs from Plan B-1 in that B-2 allows aged filers and their aged spouses double the amount of exemptions and deductions (EX-MSD). It is assumed here that 50 percent of households with an aged head had a spouse under 65. The 50 percent assumption is based on data from U.S. Department of the Treasury, Internal Revenue Service, *Statistics of Income, Individual Income Tax Returns, 1962*, Table 25, p. 124, which reported that a little less than 50 percent of joint returns filed by the aged showed that both spouses were over 65 years of age. [b] Computed on the assumption of an eight-member family. [c] See Table D-1, line 6.

191

TABLE D-3. Cost Estimates for Hypothetical Social Dividend Plan D-1, 1964[a]

Item[b]	Number of Members in Family							Totals
	One	Two	Three	Four	Five	Six	Seven or More[c]	
Features of Plan D-1 (dollars):								
(1) Basic allowance, by family size	1,500	2,000	2,500	3,000	3,500	4,000	5,000	
(2) Breakeven level of income	3,000	4,000	5,000	6,000	7,000	8,000	10,000	
Number of Families (by size):								
(3) All families in population (thousands)	12,057	15,713	10,045	9,137	6,224	3,284	3,432	59,892
(4) Eligible for net allowances (thousands)	7,536	6,222	3,194	3,097	2,795	1,882	2,732	27,458
(5) Eligible as percentage all families, (4)÷(3)	62.5	39.6	31.8	33.9	44.9	57.3	79.6	45.8
Income, Guarantees, and Costs ($ millions):								
(6) Total guarantee to eligible families, (1)×(4)	11,304	12,444	7,985	9,291	9,782	7,528	13,660	71,994
(7) Total income of eligible families	9,321	14,020	9,573	11,860	12,536	9,440	14,757	81,507
(8) Revenue from 50% tax on income of eligible families, [.50×(7)]	4,661	7,010	4,787	5,930	6,268	4,720	7,379	40,754
(9) Net cost of plan, (6)–(8)	6,644	5,434	3,198	3,361	3,514	2,808	6,281	31,240

Source: Census, CPS for 1964, Table 4, p. 25.
[a] Plan D-1 is described in Chapter IX.
[b] The term "eligible families" is used in this table and in Table D-4 as a short form for "families with income below breakeven levels." In principle, all families are eligible for social dividends, no matter what the level of income. What they receive in net allowances is, of course, a different matter. In estimating the net cost of the plan (as opposed to the gross cost discussed in Chapter VI), it is useful to look only at families below the breakeven levels of income.
[c] Computed on the assumption of an eight-member family.

TABLE D-4. Cost Estimates for Hypothetical Social Dividend Plan D-2, 1964[a]

Item[b]	Number of Members in Family							Totals
	One	Two	Three	Four	Five	Six	Seven or More[c]	
Features of Plan D-2 (dollars):								
(1) Basic allowance, by family size	1,500	2,000	2,500	3,000	3,500	4,000	5,000	
(2) Breakeven level of income	4,500	6,000	7,500	9,000	10,500	12,000	15,000	
Number of Families (by size):								
(3) All families in population (thousands)	12,057	15,713	10,045	9,137	6,224	3,284	3,432	59,892
(4) Eligible for net allowance (thousands)	9,121	9,160	5,761	5,998	4,709	2,784	3,211	40,744
(5) Eligible as percentage all families, (4)÷(3)	75.6	58.3	57.3	65.6	75.6	84.8	93.6	68.0
Income, Guarantees, and Costs ($ millions):								
(6) Total guarantee to eligible families, (1)×(4)	13,681	18,320	14,403	17,994	16,481	11,136	16,055	108,070
(7) Unadjusted: total income of eligible families[d]	15,224	28,702	25,576	33,088	28,815	18,322	20,527	170,254
(8) Revenue from $33\frac{1}{3}\%$ tax on unadjusted income, [$33\frac{1}{3}\%\times$(7)]	5,074	9,566	8,524	11,028	9,604	6,107	6,842	56,745
(9) Unadjusted: net cost of plan, (6)–(8)[d]	8,607	8,754	5,879	6,966	6,877	5,029	9,213	51,325
(10) Adjusted: total income of eligible families[e]								200,004
(11) Revenue from $33\frac{1}{3}\%$ tax on adjusted income, [$33\frac{1}{3}\%\times$(10)]								66,668
(12) Adjusted: net cost of plan, (6)–(11)[e]								41,402

Source: Census, CPS for 1964, Table 4, p. 25.

a Plan D-2 is described in Chapter IX.
b See Table D-3, footnote b for explanation of use of term "eligible families."
c Computed on the assumption of an eight-member family.
d Unadjusted for underreporting of income in the Census Bureau's CPS for 1964.
e Census data adjusted for underreporting. Adjustment is necessary because the $33\frac{1}{3}$ percent tax rate is that rate which when applied to total money income will raise $155 billion, the gross cost of Plan D-2 (and also the gross cost of Plan D-1). The data indicate that TMI in 1964 was $470 billion, or $70 billion more than reported in the Current Population Survey. Since in Plan D-2 families with income below the breakeven level had 42.5 percent of all TMI ($170.3 billion ÷ $400 billion), it is assumed that 42.5 percent (or $29.75 billion) of $70 billion should be added to the $170.3 billion.

TABLE D-5. Cost Estimates for Hypothetical Plan F, the Tobin Plan, 1964[a]

Item	Number of Members in Family							Totals
	One	Two	Three	Four	Five	Six	Seven or More[b]	
Features of Plan F (dollars):								
(1) Basic allowance, by family size	400	800	1,200	1,600	2,000	2,400	2,700	
(2) Breakeven level of income [(1)÷33⅓%]	1,200	2,400	3,600	4,800	6,000	7,200	8,100	
(3) Tie-in level of income[c]	1,422	3,000	4,636	6,306	8,050	9,928	10,196	
Number of Families (by size):								
(4) All families in population (thousands)	12,057	15,713	10,045	9,137	6,224	3,284	3,432	59,892
(5) Eligible for net allowances (thousands)[d]	3,916	3,313	1,954	2,014	2,079	1,607	2,258	17,141
(6) Eligible for tax reductions (thousands)[e]	1,953[e]	2,769[e]	1,850	2,493	2,627	1,733	1,278	14,703
(7) Eligible for both net allowances and tax reductions (thousands)	1,095[e]	1,572[e]	982	1,110	1,177	952	777	7,665
(8) Eligible for either net allowances or tax reductions (thousands), (5)+(6)−(7)	4,774	4,510	2,822	3,397	3,529	2,388	2,759	24,179
Income of Eligible Families ($ millions):								
(9) Breakeven level times number of eligible families, (2)×(5)	4,699	7,951	7,034	9,667	12,474	11,570	18,290	71,685
(10) Total money income	2,426	4,850	4,208	5,995	7,882	7,343	10,369	43,073
(11) Income gap, (9)−(10)[f]	2,273	3,101	2,826	3,672	4,592	4,227	7,921	28,612
Allowances, Taxes, and Costs ($ millions):								
(12) Net allowances [(11)×33⅓%]	758	1,034	942	1,224	1,530	1,409	2,640	9,537
(13) Taxable income when money income is below tie-in level[g]	441	1,961	2,322	4,659	6,256	4,504	2,551	22,694
(14) Taxes paid when money income is below tie-in level	62	290	333	685	939	691	364	3,364
(15) Taxes paid under Tobin 33⅓% schedule[h]	31	150	160	331	456	309	171	1,608
(16) Tax reductions, (14)−(15)	31	140	173	354	483	382	193	1,756
(17) Cost of plan, (12)+(16)	789	1,174	1,115	1,578	2,013	1,791	2,833	11,293

Source: Census, CPS for 1964, Table 4, p. 25.

a Plan F is described in Chapter IX and the Tobin plan, upon which it is based, is discussed in Chapter IV. The aged are included in the estimates in this table and in Table 9-1, whereas Tobin himself would have assured each aged person a minimum of $400 in old-age, survivors and disability insurance.   b Computed on the assumption of an eight-member family.   c This means that income tax liability under the present income tax schedule is equal to that under the 33⅓ percent tax schedule suggested by Tobin.   d These are families whose total money income is below the breakeven levels of income.   e These are overestimates because many one-member and two-member families are headed by aged persons who are allowed double the amount of personal tax exemptions and minimum standard deductions (EX-MSD).   f The sum of the positive differences between breakeven income levels and family money income.   g It is assumed that all income in excess of a family's EX-MSD is taxable.   h Tax on income above the breakeven income level and below the tie-in income level.

194

BIBLIOGRAPHY

Bibliography

Books and Monographs

Ayres, C. E. *The Industrial Economy*. Boston: Houghton-Mifflin Co., 1952.

Barlow, Robin, Harvey E. Brazer, and James N. Morgan. *Economic Behavior of the Affluent*. Washington: Brookings Institution, 1966.

Blum, Walter J., and Harry Kalven, Jr. *The Uneasy Case for Progressive Taxation*. Chicago: University of Chicago Press, 1953.

Buchanan, James M. *The Public Finances*. Homewood, Ill.: Richard D. Irwin, 1960.

Condliffe, John B. *The Welfare State in New Zealand*. London: George Allen and Unwin, 1959.

Dalton, Hugh. *Principles of Public Finance*. 4th ed. London: Rutledge, 1957.

Eldridge, Hope T. *Population Policies: A Survey of Recent Developments*. Washington: The International Union for the Scientific Study of Population, 1954.

Freedman, Ronald, Pascal K. Whelpton, and Arthur A. Campbell. *Family Planning, Sterility and Population Growth*. New York: McGraw-Hill, 1959.

Friedman, Milton. *Capitalism and Freedom*. Chicago: University of Chicago Press, 1962.

Friedman, Rose. *Poverty: Definition and Perspective*. Washington: American Enterprise Institute, 1965.

Gillespie, W. Irwin. "Effect of Public Expenditures on the Distribution of Income," *Essays in Fiscal Federalism*, ed. Richard A. Musgrave. Washington: Brookings Institution, 1965.

Goode, Richard. *The Individual Income Tax*. Washington: Brookings Institution, 1964.

Groves, Harold M. *Federal Tax Treatment of the Family*. Washington: Brookings Institution, 1963.

Harrington, Michael. *The Other America*. New York: Macmillan, 1962.

MacIntyre, Duncan M. *Public Assistance: Too Much or Too Little?* Ithaca: New York State School of Industrial and Labor Relations, Cornell University, December 1964.

May, Edgar. *The Wasted Americans*. New York: Harper and Row, 1964.

Meriam, Lewis. *Relief and Social Security*. Washington: Brookings Institution, 1946.

Morgan, Daniel C. *The Retail Sales Tax*. Madison: University of Wisconsin Press, 1964.

Morgan, James N., *et al. Income and Welfare in the United States*. New York: McGraw-Hill, 1962.

Musgrave, Richard A. *The Theory of Public Finance*. New York: McGraw-Hill, 1959.

Peacock, Alan. *Economics of National Insurance*. Edinburgh: W. Hodge, 1952.

Pechman, Joseph A. *Federal Tax Policy*. Washington: Brookings Institution, 1966.

Pigou, A. C. *The Economics of Welfare*. 4th ed. London: Macmillan, 1952.

Polanyi, Karl. *The Great Transformation*. New York: Rinehart, 1957.

Rhys-Williams, Lady Juliette. *Something to Look Forward To*. London: MacDonald and Co., 1943.

————. *Taxation and Incentive*. New York: Oxford University Press, 1953.

Rolph, Earl. *The Theory of Fiscal Economics*. Berkeley: University of California Press, 1954.

Rolph, Earl, and George Break. *Public Finance*. New York: Ronald Press, 1961.

Sanders, Thomas. *Effects of Taxation on Executives*. Boston: Graduate School of Business Administration, Harvard University, 1951.

Seligman, E. R. A. *Progressive Taxation in Theory and Practice*. Vol. 9, Nos. 1 and 2. Publication of the American Economics Association, 1894.

Simons, Henry C. *Personal Income Taxation*. Chicago: University of Chicago Press, 1938.

Stolnitz, George J. "The Demographic Transition: From High to Low Birth Rates and Death Rates," *Population: The Vital Revolution*, ed. Ronald Freedman. New York: Anchor Books, 1964. Chapter 2.

Theobald, Robert (ed.). *Free Men and Free Markets*. New York: C. N. Potter, 1963.

————. *The Guaranteed Income: Next Step in Economic Evolution?* Garden City, N.Y.: Doubleday, 1966.

Turnbull, John, C. Arthur Williams, and Earl Cheit. *Economic and Social Security*. 2nd ed. New York: Ronald Press, 1963.

Vadakin, James. *Family Allowances*. Miami: University of Miami Press, 1958.

Vickrey, William. *Agenda for Progressive Taxation*. New York: Ronald Press, 1947.

Weststrate, C. *Portrait of a Modern Mixed Economy: New Zealand*. Wellington: New Zealand University Press, 1959.

Articles, Periodicals, and Conference Proceedings

Break, George F. "Income Taxes and Incentives to Work: An Empirical Study," *American Economic Review*, Vol. 47 (September 1957), pp. 529-49.

Brehm, C. T., and T. R. Saving. "The Demand for General Assistance Payments," *American Economic Review*, Vol. 54 (December 1964), pp. 1002-18.

"Broadening the Base of Tax Cuts," *Business Week* (July 10, 1965), pp. 28-29.

Burns, Eveline. "Social Security in Evolution: Towards What?," Industrial Relations Research Association, *Proceedings of the Seventeenth Annual Meeting,* Chicago, December 1964, pp. 20-29.

Dale, Edwin. "Subsidizing the States." *New Republic* (November 28, 1964), pp. 11-12.

Fagan, Elmer F. "Recent and Contemporary Theories of Progressive Taxation," *Journal of Political Economy*, Vol. 46 (August 1938), pp. 457-98.

Farber, Joseph. "The Individual Subsidy Plan," *Feedback* (publication of the Institute for Cybernetic Research), Vol. 4 (January-February 1966).

Freedman, Deborah S. "The Relation of Economic Status to Fertility," *American Economic Review*, Vol. 53 (June 1963), pp. 414-22.

Friedman, Milton. "Poverty: A Direct Approach," *Context*, Vol. 2 (Winter 1964), pp. 1-3.

Gallaway, Lowell E. "Negative Income Tax Rates and the Elimination of Poverty," *National Tax Journal*, Vol. 19 (September 1966), pp. 298-307.

Green, Christopher, and Robert J. Lampman. "Schemes for Transferring Income to the Poor," in "A Symposium: Negative Income Tax Proposals," *Industrial Relations*, Vol. 6 (February 1967), pp. 121-37.

Groves, Harold M. "Income-Tax Administration," *National Tax Journal,* Vol. 12 (March 1959), pp. 37-53.

———. "Toward a Social Theory of Progressive Taxation," *National Tax Journal*, Vol. 9 (March 1956), pp. 27-34.

Hildebrand, George. "Second Thoughts on the Negative Income Tax," in "A Symposium: Negative Income Tax Proposals," *Industrial Relations*, Vol. 6 (February 1967), pp. 138-54.

Hitch, Thomas K. "Why the Negative Income Tax Won't Work," *Challenge,* Vol. 14 (July-August 1966), pp. 13-15.

Kahn, Gerald, and Ellen J. Perkins. "Families Receiving AFDC: What Do They Have to Live On?," *Welfare in Review*, Vol. 2 (October 1964), pp. 7-15.

Lampman, Robert J. "Approaches to the Reduction of Poverty," *American Economic Review, Papers and Proceedings*, Vol. 55 (May 1965), pp. 521-29.

———. "Prognosis for Poverty," National Tax Association, *Proceedings of 57th Annual Conference*, Pittsburgh, September 1964, pp. 71-81.

Merriam, Ida C. "Social Welfare Expenditures, 1964-65," *Social Security Bulletin*, Vol. 28 (October 1965), pp. 3-16.

Morgan, James N., Robin Barlow, and Harvey E. Brazer. "A Survey of Investment Management and Working Behavior Among High-Income Individuals," *American Economic Review, Papers and Proceedings*, Vol. 55 (May 1965), pp. 252-64.

Notestein, Frank. "The Fertility of Populations Supported by Relief," *The Milbank Memorial Fund Quarterly*, Vol. 14 (January 1936), pp. 37-49.

Orshansky, Mollie. "Children of the Poor," *Social Security Bulletin*, Vol. 26 (July 1963), pp. 3-13.

———. "Counting the Poor: Another Look at the Poverty Profile," *Social Security Bulletin*, Vol. 28 (January 1965), pp. 3-29.

———. "More About the Poor in 1964," *Social Security Bulletin*, Vol. 29 (May 1966), pp. 3-38.

———. "Recounting the Poor—A Five-Year Review," *Social Security Bulletin*, Vol. 29 (April 1966), pp. 20-37.

———. "Who's Who Among the Poor: A Demographic View of Poverty," *Social Security Bulletin*, Vol. 28 (July 1965), pp. 3-32.

Reagan, Michael D. "Washington Should Pay Taxes to the Poor," *New York Times*, Magazine Section, Sunday, February 20, 1966.

Rolph, Earl. "The Case for a Negative Income Tax Device," in "A Symposium: Negative Income Tax Proposals," *Industrial Relations*, Vol. 6 (February 1967), pp. 155-65.

Schorr, Alvin. "The Family Cycle and Income Development," *Social Security Bulletin*, Vol. 29 (February 1966), pp. 14-25.

———. "Income Maintenance and the Birth Rate," *Social Security Bulletin*, Vol. 28 (December 1965), pp. 22-30.

Schwartz, Edward E. "A Way to End the Means Test," *Social Work*, Vol. 9 (July 1964), pp. 3-12.

Smith, D. B. "A Simplified Approach to Social Welfare," *Canadian Tax Journal*, Vol. 13 (May-June 1965), pp. 260-65.

Stigler, George. "The Economics of Minimum Wage Legislation," *American Economic Review*, Vol. 36 (June 1946), pp. 358-65.

Storrow, Hugh A. "Money As a Motivator," *Public Welfare*, Vol. 20 (October 1962), pp. 199-205.

Tobin, James. "Improving the Economic Status of the Negro," *Daedalus*, Vol. 94 (Fall 1965), pp. 878-98.

Public Documents

Economic Report of the President, January 1965, and *ibid., January 1966*. Washington: Government Printing Office, 1965 and 1966.

Gallaway, Lowell E. *The Retirement Decision: An Exploratory Essay*. U. S. Department of Health, Education, and Welfare, Research Report No. 9. Washington: Government Printing Office, 1965.

Musgrave, Richard A. "The Incidence of the Tax Structure and Its Effects on Consumption," Joint Committee on the Economic Report, *Federal Tax Policy for Economic Growth and Stability*. Papers submitted by panelists appearing before the Subcommittee on Tax Policy, 84 Cong. 1 sess., 1955.

New Zealand Official Yearbook. Wellington: Public Printer, 1961.

Schultz, T. Paul. *Statistics on the Size Distribution of Personal Income in the United States.* Joint Economic Committee, 88 Cong. 2 sess., 1964.

State of Colorado. *The Incentive Budgeting Demonstration Project.* Final report. Colorado State Department of Public Welfare and the Denver Department of Welfare, December 1961.

U. S. Congress, Joint Economic Committee. *European Social Security Systems.* Paper No. 7, Economic Policies and Practices. 89 Cong. 1 sess., 1965.

U. S. Department of Commerce, Bureau of the Census. *Current Population Reports.* Series P-60, No. 47. "Income in 1964 of Families and Persons in the United States." 1965.

——. *Current Population Survey for 1964.*

U. S. Department of Health, Education, and Welfare, Advisory Council on Public Welfare. *Having the Power, We Have the Duty.* Washington: Government Printing Office, June 1966.

——, Bureau of Family Services. "Characteristics of Families Receiving Aid to Families with Dependent Children, November-December, 1961." April 1963.

——, Social Security Administration. Annual Statistical Supplement, 1963, of *Social Security Bulletin.*

——, Welfare Administration. Statistical Supplement, 1965, of *Welfare in Review.*

U. S. Department of the Treasury, Internal Revenue Service. *Statistics of Income, Individual Income Tax Returns, 1962.*

——, Office of Tax Analysis. Special tabulations of the Survey of Consumer Expenditures, 1960-61, of the Bureau of Labor Statistics, U. S. Department of Labor.

Unpublished Material

Hausman, Leonard. "Incentive Budgeting for Welfare Recipients." Unpublished paper, University of Wisconsin, January 1965.

Hildebrand, George. "The Negative Income Tax and the Problem of Poverty." Unpublished paper, U. S. Department of Labor, Winter 1965.

Lampman, Robert J. "The American System of Transfers. How Does it Benefit the Poor?" Unpublished paper, Fall 1965.

——. "The Guaranteed Minimum Income: Is it Worth What it Would Cost?" Paper prepared for delivery at Conference on the Guaranteed Minimum Income. The School of Social Service Administration, University of Chicago, January 14-15, 1966.

——. "Negative Rates Income Taxation." Unpublished paper prepared for Office of Economic Opportunity, August 1965.

McGuire, Patricia. "Family Allowances in the United States." Unpublished paper of the Office of Policy Planning and Research, U. S. Department of Labor, April 27, 1964.

Shutz, Robert Rudolph. "Transfer Payments and Income Inequality." Unpublished doctoral dissertation, University of California, 1952.

Tobin, James. "Memorandum on Basic Income Allowances." Unpublished paper, Yale University, Summer 1965.

Index